The Palgrave Macmillan Animal Ethics Series

Series editors: **Andrew Linzey** and **Priscilla Cohn**

In recent years, there has been a growing interest in the ethics of our treatment of animals. Philosophers have led the way, and now a range of other scholars have followed from historians to social scientists. From being a marginal issue, animals have become an emerging issue in ethics and in multidisciplinary inquiry. This series explores the challenges that Animal Ethics poses, both conceptually and practically, to traditional understandings of human-animal relations.

Specifically, the Series will:

- provide a range of key introductory and advanced texts that map out ethical positions on animals;
- publish pioneering work written by new, as well as accomplished, scholars, and
- produce texts from a variety of disciplines that are multidisciplinary in character or have multidisciplinary relevance.

Titles include:

ANIMAL SUFFERING: PHILOSOPHY AND CULTURE
Elisa Aaltola

ANIMALS AND PUBLIC HEALTH
Why Treating Animals Better Is Critical to Human Welfare
Aysha Akhtar

AN INTRODUCTION TO ANIMALS AND POLITICAL THEORY
Alasdair Cochrane

ANIMAL CRUELTY, ANTISOCIAL BEHAVIOUR, AND HUMAN AGGRESSION
More Than a Link
Eleonora Gullone

ANIMALS IN THE CLASSICAL WORLD
Ethical Perspectives from Greek and Roman Texts
Alastair Harden

POWER, KNOWLEDGE, ANIMALS
Lisa Johnson

THE COSTS AND BENEFITS OF ANIMAL EXPERIMENTS
Andrew Knight

AN INTRODUCTION TO ANIMALS IN VISUAL CULTURE
Randy Malamud

CHRISTIAN THEOLOGY AND THE STATUS OF ANIMALS
Ryan McLaughlin

POPULAR MEDIA AND ANIMALS
Claire Molloy

The Palgrave Macmillan Animal Ethics Series
Series Standing Order ISBN 978–0–230–57686–5 Hardback
                              978–0–230–57687–2 Paperback
(*outside North America only*)

You can receive future titles in this series as they are published by placing a standing order.
Please contact your bookseller or, in case of difficulty, write to us at the address below with
your name and address, the title one of the series and the ISBNs quoted above.

Customer Services Department, Macmillan Distribution Ltd, Houndmills, Basingstoke,
Hampshire RG21 6XS, England.

Christian Theology and the Status of Animals

The Dominant Tradition and Its Alternatives

Ryan Patrick McLaughlin
Department of Theology, Duquesne University, USA

First published 2014 by
PALGRAVE MACMILLAN

Palgrave Macmillan in the UK is an imprint of Macmillan Publishers Limited,
registered in England, company number 785998, of Houndmills, Basingstoke,
Hampshire RG21 6XS.

Palgrave Macmillan in the US is a division of St Martin's Press LLC,
175 Fifth Avenue, New York, NY 10010.

Palgrave Macmillan is the global academic imprint of the above companies
and has companies and representatives throughout the world.

Palgrave® and Macmillan® are registered trademarks in the United States,
the United Kingdom, Europe and other countries

ISBN: 978–1–137–34457–1

This book is printed on paper suitable for recycling and made from fully
managed and sustained forest sources. Logging, pulping and manufacturing
processes are expected to conform to the environmental regulations of the
country of origin.

A catalogue record for this book is available from the British Library.

A catalog record for this book is available from the Library of Congress.

Contents

List of Illustrations

Tables

Figures

Series Editors' Preface

This is a new book series for a new field of inquiry: Animal Ethics.

In recent years, there has been a growing interest in the ethics of our treatment of animals. Philosophers have led the way, and now a range of other scholars have followed from historians to social scientists. From being a marginal issue, animals have become an emerging issue in ethics and in multidisciplinary inquiry.

In addition, a rethink of the status of animals has been fuelled by a range of scientific investigations which have revealed the complexity of animal sentiency, cognition and awareness. The ethical implications of this new knowledge have yet to be properly evaluated, but it is becoming clear that the old view that animals are mere things, tools, machines or commodities cannot be sustained ethically.

But it is not only philosophy and science that are putting animals on the agenda. Increasingly, in Europe and the United States, animals are becoming a political issue as political parties vie for the "green" and "animal" vote. In turn, political scientists are beginning to look again at the history of political thought in relation to animals, and historians are beginning to revisit the political history of animal protection.

As animals grow as an issue of importance, so there have been more collaborative academic ventures leading to conference volumes, special journal issues, indeed new academic animal journals as well. Moreover, we have witnessed the growth of academic courses, as well as university posts, in Animal Ethics, Animal Welfare, Animal Rights, Animal Law, Animals and Philosophy, Human-Animal Studies, Critical Animal Studies, Animals and Society, Animals in Literature, Animals and Religion – tangible signs that a new academic discipline is emerging.

Animal ethics is the new term for the academic exploration of the moral status of the nonhuman – an exploration that explicitly involves a focus on what we owe animals morally, and which also helps us to understand the influences – social, legal, cultural, religious and political – that legitimate animal abuse. This series explores the challenges that animal ethics poses, both conceptually and practically, to traditional understandings of human-animal relations.

The series is needed for three reasons: (i) to provide texts that will support the new university courses on animals, (ii) to support the increasing number of students studying and academics researching in animal-related fields, and (iii) because there is currently no book series whose focus is multidisciplinary research in the field.

Specifically, the series will

- provide a range of key introductory and advanced texts that map out ethical positions on animals;
- publish pioneering work written by new, as well as accomplished, scholars;
- produce, from a variety of disciplines, texts that are multidisciplinary in character or have multidisciplinary relevance.

The new Palgrave Macmillan Series on Animal Ethics is the result of a unique partnership between Palgrave Macmillan and the Ferrater Mora Oxford Centre for Animal Ethics. The series is an integral part of the mission of the Centre to put animals on the intellectual agenda by facilitating academic research and publication. The series is also a natural complement to one of the Centre's other major projects, the *Journal of Animal Ethics*. The Centre is an independent think tank for the advancement of progressive thought about animals and is the first centre of its kind in the world. It aims to demonstrate rigorous intellectual enquiry and the highest standards of scholarship. It strives to be a world-class centre of academic excellence in its field.

We invite academics to visit the Centre's website, www.oxfordanimalethics.com, and to contact us with book proposals for the series.

Andrew Linzey and Priscilla N. Cohn
General Editors

Foreword

During the last 30 years, we have witnessed an increasing number of Christians concerned with the protection of animals. They are often perplexed by the traditional indifference on the part of the churches and cannot comprehend how they can remain silent on issues of abuse and plain cruelty. Understandably, they often write letters of protest to priests and bishops, but often they appear to get nowhere.

These protests invariably fall on deaf ears for one simple reason: the protesters haven't understood the theology that still justifies animal abuse. The historic ideas are quite simple: animals are put here by God for our use; they have no immortal souls or inherent value, and exist solely as means to human ends. And these ideas still variously pervade even secular culture.

Christian animal protectionists can only make progress if they are prepared to learn the grammar of Christian thinking and engage with the dominant theology that justifies abuse. Protests by themselves are not enough – they don't touch the basic issue – and they alone won't persuade fellow churchpeople and church authorities.

This excellent book is what every Christian concerned for animal protection needs, though at first some may not appreciate its vital importance. It explains and documents the dominant ways of Christian thinking that are negative toward animals, while, at the same time, showing how deficient these positions are, and how alternative traditions can and should have supplanted them. People don't always appreciate that the Christian tradition is not a closed book but (to mix metaphors) is rather like a vast living river that comprises different swells, movements, and tributaries. It is always moving on, adapting itself to new circumstances, but in some cases it becomes stagnant and needs revitalizing.

As E. L. Mascall once wrote: "The Church's tradition is a great living inheritance of thought and life, most of whose content has hitherto been undiscerned and most of whose potentialities have hitherto been unactualised.It is by bringing this great living inheritance into impact upon the world in which we live that our task towards the world will be achieved" (*Theology and the Gospel of Christ*, 1977, p. 62).

This, then, is the challenge for Christian animal protectionists: to become their own theologians, to *think* about their tradition, to engage with it, and, by the Holy Spirit, to discern its potentialities and help realize them.

Personally, I have waited a long time for this book. I have been working in the area of animal theology for more than 40 years, and I have long hoped that theologians would take the issue of animals seriously. Now, thankfully, there are serious signs of a new intellectual awakening, and many new books are appearing. But Ryan McLaughlin's book is undoubtedly one of the very best – of the top class. He takes up many of the ideas I have developed in my own work, builds upon them, criticizes them, and thus pushes theological thinking in new creative ways. This is a commanding work of constructive theology which should inspire and invigorate us all.

Andrew Linzey
Oxford Centre for Animal Ethics

Acknowledgments

I express my utmost gratitude to all those who have aided in the development of this book. Special thanks go to Andrew Linzey, without whom it would not exist. I also thank my wife, Melissa, who graciously read much of this book and provided editorial feedback. More than that, she has been my greatest source of encouragement. Also, I thank other family members, whose support has been immeasurably valuable in my education and research. I am also grateful to Brenda Colijn, whose mentorship and friendship have been worth more to me than I can say.

In addition, I express my appreciation to the faculty members at Duquesne University, particularly Daniel Scheid, James Bailey, Elizabeth Cochrane, Aimee Light, and Marie Baird. I also acknowledge that the creative inspiration for much of what follows burgeoned out of many a lunchtime discussion with fellow doctoral students at Duquesne. I am ever appreciative of the camaraderie I encountered there.

I would also like to offer thanks to the University of Illinois Press, Cambridge University Press, and Wiley-Blackwell Publishing for permission to make use of material previously published through them. Lastly, I would like to thank Palgrave Macmillan, for providing a reputable venue within which to dialogue through publishing.

Introduction

I was the youth pastor at a church in rural Ohio. One of the teens from my group decided to attend a youth worship rally at another local church. I encouraged such activities, being a lover of ecumenism. However, on this particular occasion, the teen returned with a disturbing tale. The youth pastor at the rally gave a sermon on the connection between choice and consequence. His main point, as the teen from my group told it, was that God was not responsible for the bad things that result from human beings succumbing to temptation. We are responsible for the negative consequences of our injudicious decisions.

Like many another pastor, this youth pastor decided to use an illustration to instill his point in the teens. Earlier that day, the pastor purchased a hamster from a local pet store. During his sermon, his wife brought out the animal in a cage. The pastor told the teens two things about the hamster. First, the animal had no food available to it all day, ensuring that the creature was quite hungry. Second, the sales person at the pet store said that this particular hamster was "evil" – presumably he meant uncooperative and domineering.

After making these points, the pastor took out a mouse trap in which he had placed food for the hamster. He told the onlookers, "I'm not forcing this hamster to eat this food. He's going to make that decision on his own. But his decision will come with consequences." Then he placed the trap into the cage while everyone watched to see what happened.

Much to the pastor's chagrin, the hamster avoided the trap. So much for a memorable illustration. Determined to make his point, he signaled his wife, who took the cage out of the room. She returned a few minutes later. The hamster was now struggling in the trap, and the teens gathered around to watch the creature die.

1

I have shared this story with Christians in both ecclesial and academic settings. While it seems like an appeal to emotion, I do not actually intend it as such. I realize it tends to stir emotions in those who hear it, but my reason for telling the story is different.

Most people who hear the tale are appalled. This reaction typically leads to a dialogue that reveals the actual reason I share the story. In general, the dialogue goes as follows:

"What that pastor did is so terrible!" the listeners say. "He's evil!"

I respond: "Aside from the reality that the illustration is perhaps one of the worst analogies I have encountered – seriously, is the point that God starves us, then offers us food in the form of certain peril, and then blames us for the consequences of trying to sustain our life by eating – why is the pastor's action 'so terrible'? Is it terrible because the pastor caused the animal to suffer? Is it terrible because he caused the animal to die? Is it terrible because he made a spectacle of the animal's travail in front of impressionable teens? Is it terrible because such cruelty is against the social contract of American citizens? What makes it terrible?"

"It's terrible," someone will reply, "because the pastor didn't have to harm the animal. The hamster didn't deserve what happened to it."

To this I respond: "But the pastor had a good reason for harming and killing the animal. He wanted to instill a spiritual truth in the observing youth. He wanted to make them better understand their faith and live as more responsible people in the world."

"I guess," a listener concedes. "But that doesn't justify what he did."

"But consider," I retort, "don't most people cause harm and death to animals every day when they use cosmetics that are tested on them? When they eat the flesh of animals? When they consume eggs and dairy products produced by animals who don't have room to move? When they wear leather and wool from animals kept in conditions meant to maximize profit for the animals' owners? When they hunt animals for sport?"

"Are the reasons people do these things better than a youth pastor's reason: concern for the spiritual understanding of the teens he is addressing? Is not his mind-set the same as most people's: that they are justified in causing animals harm and death because they receive some benefit – enjoyment, dietary satisfaction, more beautiful skin, or whatever – from doing so? Is it right for such people to judge the youth pastor because he causes an innocent animal to suffer and die when their everyday actions condone the very mind-set they seem to deplore in the story? Who can judge the pastor for transparently revealing the suffering and death of that hamster when they are happy to have the suffering and death they cause veiled behind the closed doors of the meat and cosmetic industries?"

The ultimate point I seek to make in sharing the story is that while most people tend to find the pastor's actions despicable, they also tend – albeit without much conscious recognition – to subscribe wholly to the principle that justifies his action. That is, the one who eats the flesh of a cow raised under the horrid conditions on a factory farm seems to operate under the influence of the same principle whereby the youth pastor causes the suffering and death of a hamster to instill his spiritual point in his listeners. This principle is as follows: Animals exist primarily for the benefit of human beings. Such being the case, humans can use them, even cause them harm and death, if the purpose of such use is the well-being of the human community.

Typically, scholars use the word "anthropocentrism" to refer to this principle. This term's import is that humans are the measure of all else in the world. They are the only creatures that exist for their own sake. They are persons in the midst of things. As such, they are justified in using these things – including animals – inasmuch as human well-being is the greatest good in the world.

Today, the principle is vibrantly alive in the church, though for many its affirmation is a subconscious or unexamined affair. Only when a shocking story arises out of a particularly heinous application of the principle do the sensibilities of default advocates of anthropocentrism stir in the form of offense. Americans hate the idea of dogs being forced to fight one another but vehemently defend people's right to shoot deer with a bow and arrow. My experience yields the conclusion that, when pressed, most Christians will say they are justified in eating meat because nonhuman animals exist for human benefit. One parishioner even asked me, "What else would that meat [that is, *living animals*] be doing out there?" Even more disturbing, a senior pastor friend of mine chastised a vegetarian friend of mine, arguing, "There is no justification in either scripture or theology for vegetarianism."

The aim of the present work

What is a Christian to make of these anthropocentric views? In the face of the recent explosion of concern for the environment and new movements in the fields of animal welfare and animal rights, anthropocentric attitudes like those I describe above and their theological roots in Christianity have become the focus of critical examination. Indeed, some scholars have followed the path blazed by Lynn White in accusing Western Christianity especially of providing the founda-tions for facets of the present ecological crisis. As I note in Chapter 1, these accusations have evoked responses from Christian historians and theologians. Some offer defenses against the accusations, while others offer critical retrievals of the tradition, applying certain princi-ples found in Christian theology to today's context of environmental concern.

This book is concerned with these responses, especially with regard to nonhuman animals. More specifically, it has two aims. The first is to evaluate the accusation that Christianity provides the anthropocentric foundations for harmful practices toward animals. I argue that the domi-nant tradition in Christian (especially Western Christian) thought is indeed anthropocentric. In eliciting an instrumental view of nonhuman animals, this tradition thereby justifies human use of them – even when such use results in suffering, death, or both. However, this dominant tradition is at times caricatured by opposing voices. While the tradition's anthropocentrism does indeed ground a utilitarian view of animals, it also contains moral limits to human use of the nonhuman creation. These limits may be said to be indirect, inasmuch as they are concerned more with either the just distribution of nonhuman resources among the human community or with the adverse affects that wanton cruelty toward animals may have on humans than with the well-being of those resources. Even so, they provide grounds for reform in modern practices that are harmful to nonhuman animals. While such reform is not in itself directed toward the well-being of animals, it is nonetheless condu-cive to their welfare, in that as it encourages the virtue of moderation, it thereby calls for conservation of the nonhuman world for the sake of all humans, including those not yet born.

The book's second aim is, through critical retrieval and historical inves-tigations, to delineate foundations that provide space for alternatives to the dominant tradition in Christian theology. These alternatives tend to challenge the form of anthropocentrism in which humans are the only bearers of intrinsic value. Some of them also challenge the ethics of conservation that accompany the dominant tradition by permitting nonhuman animals a place in the new creation, even acknowledging the need for cosmic transfiguration in the wake of human sin. Such alter-natives highlight the proposition that the dominant view in Christian history is not the only view. Indeed, contra the aforementioned pastor's chastisement, there is justification for direct moral concern for animals (vegetarianism being one such expression) in the variegated voices of Christianity's past and present. However, it is my contention that such a move would require not merely retrieving but *rejecting* certain tenets of the dominant tradition.

Methodological qualifications of the present work

This book's aims thus seek to provide means to escape the dominant tradition of Christian theology with regard to animals. However, I want to make clear that I am not here arguing that the dominant tradition is *wrong*. Personally, I find it deeply unsatisfying – no doubt this is a bias I bring to the table in my research – but even so, I am not interested in arguing that the views I prefer are *the* Christian view, while the views that make me uncomfortable have no grounding in Christian thought. My argument, rather, is simply that the dominant tradition is not *the* Christian view either. There are open spaces in Christian theology for those dissatisfied with it. For my part, I want to shed light on those spaces. Thus, while my discomfort with and disapproval of the dominant tradition will be evident to the reader, I am not so naive as to claim that my feelings regarding this tradition are tantamount to its being incorrect.

Another clarification I offer pertains to method. Many of the following chapters represent interpretations – of the work of theologians, of ecclesial documents, and of the Bible. I make no pretense that I am "starting with the text" in any of these cases. There is, for each text I engage, a particular "I" that is reading them. I have a narrative and a context, both of which affect my interpretations. As such, I want to acknowledge these facets of my identity.

I am a white male who was born and raised in the United States of America. I currently am a member of the Church of the Nazarene, although my personal and educational backgrounds are ecumenically diverse. Furthermore, I am a strict vegetarian and (admittedly slightly less strictly) a vegan. My decision, made around eight years ago, to become a vegetarian burgeoned out of developments of my understanding of the doctrine of God and my personal experiences of being moved by the plight of nonhuman animals. All of these facets of my narrative bear on the present work. While in what follows I try to remain honest and fair, there is no doubt that part of the "I" that is me is in this text.

Outline of the present work

This book came to fruition through the urging of Andrew Linzey to gather some of my published articles into a monograph. Thus, four of the eight chapters (1, 3, 4, and 8) were previously published. Each was originally intended to stand on its own. For the sake of continuity and cohesiveness, I have reworked each of them toward a coherent whole. The other four chapters (2, 5, 6, and 7) are new. Parts of these chapters represent previous (unpublished) research; other parts have been written with the present work in mind.

Chapter 1 establishes the parameters of the dominant tradition by engaging the masterful work of Saint Thomas Aquinas. I contend that where Aquinas's view of nature and teleology intersect, one detects a theocentric cosmology that grounds, in the temporal realm, an anthropocentrism in which all corporeal nonhumans exist for the well-being of the entire human community. Thus, humans must conserve the cosmos as whole for the sake of other humans.

Chapter 2 examines the extent to which the parameters of the dominant tradition are maintained in modern thought. In this chapter I focus on magisterial pronouncements of the Roman Catholic Church. While these documents betray some ambiguity on issues where Aquinas does not, they nonetheless on the whole promulgate the dominant tradition. They refer to animals as resources that must be justly distributed among the entire human community, of both the present and the future.

Chapter 3 offers a vision, one grounded in the tradition and taken up by various modern scholars, in which the uniqueness of humans does not so much secure a status that raises them above the rest of the created order as render them uniquely responsible for the well-being of the "lesser" creation. This functional understanding of the human position in the cosmos is anthropocentric in the sense that the well-being of the created order is partly predicated upon human work. However, this form of anthropocentrism is a far cry from the denial of intrinsic value to nonhumans. Indeed, the importance of human beings reveals the importance of the cosmos, because the former are significant in part *for the sake of the latter*, including animals.

Chapter 4 examines two Church Fathers, Irenaeus of Lyons and Ephrem the Syrian, in an effort to establish early Christian roots for alternatives to the dominant tradition. Both Fathers imply that the original peace of the protological Eden will be restored in the eschatological consummation of the world. Furthermore, both maintain that the cosmos is on its way – *in via* – toward this future such that there are glimpses of it in the wake of the Christ event. When this framework is combined with the peace between saints and animals depicted in various hagiographies, it is possible to claim that the righteous person ought to practice peace toward animals as a witness to the eschatological hope of the cosmos.

Chapters 5 and 6 provide exegetical explorations of two passages in the Hebrew Scriptures; they thus go back farther than the Fathers into the Jewish roots of Christianity. Chapter 5 engages Genesis 1:26–29 in conjunction with Genesis 9:1–3. Chapter 6 examines Isaiah 11:1–9. I argue that both passages provide challenges to the dominant tradition. The Genesis text does so in its connection of *imago Dei* with dominion, both of which lead to God's prescription of a vegetarian diet for humans. When compared with Genesis 9, where God permits the consumption of meat after the arrival of sin and the flood, Genesis 1 suggests that God's intent for humanity was not to harm animals nor view them through a strictly utilitarian lens. Rather, humanity's unique status leads to its grave responsibility of revealing God to the animals. Isaiah's peaceable kingdom strikes at the heart of both anthropocentrism and the exclusion of animals from the future hope of the cosmos. It provides further credence to the notion that humanity is responsible for the well-being of animals. It also suggests that humans and animals will participate together in a future that entails the cessation of violence, a future in which peace among all creatures will reign.

Chapter 7 examines the notion of the sacramentality of the cosmos and evaluates the extent to which it departs from the dominant tradition. The notion finds its strongest representation in Orthodox theology, but it is not without a voice in Roman Catholic thought. I argue that this tradition, while breaking with the conservationist strand of the dominant tradition, nonetheless tends to perpetuate its anthropocentric slant. However, I maintain that cosmic sacramentality provides powerful foundations to challenge the anthropocentrism of the dominant tradition by portraying a sacramental reciprocity between humans and animals in which they reveal God in their own way to each other.

Finally, Chapter 8 provides a glimpse into how alternative strands of Christian theology regarding nonhuman animals open new spaces for interreligious dialogue. I examine the foundations for nonviolence toward animals in Mahatma Gandhi and Albert Schweitzer. There are strong similarities in these foundations, similarities that would not exist if Schweitzer had not broken from the anthropocentrism of the dominant tradition.

Collectively, these critical investigations suggest that while the anthropocentrism evident in Aquinas's work is indeed Christian theology's dominant tradition, that theology is not without strands of discontents. By delineating these strands, one reveals alternatives to the dominant tradition, alternatives that open the door to a reenvisioning of the status of animals in Christianity.

1
Thomas Aquinas and the Dominant Tradition

There can be little doubt that Saint Thomas Aquinas has left a profound and lasting impact on the landscape of Christian philosophy and theology. His appropriation of Aristotelian philosophy and his engagement with the thinking of such figures as Augustine, John Damascene, the Jewish philosopher Maimonides, and the Islamic philosopher Averroes are nothing short of brilliant. Contemporary scholars, however, have raised questions regarding Aquinas's legacy in relation to creation care. These questions warrant investigation into his eco-theological position.

In this chapter I argue that Aquinas represents, in a coherent and cohesive manner, a view concerning nonhuman animals that is the dominant tradition in Christian history. In this view animals are essentially reduced to resources for human well-being in the temporal realm, including bodily nourishment and spiritual knowledge. These resources belong to the entire human community and thus must be used in a manner conducive to the welfare of that community. This emphasis on the common good renders Aquinas's position a potentially powerful voice for ecological concern but only within a framework that is ultimately indirect, anthropocentric, and conservationist. Humans must preserve the cosmos as it is for the sake of the entire human community. Such is the dominant tradition – one that posits only indirect moral concern for nonhuman animals and effectively denies them intrinsic value.

The question of Aquinas's eco-theological legacy

In his frequently cited 1967 essay, Lynn White writes: "Especially in its Western form, Christianity is the most anthropocentric religion the world has seen."[1] As we will see, White's contention is not without dissent. Even so, many scholars' sentiments echo White's regarding at least the dominant strand of thought in Western Christianity. These scholars, both secular and religious, often trace this strand to the writings of Aquinas.

For example, regarding Aquinas's position regarding nonhuman animals, Peter Singer states, "No argument could reveal the essence of speciesism more clearly."[2] Richard Ryder laments that Aquinas's anthropocentrism is responsible for the justification of "several centuries of outstanding cruelty" toward animals.[3] Gary Steiner categorizes Aquinas as "the apex of medieval anthropocentrism."[4] Robert Wennberg argues that Aquinas, like Immanuel Kant, adheres to a moral theory "that has no place for animals."[5] Andrew Linzey charges that Aquinas's speciesist viewpoint in which nonhuman creatures have no claim of direct moral concern "has left a bitter legacy in Christian theology."[6] Finally, Paul Santmire detects an anthropocentrism in Aquinas in which "nature is seen more as an object for human use, which satisfies biological needs and serves spiritual knowledge, than as a subject in its own right."[7]

In responding to these negative readings, defenders of Aquinas have frequently pointed to his historical context and the overarching scope of his theology in order to reveal the aforementioned critiques as overly simplistic. For example, John Berkman writes that, for Aquinas, "the entire physical universe (for example plants, birds, nonhuman and human animals) is ordered towards 'ultimate perfection', which is in turn ordered to God, and by its perfection gives glory to the goodness of God."[8] With this claim, Berkman argues that, for Aquinas, "God's plan in creation…is by no means anthropocentric."[9] Anne Clifford argues that negative interpretations of anthropocentric passages in Aquinas can only stand when they are "read in total isolation from other passages in which he affirms the inherent goodness of all creatures as unique manifestations of the Trinity and if his theology is interpreted ahistorically."[10] Celia Deane-Drummond, while noting certain problems with Aquinas's biology, nonetheless defends him against overgeneralized accusations of anthropocentrism by acknowledging the interplay between grace and nature in his thought.[11] Jame Schaefer offers a similar qualified defense.[12] William French, likewise a critical advocate of Aquinas, notes, "Many who know little of Catholicism cite certain unfortunate parts of a long and varied tradition to dismiss it as holding no helpful resources for promoting responsible care of animals or the eco-system."[13] Mark Wynn argues that Aquinas's position is more nuanced than his detractors acknowledge. To make this point, he draws on Aquinas's understanding of God's subsistent existence in order to highlight his theological cosmocentrism.[14] Willis Jenkins maintains that Aquinas "escapes facile categorization by cosmological centrisms." In Jenkins's view, Aquinas resists appeals to "anthropocentrism, theocentrism, and ecocentrism...because he sees that God chooses to move creation to Godself by inviting humans into a friendship shaped by their intimacy with all creation."[15]

Even given the disparate voices, there can be little doubt that Aquinas has greatly impacted the theological landscape of Christian history. What remains in dispute is the nature of his eco-theological legacy. Does Aquinas provide the foundations for an unhindered degradation of the nonhuman creation? Or does his theocentric framework and historical context either mitigate or flatly disprove such accusations?

It is my position that regarding nonhuman animals in particular, Aquinas's position can be described as both anthropocentric and conservationist. These facets of his thought are grounded in – as opposed to exonerated by – his theocentric framework. To back this position, in this chapter I explore the intersection of nature and teleology in Aquinas's summas. I argue that his appropriation of these ideas establishes a cosmological theocentrism that grounds, in temporal practice, an eco-theological ethics in which the telos of corporeal nonhuman entities is exhausted in the temporal realm and is directed to the well-being of the entire human community. Because this ethics understands the value of the nonhuman creation with reference to humanity, it is anthropocentric. Because this value exists for the sake of *all* humans, including future generations, Aquinas's ethics calls for conservation of the natural order. In my view, such is Aquinas's eco-theological legacy. This legacy, as I argue in Chapter 2, is evident today in contemporary magisterial pronouncements of the Catholic Church.

Aquinas's theological framework and nonhuman animals

For Aquinas, the created order embodies a multiplicity of formal distinctions. All of these forms, whether human or nonhuman, are good.[16] However, as "formal distinction always requires inequality," the multiplicity in creation entails also a hierarchy of created things in which some are more perfect than others.[17] Regarding the forms of life in these distinctions, Aquinas posits three hierarchically arranged classifications of souls: vegetative, sensitive, and rational.[18] At the lowest rung of the hierarchy of souls is the vegetative soul, which lacks both sentience and rationality but possesses the powers of nutrition, augmentation, and generation.[19] At the second rung is the sensitive soul. It is here that

Aquinas places all nonhuman animals, in that in addition to vegetative qualities, they possess the exterior and interior senses but lack rationality.[20] Aquinas maintains that forms of higher perfection contain the lower forms. That is, "What belongs to the inferior nature pre-exists more perfectly in the superior."[21] Hence, the human soul possesses the qualities of both the vegetative and sensitive souls; but in its rationality it excels them.[22] Aquinas claims that it is this unique rational dimension of the human creature that constitutes the *imago Dei* ("image of God"). All nonhuman creatures and the animalistic dimensions of human beings bear a likeness to God in that they reveal a trace of God's design "just as the shape of a house points to the idea of the architect."[23] However, only the rational component (the mind) of humans bears the likeness of God as image: "This image of God is not found even in the rational creature except in the mind." That is, "[t]he intellect or mind is that whereby the rational creature excels other creatures."[24]

I return to Aquinas's depiction of the hierarchy of beings below, but my immediate concern is the link between the nature and telos of a creature. What is the proper end of the human creature that, with its rational soul, occupies the highest tier of the corporeal hierarchy? In Aquinas's thought, the answer is twofold.[25] The first end proper to the human creature pertains to temporal matters. The second is the ultimate telos of humanity, which Aquinas defines as "happiness."[26] For Aquinas, "God alone constitutes man's happiness."[27] Hence, while all creatures have God as their end, "happiness" denotes the particular way in which humanity is directed toward God as ultimate end. This telos of happiness is a shared life with God in which the rational soul contemplates the divine.[28] In short, for Aquinas, the ultimate telos appropriate for the nature of the human creature is the Beatific Vision. Thus, he states: "Final and perfect happiness can consist in nothing else than the vision of the Divine Essence,"[29] which Aquinas elsewhere links to union with God.[30] While this telos is appropriate to humanity's rational core, human nature also requires a gracious augmentation to perfect it for the Beatific Vision.[31]

Regarding the temporal telos of humanity, Aquinas posits that an imperfect happiness is possible in the temporal realm. This happiness "depends, in a way, on the body."[32] Furthermore, "For imperfect happiness, such as can be had in this life, external goods are necessary, not as belonging to the essence of happiness, but by serving as instruments to happiness, which consists in an operation of virtue."[33] This passage indicates that the temporal ends of humans (1) include a dependence on their animal bodies, which requires meeting the needs of their vegetative soul, among which are nutrition, augmentation, and generation;[34] and (2) are directed toward their ultimate end.[35] It also reveals the centrality of teleology in Aquinas's understanding of virtue.[36]

For a human to live virtuously in the temporal realm is for that human to live toward his or her proper telos, whether temporal or ultimate. Thus like Aristotle, Aquinas holds that the cardinal virtues, which exist for Christians and non-Christians alike, are directed toward temporal ends.[37] However, Aquinas differs from Aristotle in arguing that in Christians, who are infused with the theological virtues, the cardinal virtues are perfected beyond what is possible for those who lack the former.[38] The theological virtues' presence perfects other virtues. Pinckaers expresses this point when he writes, "The virtues form an organism whose head is constituted by the theological virtues."[39]

A Christian infused with the theological virtues will exercise prudence differently – at least on some occasions – than someone without them. Pope goes as far as to say that "the cardinal virtues are also 'infused' by divine grace in those who have been blessed with the theological virtues."[40] Therefore, a prudent Christian with the theological virtues will engage in certain forms of abstinence that fail to meet the criteria of prudential temperance for non-Christians.[41] In Bonnie Kent's estimation of Aquinas, "What would be prudent for a Christian might...appear, or even be, imprudent for a non-Christian."[42] The perfection of the cardinal virtues occurs because, in conjunction with the theological virtues, they are redirected from merely temporal ends to humanity's ultimate telos.[43] The acquired virtues are still properly directed to natural ends; but they are so directed *in light of the ultimate telos of the human creature*. For Aquinas, to "have the character of virtue, truly and perfectly," virtues must "produce good works in proportion to a supernatural last end."[44] As David Hollenbach succinctly notes, "Everything human beings are to do, in both personal and social life, should be directed to one end: union with the God who is their maker and redeemer."[45] The point to be made here is that what it means for a person to be virtuous is predicated upon the *ultimate* end proper to that person. This understanding of virtue will bear significance regarding whether or not humanity's ultimate telos is shared with nonhuman animals.

As noted, Aquinas sees the nature of human beings directing them to a particular temporal and eternal telos. What about the telos of the nonhuman creation, including animals? The two ends of humanity do not exhaust Aquinas's teleology. All life is teleological by nature.[46] For Aquinas, the telos of a creature is its good,[47] and God is the ultimate good for the entirety of creation.[48] Therefore, the entire creation has God as its end.[49] In this teleological sense, there is a commonality between humans and nonhumans. In acting according to their distinct natures – and thus toward the ends proper to those natures – all creatures in their multiplicity glorify God.[50] Says Aquinas, "The whole universe together participates in the divine goodness more perfectly, and represents it better than any single creature whatever."[51]

God is the ultimate good of the entire creation because God provides creatures with variegated natures predisposing each toward the appropriate telos for which it lives. In living thus, the created order, in the multiplicity of its formal distinctions, reveals the goodness of God.[52] Thus all life derives from and is directed toward God. Yet there is a sharp disparity concerning the manner in which God is the telos of different creatures.[53] This disparity is predicated upon the difference between the nature of humans and nonhumans.[54]

Of the three classes of souls Aquinas delineates (vegetative, sensitive, and rational), he applies greater goodness to the creatures with the capacities entailed by the higher souls.[55] These creatures are more perfect than those below them. Furthermore,

> From the order observed by nature... the imperfect are for the use of the perfect; as the plants make use of the earth for their nourishment, and animals make use of plants, and man makes use of both plants and animals. Therefore it is in keeping with the order of nature, that man should be master over animals.[56]

Because of their lower disposition in the hierarchy of the created order, nonrational animals are "naturally under slavery."[57] Thus Aquinas follows Aristotle in claiming that humans can hunt nonhuman animals as a "natural right" – that is, by virtue of being human.[58] Aquinas sees an affirmation of his position in the language of the biblical creation narratives: "In describing man's production, Scripture uses a special way of speaking, to show that other things were made for man's sake."[59]

These passages appear to be anthropocentric. Yet John Berkman states:

> If we look at Aquinas' larger picture, we see that for Aquinas the entire physical universe... is ordered towards "ultimate perfection," which is in turn ordered to God, and by its perfection gives glory to the goodness of God. Each creature manifests the goodness of God by living according to its own *telos*. Furthermore, all species by existing according to their own degree of goodness make a

necessary contribution to the perfection of the universe....Thus, for Aquinas, God's plan in creation, while hierarchical, is by no means anthropocentric.[60]

In a fashion similar to that of other defenders of Aquinas, Berkman argues that those who provide an essentially anthropocentric interpretation of Aquinas miss the theocentric heart of his theology. Some boilerplate readings of Aquinas do make this error. However, many retrievals of Aquinas's theocentrism likewise fail to acknowledge (or at least they firmly downplay) that his affirmation that the entire nonhuman creation has God as its end is true only inasmuch as the nonhuman creation has God as its end *for the sake of humanity*. Says Aquinas, "The intellectual nature is the only one that is required in the universe, for its own sake, while all others are for its sake."[61]

In short, the nonhuman creation is *for God, through humanity*. In this sense, Aquinas's cosmological theocentrism actually reinforces an ethical anthropocentrism. The justification of humanity's use of nonhuman animals is solidified by the providential ordering of the cosmos. For this reason, I concur with David Kinsley's claim that in Aquinas's theology, "all creatures serve the good of the whole...by serving human purposes and needs."[62] Paul Santmire makes a similar claim.[63] Furthermore, Andrew Linzey notes that Aquinas exceeds Aristotle by claiming that divine providence establishes natural order: "Subordination is justifiable *because God has ordained it*."[64] Therefore, claiming that for Aquinas "God's plan in creation...is by no means anthropocentric" is as overly simplistic as exhausting his cosmology with anthropocentrism.

Aquinas's theocentrically grounded anthropocentrism is further evident in the very point that defenders of Aquinas use to exonerate him from accusations of anthropocentrism: that the entire created order, in its multiplicity, reveals the glory of God better than one life-form could.[65] It is, after all, not God who requires such a revelation. Furthermore, the revelation can have meaning only for those with the capacity to appropriate it through contemplation (that is, rational creatures).[66] Thus, for Aquinas, "Reasonable creatures...have in some special and higher manner God as their end, since they can attain to Him by their own operations, by knowing and loving Him."[67] If then, at the eschaton, humanity – for whom the multiplicity of creation has revelatory meaning – reaches ultimate happiness understood as the Beatific Vision, the nonhuman creation will be rendered superfluous with regard to this telos. That is, when humanity "sees God as God is," the nonhuman creation will lose one of its central significances – revelation of the divine for humanity. Aquinas's redactor in the supplement to the *ST*'s third part believes this point to be explicit in Aquinas's theology:

> We believe all corporeal things to have been made for man's sake, wherefore all things are stated to be subject to him. Now they serve man in two ways, first, as sustenance to his bodily life, secondly, as helping him to know God, inasmuch as man sees the invisible things of God by the things that are made (Rom. 1:20). Accordingly glorified man will nowise need creatures to render him the first of these services, since his body will be altogether incorruptible, the Divine power effecting this through the soul which it will glorify immediately. Again man will not need the second service as to intellective knowledge, since by that knowledge he will see God immediately in His essence.[68]

According to this passage – constructed from Aquinas's commentary on Peter Lombard's *Sentences* – the corporeal nonhuman creation exists for the sake of nourishing human bodies and revealing God's glory to humanity. As these functions will no longer be necessary for glorified humanity, the redactor holds that Aquinas rejects the presence of the nonhuman creation (with the exception of the simple inanimate matter) at the eschaton.[69] Regarding the presence of nonhuman animals and plants in the renewed world, the redactor states, "If the end cease, those things which are directed to the end should cease. Now animals and plants were made for the upkeep of human life...Therefore when man's animal life ceases, animals and plants should cease."[70]

Consistent with these redacted passages, Aquinas follows Augustine in claiming, "Man's last end is happiness...but 'happiness is not possible for animals bereft of reason'...Therefore other things do not concur in man's last end."[71] Of corporeal creatures only the human has a particular ultimate telos. Happiness, in the ultimate sense, is an end suited only to the nature of humans.[72] As Carlo Leget states, "In Aquinas' theology, 'eternal life' is a name for both the destination of humankind and for God."[73]

Because nonhuman animals lack a rational soul, they also lack the capacity for ultimate happiness – that is, contemplation of the Beatific Vision. In short, for nonhumans the temporal realm is the extent of their particularity.[74] The death of their bodies is the annihilation of their sensitive souls, which in Aquinas's view are necessarily and wholly dependent on their physicality.[75] That is, while the souls of humans are incorruptible, "the souls of brutes are corrupted when their bodies are corrupted."[76] Hence, referencing the incorruptibility that humanity (and the inanimate creation in service to humanity) will attain in the eschaton, Aquinas states, "The other animals, the plants, and the mixed bodies, those entirely corruptible both wholly and in part, will not remain at all in that state of incorruption."[77]

It is thus justifiable to claim that the redacted passages express explicitly what Aquinas strongly implies. The only telos proper to nonhuman animals, both generally and individually, is a temporal telos in which they exist for the sake of humanity, to nourish them and reveal God's glory for contemplative purposes. In other words, the nature of nonhuman animals excludes them from the eschatological community, an exclusion that bears ethical consequences.

This exclusion and its ethical consequences are consistent with Aquinas's understanding of virtue, in which the end informs the manner of moving toward that end. If humanity's ultimate end is one that includes other humans but excludes nonhuman corporeal creatures, the exercise of virtue, which is teleological, will reflect this exclusion. And indeed, Aquinas claims that the extension of charity to nonhuman animals is improper because "charity is based on the fellowship of everlasting happiness, to which the irrational creature cannot attain."[78] In light of these reasons, I believe Jenkins's argument that Aquinas's view demands charitable engagement of the nonhuman creation for its own sake lacks validity.[79]

In my reading, then, Aquinas does not consider nonhuman animals subjects of direct moral concern because their nature precludes them from the purview of God's redemptive scope. Indeed, it is somewhat unclear whether or not Aquinas considers nature in need of redemption even from suffering, predation, and death. He claims that predation is not a sign of the privation of good in the form and integrity of predatory animals.[80] This claim is further evident in his rejection of an edenic state of creation without predation:

> In the opinion of some, those animals which now are fierce and kill others, would, in that state, have been tame, not only in regard to man, but also in regard to other animals. But this is quite unreasonable. For the nature of animals was not changed by man's sin, as if those whose nature now it is to devour the flesh of others, would then have lived on herbs, as the lion and falcon.[81]

Even so, Aquinas does suggest some difference in the relationship between nature and humanity before and after sin. In reply to the objection that God created nonhuman animals that are harmful to humanity, Aquinas states, "Since man before he sinned would have used the things of this world conformably to the order designed, poisonous animals would not have injured him."[82] Presumably, then, sinless humanity used the nonhuman creation according to its natural order, an order that precluded harm to humanity but not harm between animals. In this sense, it is not the poisonous snake but humanity that changed, a change that elicited the harmful actions of the snake.[83]

At any rate, animals do not partake in redemption. Humans, on the other hand, are proper subjects of direct moral concern on account of their rational nature, which is directed toward their ultimate telos.[84] Thus Aquinas states that rational creatures "stand out above other creatures, both in natural perfection and in the dignity of their end."[85] Furthermore,

> There should be a union in affection among those for whom there is one common end. Now, men share in common the one ultimate end which is happiness, to which they are divinely ordered. So, men should be united with each other by a mutual love.[86]

What, then, is the temporal end proper to nonhuman animals? The well-being of humanity. Furthermore, human beings' use of nonhuman life is directed toward humanity's ultimate (and unique) telos: "Man must, of necessity, desire all, whatsoever he desires, for the last end."[87] The nature of nonhuman animals renders them resources meant to meet the needs of human creatures, both contemplative and bodily, as they journey toward God.[88] It is this point that Mark Wynn fails to address sufficiently in his defense of Aquinas. He claims that nonhuman animals have value independent of humanity in their showing forth of the divine goodness. Yet for Aquinas even this showing forth is always a showing forth *for humanity*. It is thus an anthropocentrism grounded in theocentrism. Nonhuman resources, lacking the dignity of human nature, have no grounds for direct moral concern. Thus Aquinas echoes Aristotle: "There is no sin in using a thing for the purpose for which it is [created] ... Wherefore it is not unlawful if man use plants for the good of animals, and animals for the good of man, as the Philosopher states."[89]

Aquinas's indirect protection of nonhuman animals

Aquinas's theocentrically grounded anthropocentric framework notwith-standing, he does present challenges regarding present practices toward nonhuman animals. These challenges, however, which are always directed toward concern for human well-being, take the form of conservation of the order of the cosmos. While this conservation remains anthropocentric in that the ethical concern it elicits is always directed toward the entire human community in relation to God – and thus only indirectly toward nonhumans – it nonetheless provides a possible foundation for critique of certain practices directed at nonhuman animals. This foundation elicits three central forms of indirect concern for creatures that lack a rational nature.

First, Aquinas expresses concern that humans causing gratuitous harm to nonhuman animals might lead to the desensitization of the one causing the harm. This desensitization, in turn, could lead to violence against other humans. Says Aquinas,

> Indeed, if any statements are found in Sacred Scripture prohibiting the commission of an act of cruelty against brute animals...this is said either to turn the mind of man away from cruelty which might be used on other men, lest a person through practicing cruelty on brutes might go on to do the same to men; or because an injurious act committed on animals may lead to a temporal loss for some man.[90]

In other words, causing harm to sensitive creatures where there is no basis for direct moral concern could lead to causing harm to sensitive creatures where there is such a basis.

It is worthy of note that Aquinas defends the goodness of creation in a context untouched by Cartesian presuppositions and industrialism. It is also important to see that Aquinas does not share Descartes's mechanistic view of animals. Aquinas's context ought to provide some grounds for a gracious reading of his work. Although his moral concern for animals is indirect and essentially anthropocentric, the possibilities he nonetheless provides of developing this point in the direction of animal welfare are significant.

The second reason nonhuman animals warrant (indirect) moral concern pertains to a dimension of their temporal telos. I have already noted that, in Aquinas's thought, God is the ultimate good of the entire created order. For nonhuman animals, God is the ultimate good in the sense that they are directed toward temporal ends consistent with their natures. As these creatures seek those temporal ends, they display a multiplicity in the created order that reveals God's goodness. If humans abuse a part of the created order to the point of causing extinction, the diversity in creation lessens. Since the diversity expresses God's goodness, the lessening of that diversity is, in a sense, the lessening of the revelation of God's goodness. Said differently, human activity that lessens the diversity of creation simultaneously robs humanity of the fullest potential to contemplate the divine. As Clifford notes,

> From the perspective of an ecological theology based on Aquinas's insights, the destruction of our earthly habitat suggests that discernible traces of the Trinity are lost. When species are made extinct, a unique manifestation of the goodness of God is gone forever.[91]

Likewise, Jenkins states, "With the extinction of species and the despoiling of places we degrade our aptitude for naming and praising God."[92] Hence, Joyce Salisbury overstates her critique when she writes, "Here on earth there [is] no need to preserve animals that [are] seen as 'useless'."[93] Aquinas's understanding of the revelatory nature of the universe in its multiplicity renders no creature "useless," for all creatures participate in revealing God's goodness more fully. Furthermore, Aquinas's view suggests that his critics overstate their case when they claim that he concerns himself only with harm to animals that *may* elicit harm to humans,[94] for an act against creation that lessens divine revelation is harmful to humanity *in and of itself*. Given these points, one can rightly claim that utilization with disregard for conservation is morally reprehensible for Aquinas.[95] Again, though, the suffering caused to nonhuman animals is not directly the moral issue. On this point Aquinas's critics are correct. The detrimental result of that suffering for humanity is the issue, though the two acts occur simultaneously in this case.

A third way in which Aquinas posits moral concern for nonhuman animals regards a second dimension of their temporal telos. In Aquinas's theological framework, nonhuman animals "are ordered to man's use in the natural course of things, according to divine providence."[96] On account of this view, Aquinas maintains that humans may use nonhuman animals "without any injustice, either by killing them or by employing them in any other way."[97] However, Aquinas takes issue with the destruction of a nonhuman animal that belongs to someone else: "He that kills another's ox, sins, not through killing the ox, but through injuring another man in his property."[98] This claim, predicated as it is upon the relegation of nonhuman animals to the condition of property, certainly lacks anything akin to animal rights and would cause a level of distress in many interested in animal welfare. Nonetheless, one could develop this notion through critical retrieval along the lines of the question of property, especially regarding the earth itself.

These three points broadly frame Aquinas's position vis-à-vis the appropriate moral disposition of humans toward nonhuman animals. However, they also recall factors that highlight Aquinas's limits in this vein. On the one hand, humans must preserve the natural order in its beautiful and good multiplicity. On the other hand, for Aquinas this preservation must be for the sake of humanity *in via* toward its unique telos. Thus, while Aquinas does provide significant contributions regarding ethical concern for nonhumans, his theological framework can shelter neither claims of direct moral concern nor an eco-theological ethics that transcends anthropocentric conservation. For Aquinas, humanity, in accordance with the providential ordering of nature, bears the entitlement to benefit from the suffering and death of nonhuman animals. However, this entitlement is carefully qualified by concern for human welfare corresponding to the common good with regard to bodily and contemplative needs and to personal well-being with regard to property.

Conclusion

I have argued that at the intersection of nature, teleology, and virtue, Aquinas's thought is both anthropocentric and conservationist. To grant nonhuman animals direct moral concern would require rejecting either Aquinas's understanding of their nature (and therefore the rights attached to human nature) or the scope of his eschatology (which is based on his understanding of nature). It is difficult, then, to see how even a critical retrieval – unless it rejected points so foundational to Aquinas that it would jeopardize central pillars of his thought – could provide more than the indirect moral concern of a conservationist ethics directed toward human well-being.

If Christian theology is content with such an ethics, Aquinas is a fine resource for delineating it. However, if there are discontents with the denial of direct moral concern to nonhumans (animals in particular), if there are discontents with anthropocentrism or the ethical limits of conservationism, I do not find Aquinas particularly helpful in addressing them. For this task, it would be more helpful to look to other Christian voices – to countertraditions – of which there is no shortage. Such is the task I undertake in later chapters. Before doing so, I examine the manner in which what I have labeled the dominant tradition – evident in Aquinas's theological thought regarding nonhuman animals – has been appropriated in the magisterial documents of the Roman Catholic Church.

2
The Dominant Tradition and the Magisterium

In the previous chapter I argue that the eco-theological vision of Saint Thomas Aquinas is limited to the conservation of the nonhuman creation for the sake of all human beings, specifically for their bodily nourishment and spiritual knowledge. Aquinas grounds his anthropocentric position firmly within a cosmological theocentrism such that the latter solidifies the former. It is my claim that this understanding represents the dominant view in Christian thought.

In this chapter I seek to explore how this dominant view is taken up today in the magisterial documents of the Roman Catholic Church. To focus this endeavor, I examine documents from Vatican II to the present, including papal speeches by both John Paul II and Benedict XVI, statements from conferences of bishops in North America, and the revised *Catechism of the Catholic Church* released during the papacy of John Paul II. I believe these documents are sufficient to make the case that the magisterium has largely taken up the vision of Aquinas. However, they also highlight some interesting tensions that leave hints of ambiguity with regard to the details of the Catholic Church's eco-theological position.

Before going any further, however, I must make three points clear. First, what follows is *my* reading of these documents. I am certainly not under the impression that I have the only valid interpretation. Second – and by way of reiteration of my cautionary words in the Introduction of the present work – while I find the dominant tradition (and therefore the magisterial position) deeply unsatisfying, I am not here claiming that the Catholic Church is wrong in its position on animals. My aim is neither to indict nor convict but to clarify the dominant tradition and shed light onto its alternatives. Third, this chapter is limited to the official documents of the Roman Catholic Church. I do not claim that what follows is emblematic of any individual Catholic theologian. Indeed, devout Catholics like Thomas Berry,[1] William French,[2] and Jame Schaefer[3] have gone to great lengths to challenge the dominant tradition, especially with regard to anthropocentrism.[4]

I make these points especially because I am not Roman Catholic. On principle, I am more hesitant to engage critically a tradition of which I am not a part. Therefore, what I offer here is meant with humility – as a contribution to an ongoing conversation, not its close.

Vatican II

The documents of Vatican II are, for the most part, silent on issues of animal welfare. The historic council offers significant claims about universal human dignity, the religious other, and the nature of the church vis-à-vis the world. These were its foci. Even so, from these significant claims one can glean certain reiterations of the dominant tradition with regard to anthropocentrism. These reiterations are most clear in the council's assertions about the *imago Dei* ("image of God") and the common good. I thus begin with these themes and then offer what I believe to be solid inferences based on them about the council's view concerning animals.

The documents of Vatican II and the intentions of their authors remain hotly debated when it comes to the council's position regarding the status of non-Christians. However, far more universally accepted is the acknowledgement that the council makes a clear proclamation concerning the intrinsic value of the religious other. This proclamation derives from the affirmation that the religious other bears the image of God. Specifically, *Nostra Aetate* ("In Our Time") – the council's "Declaration on the Relation of the Church to Non-Christian Religions" – states,

> We cannot truly call on God, the Father of all, if we refuse to treat in a brotherly way any man, created as he is in the image of God. Man's relation to God the Father and his relation to men his brothers are so linked together that Scripture says: "He who does not love does not know God" (1 John 4:8). No foundation therefore remains for any theory or practice that leads to discrimination between man and man or people and people, so far as their human dignity and the rights flowing from it are concerned.[5]

Whatever ambiguities penetrate the council regarding the soteriological status of the religious other, here is a patent affirmation that he or she is intrinsically valuable and worthy of rights. The religious other bears the *imago Dei* and as such must not become the object of discrimination. In short, the divine image in all humans mandates recognition of universal human dignity, requiring that all people be treated in a "brotherly way."

Regarding the call to a universal extension of charity in the temporal realm, *Apostolicam Actuositatem* ("Apostolic Activity") – the council's decree on the apostolic work of laity in the church – states, "In order that the exercise of charity on this scale [that is, a global scale] may be unexceptionable in appearance as well as in fact, it is altogether necessary that one should consider in one's neighbor the image of God in which he has been created."[6] Hence, the council grounds the call to charity and neighborly love in the claim that all humans bear the image of God. In the same paragraph, the council links this claim to the acknowledgment of a universal "freedom and dignity of the person" in acts of both charity and justice.[7]

Gaudium et Spes ("Joy and Hope") – the council's pastoral constitution regarding the church's role vis-à-vis the world – espouses an equality for all humans based on the significance of them bearing God's likeness:

> Since all men possess a rational soul and are created in God's likeness, since they have the same nature and origin, have been redeemed by Christ and enjoy the same divine calling and destiny, the basic equality of all must receive increasingly greater recognition.[8]

Here, the council connects the possession of a rational soul – which Aquinas links to the *imago* – with the "likeness" of God, which here appears synonymous with the term "image."[9] More clearly, the *imago* denotes the affirmation of both a common human nature and the eschatological destiny of human beings. These affirmations lead to the call for the recognition of equality – here taking the contextual connotation of human dignity – for all persons.

There are other emphases of the *imago* in the conciliar documents. However, even where dignity is not the primary point of the council's use of the doctrine, it is rarely if ever excluded. For instance, the council is adamant in affirming that Christ is the image of God.[10] However, even in these instances, the reality of God incarnate further solidifies the dignity of the human creature.[11] *Gaudium et Spes* associates the *imago* with human freedom: "For its part, authentic freedom is an exceptional sign of the divine image within man."[12] The text goes on to claim that "man's dignity demands that he act according to a knowing and free choice that is personally motivated and prompted from within."[13] Hence, the council again links dignity to the *imago Dei*.

Elsewhere *Gaudium et Spes* relates human dignity to the call to communion with God: "The root reason for human dignity lies in man's call to communion with God."[14] Later, the text states,

> God, Who has fatherly concern for everyone, has willed that all men should constitute one family and treat one another in a spirit of brotherhood. For having been created in the image of God ... all men are called to one and the same goal, namely God Himself.[15]

Here, the council directly links the call to communion with God to humanity's bearing the image of God. The syllogism is simple:

1. The root reason for human dignity is humanity's call to communion with God;
2. The call to communion with God derives from humanity's creation as *imago Dei*;
3. Therefore, humanity's creation in the image of God constitutes the root reason for human dignity.

This brief survey reveals that, even when human dignity is not explicitly associated with the *imago*, the two are never far separated. (I address the doctrine of the *imago Dei* more specifically in Chapters 3 and 5. For now, I simply note that the primary intention of the council's use of the doctrine is the establishment of a universal status of dignity for all members of the human community.) The possession of the image of God renders all humans equal with regard to dignity and rights. Furthermore, the *imago* entails the common origin of and destiny for the human creature. This reading is echoed in the catechism, which states that "the dignity of the human person is rooted in his creation in the image and likeness of God."[16] Such a vision of human dignity continues in postconciliar documents. In Pope Paul VI's *Populorum Progressio*, he too states that the human creature has been endowed with unique characteristics to reach a "higher state of perfection," which is union with God.[17] In short, "Man becomes truly man only by passing beyond himself."[18] Paul VI is building on the same foundations as Pope John XXIII's *Pacem in Terris*: "All men are united by their common origin and fellowship, their redemption by Christ, and their supernatural destiny."[19] One finds these same emphases in Pope John Paul II's *Redemptoris Hominis*.[20]

The council's use of the *imago* implies that the nonhuman creation, including animals, lacks whatever dignity results from humanity's exclusive possession of the *imago*. However, on its own this conciliar emphasis on the status of dignity that all humans bear as a result of the *imago* does not necessitate a clear form of anthropocentrism in the sense that all of the nonhuman creation exists for the sake of humans. Only when one reads the status of humanity in conjunction with the council's claims about the common good does the reiteration of the dominant tradition come into sharp relief.

David Hollenbach notes that though many thinkers in the West have appealed to the notion of the common good, the definition is elusive.[21] However, one can explore how the term functions in a particular framework. With regard to the nonhuman creation, Vatican II follows the principle of the "universal destination of all goods":

> God intended the earth with *everything contained in it* for the use of all human beings and peoples. Thus, under the leadership of justice and in the company of charity, created goods should be in abundance for all in like manner. Whatever the forms of property may be, as adapted to the legitimate institutions of peoples, according to diverse and changeable circumstances, attention must always be paid to this universal destination of earthly goods. In using them, therefore, man should regard the external things that he legitimately possesses not only as his own but also as common in the sense that they should be able to benefit not only him but also others.[22]

The sense of this passage is that all of the nonhuman creation – "the earth and everything contained in it" – constitutes a network of goods that belong to the entire human community and therefore should be distributed equitably among the members of that community. In other words, the nonhuman world is essentially reduced to its instrumental value for all humans, whose dignity entitles them to benefit from these resources.[23]

At the intersection of the *imago Dei* and the common good, two categories take shape. First, there is a community comprising all human beings, each of whom bears the image of God. Second, there are goods that must be justly distributed to all members of that community. These goods include "the earth and everything contained in it." These categories betray a deep anthropocentrism very much in line with that of Aquinas.

In line with this interpretation, *Gaudium et Spes* states that humanity's destiny of communion with God is consummate with the claim that humanity "is the *only* creature on earth which *God willed for itself*."[24] The council goes on to state:

> There is a growing awareness of the exalted dignity proper to the human person, since he stands above all things, and his rights and duties are universal and inviolable. Therefore, there must be made available to all men everything necessary for leading a life truly human, such as food, clothing, and shelter.[25]

From these claims arises a clear delineation of the categories of community and resource. Humans constitute the former. Animals, it seems, fall into the latter, destined by human right for the equitable use as food, clothing, and shelter of the entire human community.

Pope John Paul II

Like the council that ended during his predecessor Paul VI's papacy, Pope John Paul II makes admirable contributions to the Catholic emphasis on human dignity and the church's mission of service in the world. However, unlike the council John Paul offers more explicit statements concerning the nonhuman creation. These statements include his 1990 message *Peace with God the Creator, Peace with All of Creation*[26] and his 2002 *Common Declaration on Environmental Ethics*, written in conjunction with the Orthodox Patriarch Bartholomew I.[27]

The pope delivered *Peace with God the Creator* at the 1990 celebration of the World Day of Peace. In it, he seeks to address the ecological crisis by arguing for the conservation of the present order of creation for the sake of humanity. He opens by claiming that world peace is threatened "by a lack of *due respect for nature*, by the plundering of natural resources and by a progressive decline in the quality of life."[28]

To address this threat, John Paul begins by drawing on the revelation of scripture to establish a foundation for ecological concern. Four basic elements constitute this revelatory framework: (1) creation is good according to its Creator; (2) human beings, bearing the image of God and all the "abilities and gifts which distinguish the human being from all other creatures," are to serve a role in creation, governing "with wisdom and love" and thus aiding in God's plan for the entire creation; (3) human sin disrupted (and continues to disrupt) God's plan for creation; (4) *all of creation* has been subjected to futility and waits for redemption and participation in "a glorious liberty together with all the children of God."[29]

While this revelatory foundation suggests that the harmonious relationships in the created order have been disrupted by sin but will be resumed in the eschaton, the pope follows this foundation with the claim that the root of the ecological crisis is "a callous disregard for the hidden, yet perceivable requirements of the order and harmony which govern nature itself."[30] One is left to wonder how the current "order and harmony" in the natural order stands in relation to the original harmony that human sin disrupted. That is, in what sense is the order of the nonhuman creation affected by the original sin of humanity? An additional question is how the current natural order differs from the eschatological hope to which John Paul refers earlier in his message. What do freedom and redemption look like for the nonhuman creation – especially if, according to Vatican II, its purpose is exhausted in its instrumental usefulness for humans?

The tension between the protological, present, and eschatological states of nature finds some relief in John Paul's emphasis on a balance between preservation and conservational utility:

> Theology, philosophy and science all speak of a harmonious universe, of a "cosmos" endowed with its own integrity, its own internal, dynamic balance. This order must be respected. The human race is called to explore this order, to examine it with due care and to make use of it while safeguarding its integrity.[31]

In both his use of the phrase "respect for life"[32] and his concern for creation, John Paul's interest ends up being an affirmation of concern for human well-being – the distribution of the earth's resources,[33] including an intelligent use of creation that preserves it for later generations. Thus, whatever the original state of creation may have been, whatever the future hope for creation might be, the present state is governed by a harmonious order – one requiring immense and gratuitous amounts of suffering and death[34] – that directs nonhuman life to human well-being. Human sin, then, appears to be nothing other than the unjust use of nonhuman resources, by which is meant their inequitable distribution, including violations of creation's integrity that threaten the system of resources for future generations.

In line with this emphasis, John Paul denounces any ecological responsibility "based on a rejection of the modern world or a vague desire to return to some 'paradise lost.'"[35] Although the pope's theological foundation recognizes something akin to a paradise lost and an eschatological hope that includes the entire cosmos, here that foundation is denied as acceptable for an ecological ethic. Given the pope's theological framework, such a move is a bit confusing. After all, if humans are to participate in God's plan for the created order, which includes an eschatological vision of harmony between all creatures, why is it theologically acceptable merely to preserve the present (and presumably fallen) order?

At any rate, John Paul summarizes his position by declaring:

> There is an order in the universe which must be respected, and that the human person, endowed with the capability of choosing freely, has a grave responsibility to preserve this order for the well-being of future generations.[36]

In the end, the concern seems not to be for the futility and suffering of creation but rather the well-being of the human community, a point quite consistent with the dominant tradition I present in Chapter 1.

In his *Common Declaration on Environmental Ethics*, John Paul writes, "Almighty God envisioned a world of beauty and harmony, and He created it, making every part an expression of His freedom, wisdom and love."[37] God gifted human beings with unique qualities: "an immortal soul, the source of self-awareness and freedom, endowments that make us in His image and likeness." This special giftedness is coupled with a special responsibility. "We have been placed by God in the world in order to cooperate with Him in realizing more and more fully the divine purpose for creation." As in his earlier message, the pope notes that the original harmony of the created order was disrupted by human sin. However, "God has not abandoned the world. It is His will that His design and our hope for it will be realized through our co-operation in restoring its original harmony."

As before, this theological framework ultimately leads to the practical claim that the human community, both present and future, should share and use the earth and its resources. Indeed, "Respect for creation stems from respect for human life and dignity." Furthermore, the pope calls people "to use science and technology in a full and constructive way, while recognizing that the findings of science have always to be evaluated in the light of the centrality of the human person, of the common good and of the inner purpose of creation."[38]

Pope Benedict XVI

Pope Benedict XVI's major eco-theological contribution is his 2010 message at the World Day of Peace, *If You Want to Cultivate Peace, Protect*

Creation.[39] The aim of his speech is the peace of the human race, which requires the conservation of the created order – most of all "the earth and the natural goods that God has given us."[40] Benedict goes on to claim, "The environment must be seen as God's gift to all people, and the use we make of it entails a shared responsibility for all humanity, especially the poor and future generations."[41] Thus, the concern for the nonhuman creation is derivative of human well-being. In other words, it is indirect. Benedict reiterates this indirect concern when he includes the "loss of biodiversity" in the category of "conflicts involving access to natural resources," all of which "are issues with a profound impact on the exercise of human rights, such as the right to life, food, health, and development."[42]

It is in this line of thinking that he writes, "Our duties toward the environment flow from our duties towards the person, considered both individually and in relation to others."[43] This passage highlights an interesting tension in Benedict's speech. At one point he makes a distinction between "natural resources" and "living creatures," the latter including nonhuman animals: "Natural resources should be used in such a way that immediate benefits do not have a negative impact on living creatures, human and not, present and future."[44] This claim sits in an uneasy tension with his previous intimation that species extinction pertains to the unjust distribution of natural resources. One is left to wonder whether animals are part of the "gift" of God to all humans or in some other undefined category.

Furthermore, Benedict echoes the ambiguity of John Paul II in relation to notions like harmony and fallenness. He notes that the original design of the cosmos is clearly depicted in Genesis 1. However,

> The harmony between the Creator, mankind and the created world, as described by Sacred Scripture, was disrupted by the sin of Adam and Eve, by man and woman, who wanted to take the place of god and refused to acknowledge that they were his creatures. As a result the work of "exercising dominion" over the earth, "tilling and keeping it," was also disrupted, and conflict arose within and between mankind and the rest of creation.[45]

This disruption includes humanity's despotic attempts to dominate the created order. The proper relationship of humanity to the earth is that of stewardship over a "gift of the Creator, who gave it an inbuilt order and enabled man to draw from it the principles needed to 'till and keep it.'"[46]

Benedict goes no further than this general claim with regard to the nature of original harmony or to what humanity's "provoking a rebellion on the part of nature" means.[47] However, it does not seem that the original harmony/order of the cosmos precluded an anthropocentric understanding of the "goods" of creation.[48] Following Vatican II, Benedict writes, "The goods of creation belong to humanity as a whole."[49] Humanity includes both all present peoples and all future generations. Thus, humans bear a moral obligation to other humans "for the protection and care of the environment."[50]

What such a mandate means for nonhuman animals is unclear. However, elsewhere Benedict excludes them from the community for which the goods of creation are due. In *Caritas in Veritate*, he defines the common good as "the good of 'all of us,' made up of individuals, families and intermediate groups who together constitute society."[51] Here animals seem to be included in the category of the goods of creation destined for human use.

Bishops' statements

In this section, I focus on two statements made by national bishop councils. I limit my focus to North America, including the United States and Canada. Each of these councils of bishops addresses problems particular to its context and seeks to apply Catholic social teaching as a remedy for ecological abuse. In doing so, both reveal certain affirmations of the dominant tradition but also echo the tensions I detected above in other magisterial pronouncements.

Renewing the Earth (United States)

In 1991 the United States Conference of Catholic Bishops (USCCB) issued a pastoral statement entitled *Renewing the Earth*.[52] In it the bishops provide a clear expression of their aims by listing six goals. They seek to "highlight the ethical dimensions of the environmental crisis"; explore the link of "ecology and poverty"; express the preferential option for the poor in ecological concerns; "promote a vision of a just and sustainable world community"; invite both Catholics and non-Catholics to "reflect more deeply on the religious dimensions" of ecological concern; and initiate "broader conversation on the potential contribution of the Church to environmental questions."[53] These aims already highlight the dominant tradition I delineate in Chapter 1. However, there are tensions within the text concerning this tradition.

In order to achieve their aims, the bishops explore facets of the Roman Catholic perspective, including Scripture and themes of Catholic social teaching. The biblical vision presented in the document emphasizes, from the Hebrew Scriptures, the goodness of the world, the praise of creation, the earth as a gift to all living creatures, the connection between ecological degradation and human sin (which "results in suffering for all creation"), and the principle of the Sabbath as an affirmation of the world's kinship before God.[54] From the Second Testament, the bishops emphasize Jesus's inauguration of the year of Jubilee, which, in line with Romans 8:18–25, brings liberation for the entire creation. They also highlight the reconciliatory nature of Jesus's work for both humans and the nonhuman creation, which reenables a true attitude of "respect" for the world.[55]

From the perspective of Catholic social teaching, the bishops delineate seven dimensions they deem pertinent for ecological concern. The first is the sacramentality of the universe, which includes the revelatory nature of the cosmos vis-à-vis humanity. The world is sacramental because it "discloses the Creator's presence by visible and tangible signs."[56]

The second is "respect" for life. The exact nature of this respect – or how the respect for nonhuman life compares to respect for humanity – is somewhat unclear. The bishops affirm Aquinas's claim that the diversity of life witnesses to God's beauty. They go on to write,

> Accordingly, it is appropriate that we treat other creatures and the natural world not just as means to human fulfillment but also as God's creatures, *possessing an independent value*, worthy of our respect and care.[57]

Here the bishops seem to break with the anthropocentrism of Aquinas by acknowledging intrinsic value in the nonhuman creation. However, this break is so brief and the meaning of it so vague that it offers little clear practical consequence for human activity. Furthermore, most of the aspects of respect listed by the letter (preservation, protection of endangered species, balance with ecosystems) entail an affirmation of the integrity of creation as it is and a balance between utility (use of the gifts of creation) and preservation (protecting the environment).[58] There is little concern offered for *individual* creatures (or even those species not endangered), who presumably would also have intrinsic value. The central concern is the conservation of systems of life – for the human community, that is.

The third dimension of Catholic social teaching the bishops examine is the common good.[59] In a global context, the letter affirms Pope John XXIII's expansion of the community to constitute that to which the good is due (thus the "common good") so as to include the global community. That is to say, in a world in which globalization is undeniable, the nation-state can no longer serve as the base unit for consideration of the common good.

This emphasis on the global common good brings up an interesting tension in the statement. Does humanity constitute the boundaries of the community to which the good is due? If so, is all that is other than human (from rocks to apes) merely part of the good? Said differently, is the world divided into persons and things, community and resources, because it is divided into human and nonhuman? Earlier in the text, the bishops seem to separate the earth from living creatures.[60] They note that animals are included in God's postdiluvian covenant. However, the result of this inclusion is the claim "We are not free, therefore, to use created things capriciously."[61] Thus a tension remains. Use is certainly not precluded, but capricious use is. But such a claim would apply to all "things" of the created order, not just animals. Thus, the specific ethical status of the nonhuman animal is left ambiguous.

However, that the phrase "common good" intimates the *human* community seems to be the intention of the bishops, who speak of a "new solidarity" – the fourth dimension – in the context of globalization.[62] The point here, ecologically speaking, is that it is no longer possible to speak of the suffering of another people as "their" suffering. The human community is now so economically interconnected that all human suffering is "our" suffering; that is, the community's suffering. As such, the new solidarity is nothing short of the recognition and embrace of the global community. It is to this community, it appears, that the goods of the earth are due, a point evident in the bishops' reiteration of the universal destination of all goods – the fifth dimension – which I address below.

The aforementioned dimensions lead to a sixth: the principle of the preferential option for the poor. The bishops state, "The poor of the earth offer a special test of our solidarity."[63] The poor have a right to express their dignity through work. They also have a right to use of the goods of the earth in a manner that meets their needs. Thus, the aim of progress must be the entire human community in the context of the created order, as opposed to only certain privileged groups. Such is the point of "authentic development" – the seventh dimension – which intimates something along the lines of virtuous development, for it "supports moderation and even austerity in the use of material resources."[64]

I have saved the fifth dimension for last because it most clearly illustrates the division of community and goods in the USCCB's letter. It is "The Universal Purpose of Created Things."[65] The bishops write, "God has given the fruit of the earth to sustain the entire human family." Therefore,

> In moving toward an environmentally sustainable economy, we are obligated to work for a just economic system which equitably shares the bounty of the earth and of human enterprise with all peoples. Created things belong not to the few, but to the entire human family.[66]

While not explicitly including animals in the category of "created things," this statement seems to imply – especially when read in conjunction with the catechism, which I explore below – that human use of animals as resources is justified provided humans exercise such use in a manner conducive to preservation and equitable distribution. Said differently, all members of the human community have a right to the "bounty of the earth," to "created things," of which animals seems to be a part.

Having delineated these theological foundations for ecological concern, the bishops also make an effort to clarify what they are *not* saying. Three particular points are made here. First, the bishops affirm divine immanence in the sense of the sacramentality of the world. However, they repudiate the position of pantheism. In line with this claim, the bishops call for an "ordered love for creation," which "is ecological without being ecocentric."[67] Second, while affirming the spiritual dimension of the created order, the bishops distance themselves from a romanticism that rejects the place of human reason in scientific discovery.[68] Finally, the bishops affirm the place of love in ecological awareness, further emphasizing the significance of virtue. However, they carefully distance themselves from the dilemma of choosing between people and the earth.[69] For them, the solution is, not either/or, but both/and.

The bishops then turn to the specific role of human beings in the cosmos. They delineate this role in terms of stewardship and the act of cocreation. The uniqueness of the human creature, while constituting great status for that creature, also entails a special and serious responsibility to care for the created order, including every single human being.[70]

**"You Love All That Exists ... All Things Are Yours, God,
Lover of Life ... " (Canada)**

In 2003, the Canadian Conference of Catholic Bishops issued a pastoral
letter addressing ecological concern in their context.[71] There are many
themes that are similar to the USCCB's letter, including both the recognition of ecological degradation in both the destruction of habitat and
loss of biodiversity and the claim that Catholic social teaching bears the
potential to stymie this degradation. Regarding the status of nonhuman
animals, however, the letter makes three key contributions.

First, the ecological crisis entails, in part, the loss of biodiversity. This
loss is problematic inasmuch as it lessens the revelation of the divine in
the vast complexity of the cosmos. Thus, "In destroying creation we are
limiting our ability to know and love God."[72] The loss is further evident
in the depleted resources for human use. It is in this sense that the
Canadian bishops can cite, as an example of the ecological crisis, "the
closing of the once overwhelmingly bountiful cod fishery in Quebec,
Newfoundland and Labrador."[73] The combination of concern for the
spiritual value of the creation and its value as economic and nutritional
sustenance suggests that the ecological crisis is first and foremost an
issue of social justice.

This claim is validated by the second important contribution added
by the Canadian bishops. They clearly list animals in the category of
resources:

> The bible ... teaches about an equitable distribution of resources,
> including sharing land, *animals* and water. This insistence on justice
> is often directed towards distributing the bounty of the earth and
> providing for those who are marginalized.[74]

This passage is among the clearest in papal statements and bishops'
letters regarding the instrumental reduction of animals. They are listed
alongside land and water as "resources" that ought to be shared justly
among the peoples of the earth.

Third, the bishops reiterate the tension between the intrinsic and
instrumental value of the nonhuman creation:

> Creation and the redemptive Incarnation of the Son of God are
> inextricably linked. Through his Incarnation, Jesus Christ not only
> entered and embraced our humanity; he also entered and *embraced all*
> *of God's creation.* Thus all creatures, great and small, are consecrated
> in the life, death and resurrection of Christ. This is why the Church

does not hesitate to bless and *make generous use of the earth's materials* in liturgical celebrations and sacraments. This is also why, in Catholic social thought, the common good should be conceived as the sustenance and flourishing of life *for all beings* and for future generations. The call for a "new solidarity" should take into consideration not only the economic needs of all people but also environmental protection *in order to provide for all*. The principle of the social mortgage on private property should include an "ecological mortgage" on *the goods of creation* (for this as well as future generations). The preferential option for the poor can be extended to include a preferential option for the earth, made poorer by human abuse.[75]

This passage raises many questions. In what manner is the Son's incarnation consecratory for "all of God's creation"? Are animals included in the phrase "the earth's materials"? If the common good "should be conceived as the sustenance and flourishing of life for all beings" – presumably for their own sake – why are those beings described as resources for human benefit or "the goods of creation"? Are they part of the community, or are they resources to be equitably distributed to that community?

These questions require further clarification. Until then, it seems acceptable to read the position of Canadian bishops as being in line with the dominant tradition. The goods of creation should be preserved for the ultimate purpose that all humans, both present and future, can benefit from them. This reading is further viable considering that the Catholic bishops of Northern Canada defended fur trapping as a justified way of life for those who derive their livelihood from the practice. Notably, the document was called *Harvesting Wildlife in the Canadian North: A Question of Cultural Survival of Aboriginal Peoples*.[76] The term "harvesting" suggests an instrumental view of animals that places them on the same plain as fruits and vegetables.

The catechism

By way of drawing this chapter toward a close, I now consider the most recent catechism of the Roman Catholic Church, issued during the papacy of John Paul II. The Anglican animal theologian Andrew Linzey engages this work, arguing that it is an example of Christian thought perpetuating cruelty. In his reading, the catechism "represents in a clear and dramatic way how unenlightened official Christian teaching still is about animal welfare."[77] Linzey's central critique is evident in his claim that the catechism acknowledges animals as God's creatures that are due kindness but also embraces "a wholly instrumentalist understanding of their status as resources for human use."[78] He also suggests, "It is absolutely vital that all who care for animals make known their opposition to this *Catechism.*"[79]

Is Linzey's assessment accurate? I remain agnostic concerning his claim that all those interested in animal welfare must oppose the catechism. Such a position seems a bit strong (I note in Chapter 1 that Aquinas's position and the dominant tradition it perpetuates bear some potential for the animal welfare movement if properly applied to the contemporary context). However, I do believe that Linzey's estimation that the catechism betrays both an anthropocentrism and an instrumentalist view of animals is correct. For this reason, I believe that the catechism helps clarify some of the tensions in magisterial documents I noted above. That is, the catechism reveals the Roman Catholic Church's ongoing approval of the dominant tradition.

Linzey rightly notes that the catechism limits its emphasis on animals to four paragraphs.[80] However, other paragraphs bear relevance to the discussion of the moral standing of animals in Roman Catholic thought. I begin with these paragraphs and end with the four that deal specifically with animals.

First, in its discussion of human beings as the image of God, the catechism reiterates and affirms the claim of *Gaudium et Spes* that the human being is the only creature "that God has willed for its own sake."[81] Already this claim suggests that all other corporeal creatures are willed for the sake of humans. Furthermore, the possession of the divine image "is the fundamental reason for [humanity's] dignity."[82] Therefore, whatever lacks the divine image – that is, all other corporeal creatures – also lacks the dignity associated with it. The catechism then goes on to delineate clearly two categories, the *imago* serving as the dividing line between the two: "Being in the image of God the human individual possesses the dignity of a person, who is not just something, but someone."[83] In line with this distinction, the text states, "God created everything for man."[84] Collectively, then, the catechism holds that only the human creature, made in the image of God and bearing the unique dignity that accompanies that status, exists for his or her own sake; all other corporeal creatures exist, not for themselves, but for the human being. Humans are persons; everything else, including animals, falls into the category of things.

Such is the manner of the divine intention for the world. This claim leads to a second point the catechism offers vis-à-vis the nonhuman creation. The original harmony, whatever it might entail, does not intimate a nonanthropocentric or noninstrumentalist view of animals. The original human was created "in harmony with himself and with the creation around him."[85] This harmony comprises part of the state of "original justice."[86] This state of harmonious justice is lost with the introduction of sin into the world.[87] The exact nature of this harmony and its disruption in the face of sin is unclear. However, since the catechism makes clear that all creation exists for the sake of human beings, one can surmise that the issue is not the pain of the created order itself but rather its consequences for the human person. Thus, the text states that the result of the Fall is that the "visible creation has become alien and hostile *to man*."[88] The catechism does maintain the notion of creation's subjection to decay but makes no clear claim about the meaning of this notion or its ethical corollaries.[89]

The third point the catechism makes clear is that nonhuman animals are best categorized as part of the good to be distributed to the human community. That is, they are resources. This point is perhaps most evident in the fact that the entire section on the integrity of the cosmos – of which the four paragraphs about nonhuman animals are a part – falls under the larger section (Article 7) on the seventh commandment: "You shall not steal."[90] Oddly, there is not a single mention of animals under the heading of the Sabbath commandment.[91] In fact, the reference to the Sabbath command from Exodus 20:8–10 (which is the citation offered by the catechism) is completely bereft of its mention of animals.[92]

The text states that the seventh commandment "forbids unjustly taking or keeping *the goods* of one's neighbor and wronging him in any way *with respect to his goods*."[93] Animals thus fall under the article dealing with the "goods" that belong to human beings. This classification highlights that the magisterium understands animals as resources. They are goods to be justly distributed to the community for which God created them.

These three points provide the proper context to discuss the catechism's specific address of the place of nonhuman animals in Catholic thought. This address begins thus: "The seventh commandment enjoins respect for the integrity of creation. Animals, like plants and inanimate beings, are *by nature destined for the common good of past, present, and future humanity*."[94] The catechism limits this claim, noting, "Use of the mineral, vegetable, and animal *resources* of the universe cannot be divorced from respect for moral imperatives."[95] Note that animals are included in the same category as plants and rocks. Furthermore, there is a clear reference to animals as resources destined for just distribution in the human community. There thus seems to be no categorical distinction between rocks and animals, a claim that recalls the position of the Jesuit Joseph Rickaby: "Animals are of the number of *things*"; therefore, "We have...no duties of charity, nor duties of any kind, to the lower animals, as neither to stocks and stones."[96]

However, the catechism also maintains that humans must not violate moral imperatives in utilizing these resources. Indeed, "Man's dominion over inanimate and other living beings granted by the Creator is not absolute."[97] What are the limitations – the moral imperatives – that accompany humanity's dominion? Humanity's use of nonhuman resources "is limited by concern for the quality of life of his neighbor, including generations to come."[98] It is for this reason that utilization "requires a religious respect for the integrity of creation."[99]

The catechism tempers this anthropocentric view in the following paragraph, stating that animals "are God's creatures" and that "by their mere existence they bless [God] and give him glory."[100] For this reason, "men owe them kindness."[101] The nature of this kindness is unclear. Also unclear is whether or not the blessing and glory that animals provide to God is enough to justify their existence theologically. Do they have an intrinsic value apart from humans?[102] The catechism's theocentric claim seems to suggest that animals could occupy a place with humanity in the category of "existing for their own sakes" (inasmuch as humanity's existence for its own sake is also grounded in a theocentric framework). But judging from the aforementioned passages, such is clearly not the case. So what is the significance of the animals' giving glory to God "by their mere existence"? It is unclear.

At any rate, humanity's kindness to animals does not preclude causing suffering or killing. Indeed, the catechism maintains that "stewardship" entails that "it is legitimate to use animals for food and clothing."[103] Furthermore, "Medical and scientific experimentation on animals is a morally acceptable practice if it remains within reasonable limits and contributes to caring for or saving human lives."[104] This claim is certainly too vague to deduce much in the way of praxis. What are "reasonable limits"? Is it possible that animal experimentation could be conducive to saving human lives but at once be outside reasonable limits?

The fourth paragraph offers a moral limitation to human dominion: "It is contrary to human dignity to cause animals to suffer or die needlessly."[105] Again, this claim is too vague to infer moral relevance. What constitutes needless suffering or death? Should Catholics not buy cosmetics tested on nonhuman animals? Should they not eat more meat than that which is vitally necessary (which in today's context in North

America is typically no meat at all)? Should they stop hunting for sport? What about fur trapping? In short, what constitutes a need sufficient to justify animal suffering and death?

The last paragraph also states, "It is…unworthy to spend money on [animals] that should as a priority go to relief of human misery."[106] Linzey astutely notes two corollaries of this claim. First, "In practice it would mean that we shouldn't spend *any* money on animal welfare until *all* human misery has been eliminated."[107] Second, "The *Catechism opposes* animal welfare to human welfare."[108] The point to be made is that giving money to alleviate animal suffering is in itself inappropriate because human misery exists. One wonders if the same could be said of *nonmonetary* resources, such as effort and time, as well. Is it unworthy or theologically inappropriate to volunteer at an animal shelter because that effort and time could be devoted to alleviate human suffering?

By way of summation and conclusion

What is one to make of the above exploration into certain magisterial documents concerning nonhuman animals? First, it is noteworthy that the documents betray a certain tension that is less evident in Aquinas's work. The central tensions I have noted are depicted in Table 2.1.

These tensions intimate a number of questions the magisterium should address. Do animals exist for the sake of human beings, or do they have worth apart from that telos? If the latter, what is the moral significance of their intrinsic worth? What was the nature of the "original harmony" between human and animals? Did it include animals suffering and dying for human welfare? How did sin disrupt this harmony such that it is no longer present today? What exactly is the "groaning" of

Table 2.1 Tensions in magisterial pronouncements concerning nonhuman animals

Animals have intrinsic worth.	Animals exist instrumentally for humans, who are the only creatures that exist for themselves.
There was an original harmony between humans and animals that was disrupted by sin.	There is an integrity and order in creation that must be preserved in human interactions with the cosmos.
The groaning of animals is part of the focus of eschatological redemption.[109]	There is nothing wrong in causing animals suffering and death for human benefit provided the integrity of creation is not violated.

nonhuman animals in the history of the cosmos if it does not include their suffering and death? In what way does eschatological redemption apply to animals?

These tensions and questions aside, for the most part I find that the magisterial pronouncements I have examined, especially the catechism, follow the dominant tradition of Aquinas. They affirm an anthropocentrism in which all corporeal creation exists for the well-being of the entire human community, both present and future. They maintain that human beings, bearing the image of God, have a special status of personhood that grants them a place in the community wherein the resources of the earth are intended for equitable distribution among its members. They perpetuate an instrumentalist view of animals in which practices that cause their suffering and death are justified.

To reiterate an earlier point, I am not here interested in arguing that the dominant tradition (or its magisterial promulgation) is wrong. There is plenty to support the dominant tradition in the Bible and the history of Christian thought. My point here is simply to highlight areas that require clarification in the contemporary Catholic position and suggest that, pending clarification that suggests otherwise, it does indeed maintain Aquinas's anthropocentric position of indirect moral concern for animals. It also maintains concern for the just distribution of nonhuman resources (including animals) for the entire human community. The magisterium thus reiterates and continues the dominant tradition in its contemporary context. However, this tradition remains one of numerous options from Scripture and the history of Christianity. It is now pertinent to explore options that deviate from this dominant tradition.

3
Theology and the Reconfiguration of Difference

The previous chapter explores the manner in which Aquinas's anthropocentrism and conservationism have been appropriated in contemporary Catholic thought. I suggest there that the magisterial teachings of the Catholic Church continue to maintain the ethics grounded in Aquinas's theology, albeit at times ambiguously so. In this chapter I seek to contribute to a perspective, already delineated by careful thinkers, that honors a traditional differentiation between humans and animals and at the same time avoids viewing the nonhuman creation strictly in terms of utility.

This perspective moves beyond an anthropocentrism that views humans as the measure of all things. However, it maintains a *functional* anthropocentrism, in which human beings role in the cosmos is unique. I argue that, theologically, unique identity entails two inseparable dimensions: status and responsibility. I begin with a brief historical consideration, showing how Christians (not only Aquinas) have established human identity in contrast to the identity of nonhumans. Next, I examine three expressions that challenge this historical view. I then explore the moral meaning of difference in systematic theology. Finally, I argue that the relationship between God and creation, as well as the intended relationship between the elect and the nonelect, establishes a paradigm for how humans ought to relate to animals.

Historical hierarchy and ecological conscientiousness

In a scene from the movie *Braveheart*, William Wallace addresses the Scottish nobles after a successful battle against their English rivals. The nobles claim it is time to declare a king and begin to argue over which clan should provide an heir to the throne. Wallace reproaches the wealthy Scotsmen, saying, "There is a difference between us. You think the people of this country exist to provide you with position. I think your position exists to provide the people with freedom. And I go to make sure they have it."[1] At its core, this scene represents a disparity in the purpose of a power hierarchy. The nobles feel their unique identity establishes a status that is maintained at the expense of those with a lesser status. For Wallace, any status derived from identity constitutes a responsibility to lead those without status to their proper end – in this case, freedom. At stake is the question: Does nobility primarily entitle or oblige?

In Christian history, many theologians and philosophers have attempted to delineate an essential boundary around humanity that excludes nonhuman animals. Often, such a boundary entails denying nonhumans direct moral concern. Immanuel Kant predicates the category of "person" on what he believes to be unique human qualities.[2] Before Kant, René Descartes argues that humans have a rational mind that separates them by nature from the mechanistic bodies of nonhuman animals. Humans are capable of expressing thoughts through communication. For Descartes, "This shows not merely that the beasts have less reason than men, but that they have no reason at all."[3] As I have already explored in great detail, before Descartes, Thomas Aquinas states, "The intellect or mind is that whereby the rational creature excels other creatures."[4] Before Aquinas, Augustine writes, "God, then, made man in His own image. For He created for him a soul endowed with reason and intelligence so that he might excel all the creatures of the earth, air, and sea, which were not so gifted."[5] Before Augustine, Jesus comforts his disciples in Luke 12:7 by declaring: "Are not five sparrows sold for two pennies? Yet not one of them is forgotten in God's sight... Do not be afraid; you are of more value than many sparrows."[6] Before Christ, the authors and redactors of Genesis 1 differentiate humanity from the rest of creation by ascribing the "image of God" to human beings alone.[7]

While this desire to maintain a sharp divide between human and nonhuman creatures is more pronounced in the West, it is not wanting in the East. Irenaeus states that humanity, "being endowed with reason, and in this respect like to God, having been made free in his will, and with power over himself, is himself the cause to himself."[8] Ephrem the Syrian writes that animals were not permitted to approach the outer area of Paradise. He also states:

> Even though the beasts, the cattle, and the birds were equal [to Adam] in their ability to procreate and in that they had life, God still gave

honor to Adam in many ways: first, in that it was said, God formed him with His own hands and breathed life into him; God then set him as ruler over Paradise and over all that is outside of Paradise; God clothed Adam in glory; and God gave him reason and thought so that he might perceive the majesty [of God].[9]

In a similar manner, Gregory of Nyssa claims that human beings are unique among the physical creation in that they bear a similarity with the divine on account of their rationality and intelligence.[10]

There are exceptions to this focus on the distinction between humans and nonhumans, especially in contemporary theology. However, the claim that humans in some way transcend the physical creation is historically normative. How should Christianity deal with this issue in an age of heightened ecological awareness? Should theologians abandon the belief that humans differ from all nonhumans in essence? Should they strengthen their resolve and reassert a hierarchical view in which anything that is less than human is at the complete service of its human overlord? Fortunately, these are not the only two options.

Foundational questions and a third option

A third possibility arises out of a consideration of the following questions: What is the purpose of the disparity in greatness within the created order? If humans are different – even if in essence – from the rest of creation, why are they different? The capacities that many Christians believe distinguish humans from animals, such as a rational soul and freedom of the will, along with the religious claim that humans alone bear the image of God, serve to constitute a uniquely human identity. Even if one accepts this distinction, the question arises: What does a uniquely human identity mean for human beings living in the context of creation? Of particular import is this question: If humans are so much greater than nonhuman animals, how should humanity exercise this greatness in relationship to these "others"?

Given the growing ecological sensitivity of our contemporary context, these questions have received more attention. This attention has in turn highlighted a third option, regarding the ethical significance of the difference between humans and animals. Here I limit my engagement to works with a theological foundation. First, I consider modern interpretations of the *imago Dei* (image of God). Second, I examine Andrew Linzey's animal theology. Lastly, I provide a very brief overview of the work of other scholars who express the third option.

The image of god

The historically dominant interpretation of the image of God (especially in Christian theology) views the concept as a metaphysical affirmation about humanity. That human beings bear the divine image means that they bear some substantive similarity to God. As already alluded to, theologians like Irenaeus, Augustine, and Aquinas posited rationality and freedom of the will as constitutive of the *imago*. Contemporary scholars refer to this interpretation as "substantive," or "substantialistic," as it focuses on the *essential* and *ontological* differences between humanity and the rest of creation.

Stanley Grenz provides a good overview of the rise and perpetuation of the substantive interpretation in Christian history. He begins by stating,

> Although most Christians today would be likely to assume that this view arises directly out of the Bible, the idea was actually introduced into Christian thought by those church fathers who were influenced by and grappled with the Greek philosophical tradition.[11]

Norman Habel links the substantialistic interpretation to Platonic dualism:

> A dualistic mindset has informed most interpretations in the past. A long tradition, that goes back to Philo who was influenced by Platonic thought, promotes the idea that the image refers to a non-physical dimension of humans, the mind, reason, consciousness or a spiritual core.[12]

Grenz notes the propensity toward the substantive view in Irenaeus. He claims Irenaeus establishes the path for his successors. In the East these include Clement of Alexandria, Gregory of Nyssa, and finally John of Damascus. In the West Augustine sets a firm groundwork for a substantive view of the *imago*. He argues that the *imago* includes rationality and sets humans over the nonhuman creation. Grenz traces Augustine's influence through Aquinas, who ascribes at least an aspect of the *imago* to all humans on account of the mind. After a lull in the substantive interpretation with such early Reformers as Luther and Calvin, subsequent Protestants return to this view. As this overview suggests, the substantive view is historically normative.[13] Furthermore, David Clough, who also traces anthropocentric readings of Genesis 1 to Philo's appropriation of Aristotelian natural philosophy, maintains that this tradition continues to impact modern readings of the text.[14]

Modern biblical scholars have questioned the exegetical basis of the substantialistic interpretation. J. Richard Middleton states, "Most patristic, medieval, and modern interpreters typically asked not an exegetical, but a speculative, question: In what way are humans *like* God and *unlike* animals?"[15] Likewise, D. J. Hall states,

> It can readily appear – if one follows the history of the interpretation of this symbol closely – that the whole enterprise of defining the *imago Dei* in our Christian conventions centers on the apparent need to show that human beings are different from all other creatures.[16]

Historically, then, the *imago* has served as tool to maintain borders. Moreover, these borders operate primarily for the purpose of exclusion. Humans are different than animals. And as Hall states, different "almost invariably implies 'higher,' 'nobler,' 'loftier,' 'better.'"[17]

The substantialistic interpretation of the *imago* remains evident in modern scholarship. Theologically, Millard Erickson favors such an interpretation.[18] Biblically, Nahum Sarna writes,

> The resemblance of man to God bespeaks the infinite worth of a human being and affirms the inviolability of the person. The killing of any other creature, even wantonly, is not murder. Only a human being can be murdered.[19]

As noted in Chapter 2, this connection between the *imago* and a unique moral status is evident in contemporary magisterial pronouncements. In addition, Benedict Ashley and other bioethicists use the *imago* to exclude animals from ethical concern in the medical field:

> The Christian view of the worth of persons who share with Jesus a human nature is based on the biblical teaching that God creates each person in his own image and likeness, different from lesser creatures in the possession of a spiritual intelligence and freewill.[20]

Hence, in the substantialistic view, the *imago* constitutes an identity that fundamentally ascribes a status to those within the boundaries of that identity.

It is precisely this "erring on the side of status" that many modern biblical scholars (and theologians) question. Based on Genesis 1, many exegetes argue that the image of God is inseparably united to the command to rule over the creatures and the earth. The exegetical arguments are complex. Here I provide an extremely truncated version of one of them.

As both Middleton and W. Sibley Towner note, the structure of Genesis 1 consistently links the act of creation to the purpose of that act.[21] That is, the object created (for example, a dome in the water, lights in the sky, humanity in the image of God) is syntactically connected to the purpose for its creation (respectively, to separate water from water, to mark seasons and give light to the earth, to have dominion). So strong is the syntax of the narrative that Towner states the Hebrew *waw* is best translated such that God creates X (the object created) *so that* Y (the purpose for its creation).[22] Hence, God creates humanity in God's image *so that* humans might have dominion over all nonhuman life on the earth.[23] As Middleton notes, "The syntax.. points to 'rule' as the *purpose*, not simply the consequence or result, of the *imago Dei*."[24] In this sense, dominion is "a necessary and inseparable purpose and hence virtually constitutive of the image."[25]

Aside from the arguments from within the text of Genesis 1, Middleton also turns to other biblical texts, including Psalm 8.[26] In addition, he examines the cultural milieu of the ancient Near East in which the authors and redactors completed Genesis 1. In other texts from that sociohistorical context, an image of a god serves as the mediator or core-gent through which the god being imaged accomplishes his or her work on earth.[27]

For my purposes, the importance of the functional interpretation of the *imago* is that it balances the focus of the term as an ascription of a unique status ("let us make humankind in our image") with an ascription of a unique calling (so that humankind may "have dominion" over all creatures). In the words of Ellen van Wolde, "The human being is created to make God present in his creation."[28] Hence, the *imago* constitutes both status (uniquely human) and responsibility (making God present to the nonhuman creation). As Terrence Fretheim states, "Human beings are not only created *in* the image of God (this is who they are); they are also created *to be* the image of God (this is their role in the world)."[29]

The ethical import of this view is evident in a consideration of the God whose image humanity bears,[30] .I explore this matter below, but for now, let it suffice to consider Towner's poignant question: "When the other creatures look upon *adam* as a royal or even god-like figure, what will they see? A tyrant, an exterminator, a satanic figure? Or will they experience the ruling hand of *adam* as something as tender and gentle as that of their Creator?"[31] Humans bear the image of a particular God, the God who is, in the words of Catherine Mowry LaCugna, "God for us," even to the point of self-sacrifice.[32] Likewise, the unique identity of humans as the image of God demands that they act as humans *for* creation, even to the point of self-sacrifice.

The functional interpretation of the *imago*, while not as historically normative as the substantive view, is not unrepresented outside biblical scholarship. Even in early Christianity the view is evident.[33] For instance, in the *Demonstration* 11, Irenaeus states that humanity is "free and self-controlled, being made by God for this end, that he might rule all those things that were upon the earth."[34] Likewise, Gregory of Nyssa, in *On the Making of Man*, frequently attaches the royal function of humanity to his substantive understanding of the *imago*.[35]

Today, many Orthodox theologians recognize the functional dimension of the *imago* and even draw out ethical implications of this view. For instance, Nonna Verna Harrison claims that the image of God constitutes a "responsibility to care for animals and for the natural world."[36] The *imago* "enables the human person to become a *mediator*" between God and animals.[37] Similarly, Kallistos Ware claims that, based on the *imago*, Greek Christians "believe in a hierarchal universe, in which humans – by virtue of their creation in the divine image – have 'dominion' over the animals."[38] Ware immediately qualifies this view by stating dominion does not sanction exploitation, but on the contrary it demands that humans "reflect the loving kindness and compassion of God."[39] Importantly, both Harrison and Ware draw upon Maximus the Confessor for their conclusions – a point I examine more closely in Chapter 7.

By way of summation, the *imago* is more than an ascription of status. It is a unique calling for humans to bear the responsibility of representing a *particular* God in and to the created order. Hence, the difference between humans and animals constituted by the image of God establishes a responsibility of the former toward the latter. Another Christian thinker to take this view of the *imago* and further develop its ethical consequences is Andrew Linzey.[40]

Andrew Linzey's animal theology

Andrew Linzey, a Christian advocate for animal rights, is the director of the Oxford Centre for Animal Ethics. His works are extensive and his approaches broad. Here I focus mainly on his theological and philosophical foundations for animal rights as developed in *Animal Theology* and *Why Animal Suffering Matters*. In particular, I am interested in his affirmation of the difference between humans and animals as a positive argument for animal rights.

The first chapter of Linzey's *Why Animal Suffering Matters* explores the common arguments used to exclude animals from moral concern. These arguments all use the same foundational approach: establish a boundary that both constitutes moral concern and is uniquely human. In this approach, the difference between humans and animals secures ethical concern to the former and denies it to the latter. Linzey's approach is not to deny that there are differences between humans and animals. In fact, he accepts the commonly proposed differences – at least for the sake of argument. His goal is to show that "the moral conclusions drawn from these differences are almost entirely mistaken and that another, completely opposed, conclusion follows."[41]

The six differences Linzey explores are interrelated. Theologically, they all fall under the general category of the image of God, which is the final difference Linzey considers. The first five differences are as follows: animals are natural slaves via a cosmic hierarchy; animals lack rationality; animals lack the communicative abilities proper to humans; animals are not moral agents; and animals do not have immortal (rational) souls.[42]

As I have already established, advocates of the substantive interpretation of the *imago* frequently posit rationality and freedom of the will as constitutive elements of the image of God. These formal features establish how the human creature is *like* God and *unlike* other creatures. Linzey notes that what follows from this distinction – which is the fundamental theological distinction – is that animals, for their lack of these elements, are naturally slaves. Their lack of a reason (or, theologically, a rational soul) makes them both unable to communicate and amoral agents. These differences may be theologically summarized as follows: because animals lack substantive elements indicative of the *imago Dei*, they are excluded from the category of moral concern, which is predicated upon those elements.

Linzey effectively takes each differentiation and reverses the moral conclusion most scholars have drawn from it. Concerning the position that animals are natural slaves, he states, "behaving morally sometimes involves acting contrary to what we perceive in nature."[43] Herein is a critique Linzey highlights in his earlier work, *Animal Theology*, in which he notes that too often the appeal to natural law becomes nothing short of an appeal to naturalism.[44] That is, humans justify their utilitarian view of nature with a religious foundation that derives from the "red in tooth and claw" observation of nature. Of course, they are careful to avoid such applications to God's relationship to humans. But one can fairly ask, if the hierarchy in creation establishes that animals are naturally the slaves of humans, why are humans not – as they are portrayed in Mesopotamian myths – slaves of God?[45]

Concerning the rationality of animals, Linzey notes, "If it is true that animals are non-rational, then it follows that they have no means of rationalising their deprivation, boredom, and frustration."[46] Hence, the lack of rationality may actually *increase* animal suffering in some cases, not diminish it. Concerning the claim that animals lack the ability to communicate as humans do, Linzey responds that this "deficiency" renders animals powerless to give consent to the suffering that humans cause them. For this reason, "our responsibility [to animals] increases" when we acknowledge their inability to communicate to us. Concerning the claim that animals are not moral agents, Linzey states, "If humans are morally superior (in the sense that we are moral agents), it more reasonably follows that our superiority should, in part at least, consist in acknowledging duties to animals that they cannot acknowledge to us."[47] Furthermore, if animals are amoral, they cannot do anything to deserve suffering and cannot be morally corrected by suffering. Hence, "It is the unmerited and undeserved nature of their [amoral animals'] suffering, and our ability to justify it by most traditional reasoning, that strengthens the case for animals."[48] Concerning the position that animals lack a rational and eternal soul, Linzey replies, "If animals are not going to be recompensed in some future life for the suffering that they have had to undergo in the present, it follows that their current suffering acquires even greater significance."[49] Finally, concerning the position that animals lack the image of God – which I maintain is theological umbrella for all the other arguments – Linzey casts his lot with the functional interpretation I delineate above.

Linzey's argument is significant in that it maintains the distinctions between humans and animals but uses these very distinctions to dismantle the justification of human exploitation of animals. He delineates this view also in his earlier work, *Animal Theology*. Here Linzey argues that the kenotic love of God establishes a "generosity paradigm," in which "the obligation is always and everywhere on the 'higher' to sacrifice for the 'lower'; for the strong, powerful and rich to give to those who are vulnerable, poor and powerless."[50] Hence, Linzey opposes the "difference-finding tendency" of the West, which serves to maintain the border between humanity and animals in order to justify exploitation of the latter by the former.[51] As a corrective question, Linzey asks, "If the omnipotence and power of God is properly expressed in the form of *katabasis*, humility and self-sacrifice, why should this model not properly extend to our relations with creation as a whole and animals in particular?"[52] In this model,

> The uniqueness of humanity consists in its ability to become the servant species. To exercise its full humanity as co-participants and co-workers with God in the redemption of the world. This view challenges the traditional notions that the world was made simply for human use or pleasure, that its purpose consists in serving the human species, or that the world exists largely in an instrumentalist relationship to human beings.[53]

Linzey's view constitutes the heart of the "third position." In a manner similar to Linzey and the advocates of the functional reading of the *imago*, one can maintain that humans bear a special status in the created order – theologically signified by the image of God – and simultaneously maintain that God grants this status *for the welfare of those without that status*. The unique status of humans theologically leads to the ascription of status for nonhumans. For human beings are special (or separate) in the same way that priests are special (or separate): to mediate the blessings of God to those outside their status.[54]

Other scholars and the third option

While Linzey provides one of the clearest delineations of the third position and consistently draws out the ethical implications of that view, many others have expressed similar ideas. Space does not permit a lengthy engagement, but I would be remiss not to mention a few of these others. My concern here is not specific ethical praxis but theological foundation.

As already mentioned, LaCugna argues that God is "God for us" even to the point of self-sacrifice. It is, in a sense, God's very nature to engage in *kenosis* (self-emptying) for the sake of the created order. This nature is expressed in God's trinitarian existence, in which each divine Person empties into the others in perichoretic love. Maintaining this view of the trinitarian God (as opposed to the view of God the Father as a monarchial and unitarian despot), Christians can avoid "deeply harmful attitudes," which, LaCugna states, "include the ruination of the earth and the destruction of 'lesser' creatures that the human being presumes to be subordinate to itself."[55] The redeemed person, in LaCugna's framework, "is free for hospitality to the stranger, nonviolence toward the oppressor, and benevolent regard for every single creature that exists."[56] In short, becoming like God means becoming loving and other-affirming, even when – perhaps especially when! – that "other" is perceived as "lesser."

In *The Ethics of Animal Experimentation*, Donna Yarri suggests a simple theological progression for ethical practice. She states, "If dominion means that God's exercise of power and influence toward all creation is mediated through human beings, then this dominion must be a reflection of the character of God."[57] Furthermore, "If, as in Christian theology, God is conceived of as loving and compassionate, then the view of dominion as benevolent stewardship seems a better understanding of the term than despotism."[58] The syllogism runs as follows:

1. Humans ought to exercise dominion in light of God's exercise of dominion.
2. God's exercise of dominion is loving and compassionate.
3. Therefore, "At the very least, humans should attempt to demonstrate the care and concern towards God's creatures that God has toward them."[59]

Norm Phelps takes a similar position when he considers the image and likeness of God. Phelps aims to avoid the "aristocracy theory," in which humans are "the aristocrats of the universe whose privileged position in the divine scheme entitles us to reduce the rest of the earth's population to serfdom."[60] As a corrective, Phelps follows those, like Linzey, who argue that dominion is most properly understood as the catalyst for service. In particular, Phelps draws an example from government, highlighting the point of my earlier quote from *Braveheart*: "We expect government officials to use their authority for the benefit of the people, not to satisfy their own lust for wealth or power."[61] Hence, the God-given status of humanity – a heightened status – does not justify harming those without that status in order to maintain it. In fact, status demands just the opposite: mediating well-being to those without it.

Another extremely important theologian I want to consider briefly is Jürgen Moltmann.[62] He clearly challenges the impassibility of God (that is, the notion that God is unable to suffer) in favor of a God who – as three persons in eternal perichoretic communion – is willing to experience death for the sake of a cosmic redemption.[63] This cosmic redemption is nothing short of the entire creation (including animals) restored and transformed.[64] Given these views in conjunction with Moltmann's political theology in which hope draws the eschaton into the present, he claims the human response is a deep "reverence for life."[65] Concerning the ethical ramifications of this response, Moltmann states,

Reverence for life always begins with respect for weaker life, vulnerable life. In the world of human beings this means the poor, the sick, and the defenseless. The same is true for the world of nature. The weaker plant and animal species are the first creatures to be threatened by extinction. Reverence for life must apply to them first of all, since they require protection.[66]

Hence, the act of protection reflects the eschatological hope of God's movement toward creation in a cosmically redemptive act.

I could consider numerous other scholars. For example, while Schweitzer proposed his ethics of "reverence for life" as a means of bridging the distance between human life and all other life-forms,[67] he also considered human beings unique in their capacity to extend reverence for their own lives to all life.[68] Likewise, in a well-reasoned article Stanley Hauerwas and John Berkman argue, "The only significant theological difference between humans and animals lies in God's giving humans a unique *purpose*."[69] The brilliance of the argument is similar to all the positions above: humanity's unique status (what makes us different from animals) is inseparably connected to humanity's unique function, which is to draw "all flesh" toward a common telos in God. In short, the difference (status and function) is ultimately given by God for the sake of commonality (telos).

All of these positions, including that of advocates for a functional reading of the *imago Dei* and Linzey, are nuanced. My inclusion of these names is simply to note the theological foundation for a third position regarding status and responsibility, not to suggest all of these thinkers agree on the ethical implications of this foundation.

Exploring differentiation in theology

Having delineated the third view, I now seek to develop further the theological case that supports it. To accomplish this development, I explore the theme of differentiation in systematic theology in order to establish a paradigm of how we ought to view "greater-than-ness." My approach here is nothing extremely novel. I merely expand upon what Linzey and others have already argued.

The issue of differentiation is not unique to the border between humans and animals. In both scripture and systematic theology, the theme of differentiation arises. Save for pantheists, all theologians posit some categorical differentiation between God and creation. Likewise, the concepts of covenant and election create categories of "us" and

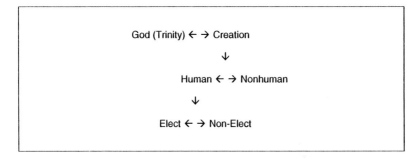

Figure 3.1   Theological differentiation

"them," in and out, elect and nonelect. Given these points, one way to think of systematic theology is as a categorization of reality and an exploration of the exchanges between its categories. From broader to narrower, the categories could read as follows: overall, God and creation; within creation, human and nonhuman; within humanity, elect and nonelect.[70] Figure 3.1 helps to clarify my point. I have separated the differentiated categories by arrows, indicating an interaction between categories.

Let us consider two of these examples of differentiation.

God and creation

First, what is the meaning of the differentiation of God and creation? The triune God is certainly categorically greater than anything in the created order. But when we consider the revelation of God in Scripture, how is God's "greater-than-ness" expressed?

Unlike the gods of certain Mesopotamian narratives, God does not create humanity to be slaves in order to ensure divine ease.[71] For instance, in the Babylonian creation myth, the *Enuma Elish*, Marduk creates human beings after a war among the gods. The purpose of humanity's creation is explicit in the words of Marduk: "He shall be charged with the service of the gods that they may be at ease!"[72] This language, unlike that of Genesis, describes the relationship of the gods and humanity as that of master and slaves. The God of Genesis 1 is, not the utilitarian enslaver of the *Enuma Elish*, but self-sacrificing and loving. Elohim does not enslave; Elohim empowers.[73]

Nor is God unmoved by the plight of the created order. In the Flood narrative, God is "grieved" by the state of creation (Genesis 6:6). The Hebrew word for "grieved" in this verse is *'âtsab*, which is the root for the word used to describe Eve's "pain" in childbirth and Adam's "struggle" to work the earth in Genesis 3:16–17 (*'itstsâbôn*). This etymological connection yields a theological significance: God experiences the suffering of the created order.[74] In Exodus, God tells Moses that he has "known" Israel's suffering. Here the Hebrew word is *yada'*, which in this context seems to denote a knowledge through experience or acquaintance.[75]

Similarly, the prophet Hosea offers a startlingly anthropomorphic image of God. The book bearing his name records a message God gave to Hosea:

> When Israel was a child, I loved him, and out of Egypt I called my son. The more I called them, the more they went from me; they kept sacrificing to the Baals, and offering incense to idols. Yet it was I who taught Ephraim to walk, I took them up in my arms; but they did not know that I healed them. I led them with cords of human kindness, with bands of love. I was to them like those who lift infants to their cheeks. I bent down to them and fed them... How can I give you up, Ephraim? How can I hand you over, O Israel?...My heart recoils within me; my compassion grows warm and tender. I will not execute my fierce anger; I will not again destroy Ephraim; for I am God and no mortal, the Holy One in your midst, and I will not come in wrath.[76]

Hosea portrays God as one who does not destroy those beneath God. How does God deal with those categorically lesser than God is? God leads them "with cords of human kindness." God bends down to care for them.

These passages portray a God who is affected by the sufferings of the created order. Furthermore, God is interested in caring for those of lesser status. God knows the suffering of creation and acts on its behalf. One is reminded of Dietrich Bonhoeffer: "Only the suffering God can help."[77]

This portrait of God only intensifies with the New Testament. Jesus weeps over Jerusalem[78] and at the tomb of Lazarus.[79] He reveals the glory of God by dying on the cross in order to draw all things to him.[80] Considering the above passages from the Old Testament, both Christ's experience of grief and his drive to self-sacrifice on behalf of those of lesser status do not stand in contrast to his divinity. As Moltmann states,

> When the crucified Jesus is called the "image of the invisible God," the meaning is that *this* is God, and God is like *this*. God is not greater than he is in this humiliation. God is not more glorious than he is in

this self-surrender. God is not more powerful than he is in this help-lessness. God is not more divine than he is in this humanity.[81]

Here we ought to make a brief comment on the famous "Christ Hymn" from Philippians 2:6–11. Paul exhorts the church at Philippi to follow the example of Christ, "Who, being in very nature God, did not consider equality with God something to be grasped, but made himself nothing, taking the very nature of a servant, being made in human likeness."[82] Concerning this passage, Gordon D. Fee states, "God-likeness, contrary to common understanding[,] did *not* mean for Christ to be a 'grasping, seizing' being, as it would for the 'gods' and 'lords' whom the Philippians had previously known."[83] Jesus does not consider his divine status something to be exploited, and this view of status reveals his divine identity. Says Markus Bockmuehl, "Christ's incarnation and voluntary death on the cross.. were the way in which he showed that 'being equal to God' was for him not a possession to be exploited for selfish ends; instead, it led him to deprive himself and serve others."[84] For Christ, identity was not a status to be maintained at the expense of others with a lesser status. On the contrary, the identity of Christ moved him to sacrifice his status on behalf of others. In short, for Christ identity meant both status and responsibility; and the former constituted the latter.

These passages reveal that in both the Old and New Testaments, God appears as one who does not hoard status at the expense of the cosmos. Instead, God repeatedly exercises status entailed by identity – God's categorical "greater-than-ness" – as a means to take responsibility for those excluded from God's identity. As Linzey states, "The God who is (in Thomist terms) the 'highest' and most 'perfect' of all expresses divine power not in lording over 'inferior' creatures, but in taking human form and suffering and dying for their sakes."[85] This view of status is also evident in Christ's teaching: "The greatest among you will be your servant."[86] In this sense, God sets the following example concerning identity: any special status understood as categorical "greater-than-ness" entailed by identity ought to serve as a catalyst for care and self-sacrifice, not as a justification for exploitation.

Elect and nonelect

For a second consideration, what is the meaning of the differentiation of elect and nonelect? At the outset of the Abrahamic narrative, God states to Abram, "I will make of you a great nation, and I will bless you, and make your name great, so that you will be a blessing.. in you all the families of the earth shall be blessed."[87] The promise God makes to Abram is not simply for the ascription of a special status. It includes such an ascription (Abram will become a great nation), but status is not simply an end. Under the umbrella of identity, status is married to function – to responsibility (as a great nation, Abram will be a blessing to all families on the earth). Abraham's status of "greater-than-ness," which constitutes his unique identity, also constitutes a unique responsibility – a specific calling. As Fretheim states, the

> divine purpose for Israel is not simply for the sake of the chosen; God has God's world in focus. God's exclusive move in choosing Abraham/Israel is not an end in itself, but a divine strategy for the sake of a maximally inclusive end.[88]

In this sense, the connection between identity and responsibility continues with the theme of covenant. The call to be God's holy people is not a call to be different strictly for the sake of a status derived from identity; rather, it is the call to be different in order to make a difference for those without that status.

Numerous narratives in Scripture evince God's displeasure when someone attempts to grasp or exploit an identity to the exclusion of responsibility. For instance, in the book of Jonah, God calls the Israelite prophet to a ministry in the Assyrian capital of Nineveh. God calls Jonah, a member of the people of God, to be an instrument of salvation for those who are not the people of God. Jonah refuses. He is not interested in including those outside his border – that is, those who are not the elect – in the benefits that are indicative of his own identity. He would rather be an instrument of destruction for Nineveh. For Jonah, the inhabitants of that foreign city do not deserve the mercy of God. His actions are in stark contrast to the Abrahamic promise of Genesis 12. Jonah refuses to mediate God's blessing to Nineveh. He clings to the status entailed by his unique identity while simultaneously denying the responsibility entailed by it. That is, he patrols the border around his identity only to maintain his special status.

After Nineveh repents and God spares the entire city, Jonah becomes angry with God. The book ends with God's question to Jonah: "Should I not be concerned about Nineveh, that great city, in which there are more than a hundred and twenty thousand persons who do not know their right hand from their left, and also many animals?"[89] God's question is nothing short of a reprimand for hoarding identity to the exclusion of responsibility.[90] Jesus provides a similar reprimand in the Gospel according to John: "If you were Abraham's children, you would be doing what Abraham did."[91] I offer the following paraphrase of this passage: "If you want to participate in the status entailed by Abraham's identity, then take up Abraham's responsibility." In short, for the elect, "greater-than-ness" is both blessing and burden.

These considerations reveal that God calls the elect to follow the example God provides in the differentiation between God and creation. God provides the elect with a special status and calls them not to hoard that status at the expense of the nonelect. Any categorical "greater-than-ness" entailed by the Abrahamic promise is inseparable from the responsibility entailed by it. Thus, Jonah's failure was fundamentally a failure to mediate the status benefits (God's mercy) entailed by the identity of the elect (Israel) to the nonelect (Nineveh).

The theological paradigm of differentiation

How do these findings affirm the third option in addressing the difference between humans and nonhumans in an age of ecological awareness? I make three major differentiations earlier in this chapter: God and creation, human and nonhuman, elect and nonelect. In the first division, the party endowed with an identity of "greater-than-ness" takes up a responsibility to care for those without that identity.[92] God experienced grief and ultimately death for the sake of the creation. In the third division, God calls the party endowed with an identity of "greater-than-ness" to follow God's example. That is, God calls the elect to mediate blessing to the nonelect, even when this calling entails self-sacrifice. Note that Figure 3.2 bears a similar structure to Figure 3.1; note too the parallelism in the interaction between the categories.

This parallelism establishes a theological paradigm of differentiation (very similar to Linzey's generosity paradigm) that ought to apply also to

God (Trinity) → sacrifices on behalf of → Creation

↓

Human → ??? → Nonhuman

↓

Elect → called to mediate the blessings of God to → Non-Elect

Figure 3.2 Theological paradigm of differentiation

the division between humans and nonhumans.[93] Too often humans seek to maintain the distinction between humans and animals strictly for the sake of human benefit. The disparity becomes an excuse for exploitive domination. It provides rights to humans but precludes providing them for animals. This approach commits the error of Jonah in that it divorces status from responsibility. If humans bear a categorical "greater-than-ness" that separates them from the rest of the created order, that status ought to serve as a catalyst for care and self-sacrifice on behalf of the rest of creation, not a justification of utilitarian mistreatment. As Linzey states,

> St. Thomas was not entirely wrong in seeing a kind of implicit moral hierarchy in the world – except that he misunderstood it at its most important and relevant point, namely, that the "higher" should serve the "lower," rather than the reverse.[94]

This theological paradigm of differentiation contributes to the Christian foundation for a discussion of how humans ought to ethically engage animals. Much of the discussion concerning the extension of ethical concern to animals has focused on whether animals can be included in a category that predicates a status worthy of certain benefits. This approach begins with a view in which identity is fundamentally about status. The only way animals can receive a moral status akin to humans' is if they fall within the boundaries of identity that predicate moral concern. Can they reason? Are they self-aware? Can they communicate? Can they suffer?[95] Do they bear the image of God? These questions are not unimportant. Yet they do not, based on the theological paradigm of differentiation, address the fundamental Christian issue of moral concern.

According to this third option, the important question is not whether humans differ from animals in degree or essence. The important question is *why* are humans different from animals? Based on the theological paradigm of differentiation, the justification of an attitude of love and self-sacrifice toward animals is not dependent upon their inclusion in a common category with humans. In fact, it is the difference between humans and animals that provides the foundation for moral concern for animals. For humans, the foundation to care about other creatures is not based upon whether or not *they* bear the image of God; it is based on the fact that *humans* bear that image. The call to sacrifice on behalf of other creatures is predicated, not on whether they can understand that call, but on the fact that humans understand that call. In short, it is the status entailed by the uniquely human identity that awakens the responsibility entailed by that identity.

Conclusion

From the perspective of the third option, the following can be concluded: If humans patrol the borders between themselves and animals strictly for the sake of maintaining the status benefits of a uniquely human identity, they desecrate the example of God and fail to do justice to God's image, which they bear. They grasp status to the exclusion of responsibility. They bear the image of God, and regard that status as something to be exploited. To avoid this failure, the desire to keep animals "in their place" must simultaneously be a calling for humans to take *their* place – not simply for the sake of perpetuating the benefits of a special identity but also for the sake of caring for those with a "lesser status" and mediating the blessings of God to them. Given this claim, humans ought to consider a cosmically oriented Golden Rule: do unto those who are "lesser" than you as you would have those who are "greater" than you do unto you. Even more to the point: treat animals as you would have God treat you. According to the third option, this axiom provides the proper outlook for a consideration of our uniquely human identity.

4

In Via toward an
Animal-Inclusive Eschaton

Admittedly, Chapter 3 focuses mainly on contemporary thinkers. The aim of this chapter is to retrieve and develop creatively a strand of Christian thought, stretching from early Christian interpretations of biblical data through the hagiographies of the saints into modern Christian thought, that provides an eschatological foundation for concern over the welfare of nonhuman animals. This strand opens a space for an alternative to the dominant tradition.

Given my methodological aim, I seek to highlight thinkers that represent a particular strand of Christian thought. To provide the framework for this strand, I explore the theologies of Irenaeus of Lyons and Ephrem the Syrian. First, I consider their positions regarding the place of nonhuman animals in protology and eschatology. Then I note their view that the created order is *in via* toward its eschatological consummation. With this framework in place, I turn to other voices in the Christian tradition, including the hagiographies of the saints, in order to further develop the framework. Ultimately I suggest that within this particular strand of Christian thought, the further a human being progresses along the path of redemption, the more he or she ought to serve as a prolepsis of eschatological hope, which includes peaceful relationships between humans and animals.

Prelapsarian views and eschatological hopes

Irenaeus clearly affirms a prelapsarian state of harmony among animals. For him, this state includes a complete absence of predatory actions, a state where all animals ate only vegetation.[1] There is no reason to assume that this harmonious coexistence excluded humans. Irenaeus makes no explicit claim that humans participated in predation prior to the Fall.

Furthermore, the claim that humans did not participate in violent activity is consistent with Theophilus of Antioch, whom Irenaeus frequently follows theologically.[2] Concerning the fifth day of creation, Theophilus states:

> But the monsters of the deep and the birds of prey are a similitude of covetous men and transgressors. For as the fish and the fowls are of one nature, some indeed abide in their natural state, and do no harm to those weaker then themselves, but keep the law of God, and eat of the seeds of the earth; others of them, again, transgress the law of God, and eat flesh, and injure those weaker than themselves: thus, too, the righteous, keeping the law of God, bite and injure none, but live holily and righteously. But robbers, and murderers, and godless persons are like monsters of the deep, and wild beasts, and birds of prey; for they virtually devour those weaker than themselves.[3]

Aside from the influence of Theophilus, Irenaeus accepts a literal translation of Isaiah 11:6–9. It is in reference to this passage that Irenaeus describes the harmony of the prelapsarian creation. Regarding Isaiah's vision, Irenaeus states:

> I am quite aware that some persons endeavour to refer these words to the case of savage men, both of different nations and various habits, who come to believe, and when they have believed, act in harmony with the righteous. But although this is [true] now with regard to some men coming from various nations to the harmony of the faith, nevertheless in the resurrection of the just [the words shall also apply] to those animals mentioned. For God is rich in all things. And it is right that when the creation is restored, all the animals should obey and be in subjection to man, and revert to the food originally given by God..that is, the productions of the earth.[4]

It is worth noting a few important aspects of this passage from Irenaeus. First, he uses a text that affirms an eschatological peace among animals. But it also includes humans in that harmonious picture. There will be no destruction on God's mountain, neither among the animals nor between humans and the animals. Second, Irenaeus explicitly denies that this eschatological hope is allegorical. Third, this eschatological future recalls a harmonious protology. Irenaeus never references Genesis 1:30, in which Elohim limits the diet of all animals to the vegetative productions of the earth. Nonetheless, Matthew Steenberg rightly notes that, given Irenaeus's familiarity with Genesis 1, "There is no reason to suppose that [he] did not draw his reflections [from that passage]."[5] If Irenaeus does draw from Genesis 1:30, he was certainly aware of the preceding verse in which Elohim provides the same dietary delimitation to the human creature. Thus, as Irenaeus utilizes an eschatological passage in which both animals and humans participate in a harmonious kingdom, as this passage recalls a protology in Genesis where that harmony existed among both humans and animals, and as these findings are consistent with Theophilus of Antioch, there is good reason to believe that Irenaeus posits harmonious relationships between humans and animals as a proleptic beginning to the created order.

As is already apparent, Irenaeus affirms an eschatological future that not only includes nonhumans – at least in the millennial reign of Christ – but also places them in peaceful relationships with humanity.[6] Hence, in *Demonstration of the Apostolic Preaching*, Irenaeus claims, "Now as to the union and concord and peace of the animals of different kinds...the Elders say that so it will be in truth at the coming of Christ, when He is to reign over all."[7] While again Irenaeus only explicitly mentions peace among animals, the same arguments that apply to his protology apply also to his eschatology. Hence, the peace on God's holy mountain will not be limited to animals but will incorporate all creation, including humans.

Ephrem the Syrian holds a similar view to Irenaeus regarding the relationships between humans and animals in the creation as God intended it. Explicating the meaning of God's bringing the animals to Adam, Ephrem writes:

> [This happened] so that God might make known the wisdom of Adam and the harmony that existed between the animals and Adam before he transgressed the commandment. The animals came to Adam as to a loving shepherd. Without fear they passed before him in an orderly fashion, by kinds and by species. They were neither afraid of him nor were they afraid of each other. A species of predatory animal would pass by with a species of animal that is preyed upon following safely right behind.[8]

In this passage, Ephrem explicitly affirms that the peace of Paradise existed between all creatures, including humans. The pristine relationship between humans and animals is predicated on love, not fear. Hence, like Irenaeus, Ephrem views humans and animals in harmonious relationships in the original creation. This passage also highlights Ephrem's view that this harmony is disrupted by human disobedience.[9]

In *Hymns on Paradise,* Ephrem depicts the future hope of a return to Eden in terms analogous to the present world. The future he envisions is a perfected world where God will heal the wounds of all creation. He writes,

> In the world there is struggle, in Eden, a crown of glory. At our resurrection both earth and heaven will God renew, liberating all creatures, granting them paschal joy, along with us. Upon our mother Earth, along with us, did he lay disgrace when he placed on her, with the sinner, the curse; so, together with the just, will He bless her too; this nursing mother, along with her children, shall he who is Good renew.[10]

In this passage, Ephrem includes all creatures in God's liberating and healing activity. It is interesting to note that, for Ephrem, animals will participate even in paschal joy with humans. Again, this passage highlights that, for Ephrem, the current struggle observable in the cosmos is a distortion of the harmony of Eden. Hence, like Irenaeus, Ephrem affirms harmonious relationships as indicative of the beginning of creation and its eschatological end.

In sum, the theologies of Irenaeus and Ephrem contain a prelapsarian state of peace between humans and animals and an eschatological return to that state. The current struggle in creation is framed by an edenic and an eschatological harmony. In short, the telos of the cosmos includes a harmony between human and animals, which constitutes at least in part the eschatological hope toward which God calls the creation.

The present: evidences of the eschaton

Given the positions of Irenaeus and Ephrem with regard to the past and future, what do they say about the present? For both thinkers, the present is not simply a path of return to protology but rather a progression beyond it. Eden was not a perfected creation; it was a creation *in via.* It was the beginning of a path toward the eschaton. Both Irenaeus and Ephrem thus view the Fall as a departure from a path. Redemption is a return to the path beyond the original Eden. This view of a creation *in via* permits the notion of a progressive movement toward eschatological hope.

I have already examined the inclusion of a protology and eschatology in Irenaeus's theology. Both include harmony between humans and animals. However, both elements of Irenaeus's theology require a further qualification: creation is *in via*. For Irenaeus, the eschaton is, not simply a return to Eden, but a progression beyond it.[11] The beginning is a prolepsis of the end, and the end will be a fulfillment of the beginning. Hence, God does not fashion a perfect creation but rather a creation *in via* toward a telos. To develop this point for the purpose of my project, I must note a few important details concerning Irenaeus's view of creation.

First, for Irenaeus, God does not create perfect and mature human beings. On the contrary, Irenaeus views Adam and Eve as existing in the capacity of innocent children needing to grow into adulthood. Thus, concerning the creation of Adam, Irenaeus writes that he "was [but] small; for he was a child; and it was necessary that he should grow, and so come to [his] perfection."[12] Later, he states of both Adam and Eve: "There was in them an innocent and childlike mind."[13] For Irenaeus, God creates children that need to mature into God-like beings. This language is further solidified in his view of the image and likeness of God, which for Irenaeus constitute a reality proper to the human creature and a calling toward God-likeness.[14] This necessity of growth explains why the eschaton is not simply a return to Eden. In the eschaton, humanity will exist in the capacity of adults, participating in the divine nature and thus inhabiting God-likeness.

A second imperative point involves Irenaeus's view of the human role in creation. Many commentators on Irenaeus's theology have limited his soteriology to the human community. Denis Minns writes,

> The central focus of the economy is the creature formed from mud by the hands of God... Everything else in creation derives its significance from its relationship to humankind, for whose benefit it exists. For all practical purposes, then, the "stages" of the divine economy are all stages of the development of humankind toward its divine perfection.[15]

This emphasis on the salvation of the human creation is not without warrant. After all, Irenaeus does claim that "creation is suited to [the wants of] man; for man was not made for its sake, but creation for the sake of man."[16] However, if commentators are blind to the implications of salvation for the rest of the created order, their view of Irenaeus's soteriology is incomplete. For Irenaeus, the human creature bears a role – a special responsibility – in the created order. Hence, in *The Demonstration* Irenaeus writes that God endowed humans with certain faculties "that [they] might rule all those things that were upon the earth."[17] In light of this passage, Steenberg notes that the anthropocentrism of Irenaeus has been subject to a "misapprehension by a whole variety of interpreters" and provides a corrective to the dominant interpretation of Irenaeus's anthropocentric soteriology. He writes,

> Humanity and the cosmos are to exist in *mutual interaction and exchange*, through which *both* come to exist fully according to the intention revealed by God at creation, who himself manifests divine glory on both the cosmos and humankind in this *harmonious exchange*.... Creation is at the service of its human lord – it is subservient; but this is a service of growth, not a slavery of submission. The service of creation to the human race is to advance *both* parties fully into their *teloi* at the fulfilment of the economy.[18]

As Steenberg rightly notes, one cannot limit the economy of salvation to only human concerns. In fact, the importance of human beings is at least partly predicated on their role in leading the *nonhuman creation* into perfection. In this sense, God calls the human creature to mature and lead all of creation into its divinely ascribed end. Hence, when Irenaeus states, "It is fitting .. that the creation itself, being restored to its primeval condition, should without restraint be under the dominion of the righteous," he prefaces this sentence with the affirmation that "God is rich in all things, and all things are His."[19] The anthropocentrism of Irenaeus is always couched in theocentrism and, based on this theocentrism, tends toward a functional anthropocentrism. The creation is not humanity's toy but rather humanity's God-given responsibility. Furthermore, all things belong to God. And God calls all things, through the agency of the human creature, into God's peaceful kingdom. As such, Irenaeus quotes Romans 8 and claims that the dominion of humanity will result in the deliverance of all creation "from the bondage of corruption into the glorious liberty of the sons of God."[20] God calls the human creature to lead the entire creation toward the telos into which God draws humanity.

These points elucidate another important aspect of Irenaeus's view of creation: the Fall. First, the Fall of humanity is not a fall from perfection. It is rather a fall from the path to perfection.[21] Hence, for Irenaeus, the Fall is not a single act serving as a fulcrum between two states of existence. Rather, as Steenberg notes, "The misdirection of the divine economy is .. a departure from the pathway on which Adam and Eve were originally set, and there is in this departure a genuine loss of the possessions held there."[22] Further, this loss is a "loss of potential, rather than the loss of actualised realities."[23] Second, the Fall of humanity has an adverse effect on all of creation in the sense that humanity's fall from that path to perfection also constitutes creation's fall from the path to perfection. In short, the entire creation *in via* is misdirected and subjected to frustration.[24]

However, for Irenaeus, the incarnation of the Logos remedies the Fall by undoing the systemic harm from the original disobedience. The obeisance of Mary surmounts the sacrilege of Eve. The obedience of Christ conquers the failure of Adam. The cross triumphs over the tree of the knowledge of good and evil.[25] In this way, states Irenaeus, Christ "achieved our redemption, and fulfilled the promise of the fathers, and abolished the old disobedience."[26] It is thus through Christ that humanity returns to the path toward perfection.

If the Fall results in a disruption of humanity's progressive growth but Christ restores humanity, not to a state of perfection, but to that path of progressive growth, should not humans bear proleptic signs of the eschatological hope as we mature? As Steenberg writes,

> The *telos* towards which humanity is moving, the adulthood for which the child strives, is nothing other than the completion of the one creative movement of God which commenced "in the begin-ning", which was revealed in its fullness in the incarnate Christ, and which will find fulfilment in the eternal kingdom.[27]

Steenberg goes on to claim that, for Irenaeus, the eschatological hope is the finality of that toward which humanity strives. This denotes a "progressive development toward and into Christ."[28] Here, my inference is that, as harmonious relationships are indicative of the eschatological future as well as the proleptic beginning, humans moving forward on the path toward perfection should reflect those realities to whatever extent possible.

Like Irenaeus, Ephrem holds that Christ restored humanity to a path that leads beyond Paradise. He writes, "The ultimate aim of the incarnation...was not just to restore...humanity to Paradise, but to raise humanity to the position of honor that Adam and Eve would have been granted had they kept the divine commandment."[29] In this passage, Ephrem notes a need for restoration. At the Fall, something is lost. However, for Ephrem, salvation does not equate to becoming as Adam and Eve; rather, it equates to becoming as Adam and Eve would have become. It is becoming like Christ. In this sense, Adam and Eve were on the path to the likeness of God. The Fall disrupts their journey and requires restoration. Hence, the eschatological destination of fallen humanity is the same eschatological destination Adam and Eve would have achieved in the absence of their trespass. Thus, as with Irenaeus, for Ephrem the Fall is a departure from the path toward humanity's eschatological telos. This departure requires restoration. But what does this restoration include? To answer this question with regard to my particular focus, I look first to Ephrem's view of human and animal relationships in a postlapsarian world and second to Ephrem's emphasis on humanity's clothing of glory.

I have already shown that Ephrem holds that humans and animals enjoyed peaceful relationships prior to the trespass of Adam and Eve.[30] However, concerning the time of the deluge, Ephrem refers to the peace between the animals entering the ark as a "novel sight."[31] Between life in Eden and life outside of Eden, the normative experience of animals coming to humanity "as to a loving shepherd" and "without fear"[32] degrades.[33] The inescapable assumption is the introduction of predatory relationships in a postlapsarian world. Furthermore, predation is so normative by the time of Noah that the peace of animals is a "novel sight."

Hence, unlike Adam in Eden, Noah lives within a world of disharmony. Yet regarding the animals gathering to the ark and the humans watching, Ephrem writes,

When those of [the generation of Noah][34] gathered [to see] this novel sight, it was not to repent, but rather to amuse themselves. Then, in their very presence, the lions began to enter the ark and the bulls, with no fear, hurried in right on their heels to seek shelter with the lions. The wolves and the lambs entered together and the hawks and the sparrows together with the doves and the eagles.[35]

Ephrem's description of the animals coming to Noah is quite similar to his description of how they came to Adam. In this sense, the interaction between Noah and the animals on the ark recalls the prelapsarian harmony of Eden.[36] Furthermore, Tryggve Kronholm notes the connection between the language of Ephrem's passage and the eschatology of Isaiah 11.[37] The resemblance of Eden coupled with the language of Isaiah's future prophecy suggests that this postlapsarian episode not only recalls a prelapsarian harmony but also serves as a prolepsis of the eschatological future in which that harmony will be reestablished.

Kronholm also notes that in Ephrem's hymns, the ark is a typological expression of the Church and the animals are typological expressions of various kinds of humans living in harmony within the Church.[38] While this reading does appear in Ephrem's hymns,[39] in his commentary on Genesis Ephrem envisions the peace between the animals and Noah as literal – evincing Noah's righteousness and calling the wicked to repentance. Hence, Ephrem writes that God administered judgment when "those of that generation were still not persuaded, neither by the gathering of all the animals at that time nor by the love that instantly grew between [the animals]."[40] In other words, in the deluge narrative, Noah evidences eschatological hope with righteous living. His righteous living, in turn, leads to an image that both recalls the harmony of Paradise and adumbrates the peaceful kingdom of Isaiah 11. In this manner, Noah is a postlapsarian example of righteous humanity evidencing the harmonious relationships of the eschaton prior to eschatological fulfillment.

The deluge thus provides an example of evidencing the eschaton in the Old Testament. For Ephrem, however, the Incarnation is essential for a normative return to the path toward the eschaton. This point is clear when considering the theophanic language of humanity's clothing of glory.[41] Ephrem writes that, in Eden, Adam and Eve were clothed in the glory of God, who "set [Adam] in the garden to dwell, clothed him in glory and made him ruler over all the trees of Paradise."[42] It is worth noting that Ephrem links Adam's dominion with the glory.[43] Furthermore, Ephrem writes, "It was because of the glory with which they were clothed that they were not ashamed."[44] In this passage, it is clear that Ephrem views both Adam and Eve as clothed in glory. It is also apparent that Ephrem links the language of glory with existence in Paradise. For this reason, it is not surprising that the trespass of the first humans bears a dual consequence of humanity's loss of both their glory and their place in Eden. Ephrem writes, "It was when this glory was stripped from them after they had transgressed the commandment that they were ashamed because they were naked."[45]

For Ephrem, Christ bears the glory that Adam and Eve lost. When "the wolves" stripped his garments from him during his Passion, they only revealed the glory underneath.[46] Furthermore, it is only because Christ put on the flesh of humanity that humanity may again wear the glory of God. In his hymns, Ephrem expresses this reality through a consideration of Mary, who states, "I put on the glory of Him who put on the body, the garment of His mother."[47] In a subsequent nativity hymn, Ephrem states that Christ took on the suffering and death of humanity in order to return to Adam (used here as a general symbol for humanity) the robe of glory that he lost.[48] Elsewhere, Ephrem states,

"Christ came to find Adam who had gone astray, to return him to Eden in the garment of light."[49]

In his work, *Hymns on Paradise*, Sebastian P. Brock writes a fine compendium on Ephrem's use of humanity's clothing on glory.[50] Brock notes that Ephrem creatively uses the glory theme to hold the entire cosmic drama of redemption together:

> Basically there are four main episodes which go to make up this cosmic drama: at the Fall, Adam and Eve lose the "Robe of Glory" with which they had originally been clothed in Paradise; in order to re-clothe the naked Adam and Eve (in other words, humanity), God himself "puts on the body" from Mary, and at the Baptism Christ laid the Robe of Glory in the river Jordan, making it available once again for humanity to put on at baptism; then, at his or her baptism, the individual Christian, in "putting on Christ," puts on the Robe of Glory, thus reentering the terrestrial anticipation of the eschatological Paradise, in other words, the Church; finally, at the resurrection of the Dead, the just will in all reality reenter the celestial Paradise clothed in their Robes of Glory.[51]

Drawing on Ephrem's writings, Brock admirably delineates Ephrem's view of salvation history in terms of the loss and regaining of the clothing of glory. He is also correct, in my view, in stating that while Christ renders it possible for humanity to take up the clothing of glory, the completion of this redemption is ultimately eschatological. In this sense, putting on the Robe of Glory by putting on Christ is "reentering the terrestrial *anticipation* of the eschatological Paradise." Redeemed humans are not at the eschaton, but nonetheless they can anticipate it within the confines of history.

The theophanic language of glory connects both Eden and the eschaton to the present through the incarnation. Christ has enabled a return to the path toward the eschaton and movement along that path. As with Irenaeus, for Ephrem the Fall is a departure from the path toward the eschaton; but the work of Christ permits a return to that path. Furthermore, as harmony between the animals and humans is characteristic of both protology and eschatology for Ephrem, my inference is again that a return to the path – a reclothing in glory – should progressively include peace to whatever degree possible. That is, one way of living in anticipation of the eschaton is refusing to participate in predatory relationships when such participation is not a vital necessity.

In sum, in the theologies of both Irenaeus and Ephrem, creation in Eden was *in via* toward fulfillment of its telos. Life in Paradise includes peace between humans and animals. Life in the eschaton will also include such peace. Christ enables a return to that path – a return of the garments of glory. This framework provides the opportunity to affirm that peaceful acts between humans and animals evidence the reality of Christ's work and serve as a prolepsis of eschatological hope.

Filling in the framework

I have delineated a framework from the writings of Irenaeus and Ephrem. Within this framework, the present reality of competition within creation is portrayed as an unnatural perversion of life in Paradise that will be erased in the eschatological kingdom. Furthermore, through Christ humans can proleptically witness, at least in part, to the reality of Paradise and the hope of the eschaton. As already stated, my argument is that the proleptic witnessing evident in this theological framework could – perhaps even *should* – include peaceful relationships between humans and animals to whatever degree possible. But is this inference justified? To argue that it is, I turn to other voices in the Christian tradition.[52]

I begin with a specific affirmation of my inferences in the ascetical homilies of Isaac of Nineveh. This seventh-century bishop contributes to the notion that humans can serve as a prolepsis of eschatological hope. He writes,

> Though the humble man is contemptible in his eyes, his honor is esteemed by all creation. The humble man approaches ravenous beasts, and when their gaze rests upon him, their wildness is tamed. They come up to him as their Master, wag their heads and tails and lick his hands and feet, for they smell coming from him that same scent that exhaled from Adam before the fall, when they were gathered together before him and he gave them names in paradise. This was taken away from us, but Jesus has renewed it through his coming.[53]

There are a few important elements of this passage. First, the work of Christ has returned a lost attribute to the human race. Second, for Isaac, the loss of this attribute at the Fall evidently disrupts the relationships between humans and animals. Thus, this attribute, referred to as the "scent that exhaled from Adam before the fall," is connected to the peaceful life of Paradise. Third, the return of this attribute is evident in harmonious relationships between humans and animals. As with Ephrem's reading of the deluge narrative, in this passage Isaac uses the language of Eden to describe the relationships experienced between righteous humans and animals. With Isaac, however, the occurrence is explicitly in the present and derives from the work of Christ.

The above passage suggests that the peace between humans and animals rests on the submission of animals to righteous humanity. However, Isaac views this relationship as reciprocal. In his *Mystical Treatises*, he writes,

> What is a merciful heart?...The burning of the heart unto the whole creation, man, fowls and beasts, demons and whatever exists; so that by the recollection and the sight of them the eyes shed tears on account of the force of mercy which moves the heart by great compassion. Then the heart becomes weak and it is not able to bear hearing or examining injury or any insignificant suffering of anything in creation. And therefore even in behalf of the irrational beings and the enemies of the truth and even in behalf of those who do harm to it, at all times he offers prayers with tears that they may be guarded and strengthened; even in behalf of the kinds of reptiles, on account of his great compassion which is poured out in his heart without measure, after the example of God.[54]

In this passage, Isaac views great compassion for all creation as evidence that one is on the right path toward perfection. This person does not cause unnecessary harm and laments the suffering of all, even demons. This person offers prayers on behalf of animals.

Perhaps quoting a seemingly random saint from the seventh century appears a bit of a stretch. However, after appealing to the Orthodox view that the telos of the entire cosmos is deification, Vladimir Lossky cites Ephrem's passage as indicative of the theology of the Eastern Orthodox Church.[55] Says Lossky, "*In his way* to union with God, man in no way leaves creatures aside, but gathers together in his love *the whole cosmos disordered by sin*, that it may at last be transfigured by grace."[56] Considering both of Isaac's passages, it appears that he confirms the view that peace between humans and animals is indicative of movement along the path toward eschatological hope. Furthermore, this peace begins with the work of Christ and is channeled through righteous humanity, transforming the wilderness.

There are numerous accounts validating Isaac's passages in the religious orders of the Church. Many hagiographies record narratives of miraculous peace between the saints and animals. The medieval saints provide an exceptional number of examples. Before I explore these in brief, consider two passages, one from the apocryphal New Testament, another from the book of Mark. In Pseudo-Matthew, predatory animals worship the infant Jesus and protect him and his family on their journey through the wilderness to Egypt.[57] Dragons come from a cave and frighten the group during their travel. But Jesus stands before them, and they worship him. Afterwards, Jesus stays his parents' fear by claiming that all creatures of the forest will be tame before him.[58] The subsequent chapter of the gospel validates this claim and is worth quoting at length:

> Lions and panthers adored Him [Christ] likewise, and accompanied them in the desert. Wherever Joseph and the blessed Mary went, they went before them showing them the way, and bowing their heads; and showing their submission by wagging their tails, they adored Him with great reverence. Now at first, when Mary saw the lions and the panthers, and various kinds of wild beasts, coming about them, she was very much afraid. But the infant Jesus looked into her face with a joyful countenance, and said: Be not afraid, mother; for they come not to do thee harm, but they make haste to serve both thee and me. With these words He drove all fear from her heart. And the lions kept walking with them, and with the oxen, and the asses, and the beasts of burden which carried their baggage, and did not hurt a single one of them, though they kept beside them; but they were tame among the sheep and the rams which they had brought with them from Judaea, and which they had with them. They walked among wolves, and feared nothing; and no one of them was hurt by another. Then was fulfilled that which was spoken by the prophet: Wolves shall feed with lambs; the lion and the ox shall eat straw together. There were together two oxen drawing a waggon with provision for the journey, and the lions directed them in their path.[59]

In this extraordinary account, Jesus heralds the messianic kingdom of Isaiah 11. The evidence that the kingdom is breaking into the world is found in the peaceful relationships between Jesus and the predatory animals in the wilderness. Not only do these creatures not harm Jesus and the other humans, but they also do not harm the domesticated animals in the group.

Turning from this apocryphal account, it is pertinent to consider an earlier tradition in the gospel according to Mark. In his prologue, following Jesus's baptism, Mark claims, "the Spirit immediately drove him [Jesus] out into the wilderness. He was in the wilderness for forty days, tempted by Satan; and he was with the wild beasts; and the angels waited on him" (Mark 1:12–13). In his second article in the book *Animals on the Agenda*, Richard Bauckham claims that Mark's short reference to Jesus's presence "with the wild beasts" is steeped in theological significance. First, Bauckham depicts a Jewish context echoed in the views of both Irenaeus and Ephrem:

> The Jewish tradition, in the context of which Mark 1.13 should be read, saw the enmity of the wild animals as a distortion of the created relationship between humans and animals and the result of human sin. In creation God established human dominion over the animals (Gen. 1.26; Ps. 8.6–8; Sir. 17.2–4; Wisd. 9.2–3), which should have been peaceful and harmonious, but was subsequently disrupted by violence.[60]

Second, the syntax of Mark's passage suggests that Jesus's presence transformed the wilderness:

> Mark's simple but effective phrase indicates Jesus' peaceable presence with them [the wild animals]. The expression 'to be with someone' (*einai meta timos*) frequently has the strongly positive sense of close association or friendship or agreement or assistance...and in Mark's own usage elsewhere in his Gospel, the idea of close, friendly association predominates (3.14, 5.18, 14.67; cf. 4.36). Mark 1.13 depicts Jesus enjoying the peaceable harmony with wild animals which had been God's original intention for humanity but which is usually disrupted by the threat of violence.[61]

In these two passages, Jesus serves as a prolepsis of the eschatological kingdom. Furthermore, this prolepsis is evident in the peaceful relationships (friendship!) between Jesus and the animals. Bauckham goes on to state,

> Mark's image of Jesus with the animals provides a christological warrant for and a biblical symbol of the human possibility of living fraternally with other living creatures, a possibility given by God in creation and given back in messianic redemption. Like all aspects of Jesus' inauguration of the kingdom of God, its fullness will be realized only in the eschatological future, but it can be significantly anticipated in the present.[62]

These images further contribute to an alternative tradition in Christian thought that envisions Jesus as the inaugurator of the messianic age in which humans and animals may experience a new peace. As Bauckham notes, this peace is not finalized. Nonetheless, it may be witnessed to by the righteous. Moreover, it is reciprocal. But it begins with the righteous, being channeled through them from the work of Christ.

This alternative strand is further validated by the countless narratives of saints experiencing miraculous harmony with animals. Space permits only a brief treatment of this subject.[63] Considering the messianic expectations of the reestablishment of a harmonious creation in Jewish thought and the reception of that expectation in early and later Christian writings, it is not surprising that the experience of Jesus "with the wild beasts" is taken up in the hagiographies of the saints.[64] Some, like Anselm and the later Silouan the Athonite, weep at the plight of animals.[65] Other saints, such as Denis and Giles, provide animals with safety from human hunters.[66] Still other saints administer healing practices toward animals. St. Jerome removes a thorn from a lion's paw and in return received the creature's faithful service.[67]

In an article exploring animals in the *Virtues of Saint Macarius*, Tim Vivian notes how peace between the saint and animals evidences proleptically the peaceable kingdom. In one narrative, Macarius not only heals the young of a hyena by making the sign of the cross but also later instructs the mother to not harm any other creatures but rather to eat only carrion.[68] Considering similar stories, Vivian notes,

> Macarius, through God's enlightenment and grace, [enacts] the peaceable kingdom, where he lives in peace with antelopes, hyenas, sheep – and even snakes. The chief virtue of this kingdom, it appears, is compassion: not dogma, not orthodoxy, not orthopraxis, but love and empathy and mercy for others, even non-human others.[69]

Considering these narratives of saints in light of the framework provided by Irenaeus and Ephrem, which is augmented by both Isaac of Nineveh's passages concerning the characteristics of the saint and the apocryphal reference to Jesus's inauguration of the peaceful kingdom, it is clear that a countertradition to that of Aquinas exists in Christian history. These strands of thought are not the invention of contemporary voices. In the words of Tim Vivian,

> Although monks lived in close proximity with spiders, snakes, scorpions, jackals, wolves, and lions, most of them appeared to have lived

quite peaceably with their animal companions in the desert. Such peaceful coexistence, and even community, has the power, therefore, to point our age, made ecologically sensitive by necessity, to the possibility of better relationship with the nonhuman creature with whom we share God's creation. Just as importantly, the monks can guide us toward the possibility of a peaceable kingdom, one created by God in the Garden and reenvisioned by the prophets.[70]

In sum, while a collective vision of concern for nonhuman animals is an inference within the theological framework provided by Fathers such as Irenaeus and Ephrem, it is validated by other writings and narratives in the Christian tradition. The saints frequently transfigure the wilderness with their righteousness. Furthermore, Isaac of Nineveh claims that this transformative power that makes for peace in the wilderness derives from the work of Christ. The portrait painted by these narratives strongly resembles the inferences I make for a creation *in via* toward an eschatological hope that includes peace for all creatures.

Beyond conservation in the Christian tradition

The framework provided by Irenaeus and Ephrem, among others, opens a space for more than conservationism. Within this framework, conservation of the present natural order is insufficient for the Christian witness because it is predicated on the belief that the system, in this case the cosmos, is good if the system is ordered or sustainable. Neither what the order looks like nor the cost of sustaining it seems to matter.[71] Such a view is insufficient because God charges the redeemed human with more than conservation and preservation. God charges them with the task of witnessing to the teleological hope of the transfiguration of the cosmos.[72] As this hope includes harmonious relationships in the created order, the human being should serve as a leading witness – a prolepsis – of those harmonious relationships by practicing them to the extent possible.

Drawing out this transfigurative strand of Christian thought reveals powerful sources with which Christianity can address ecological issues beyond the typical conversations of rights, utility, and conservation. It draws hope into the present by permitting God's revelation of a future peace to inform ethics in the present. It affirms the inherent value of the nonhuman creation without negating its alterity. It also implicitly addresses issues of theodicy by gathering the suffering of the entire created order into the human hope for redemption. It does perhaps invite the critique of promulgating a "wanton anticipation" of the eschaton by emphasizing a seemingly unrealistic "already" of eschatological hope. However, the emphasis of this strand of tradition is neither on constructing the eschatological kingdom of God through human efforts nor claiming a realized or realizable eschatology, but rather on witnessing to the hope of that kingdom through a transformed heart that welcomes a wider scope of mercy and compassion. This compassion is not the fullness of the eschatological kingdom but rather a proleptic witness to the future hope of the cosmos.

Conclusion

The strand of tradition that I have delineated in this chapter maintains that the present disrupted order in creation is framed by both a proleptic protology and an eschatological teleology that include harmonious relationships between humans and nonhuman animals. When this vision is combined with the belief that Christ enables movement toward eschatological hope and the notion that peaceful relationships between humans and animals evince such progress – as is evident in the lives of many saints – the theological grounds for an eschatological ethics that places nonhuman animals in a realm that grounds a moral concern beyond anthropocentrism and conservation takes shape. For this reason, one can argue from within the narrative of the Christian tradition – from sources such as Irenaeus and Ephrem to the hagiographies of the saints – that the human agent, inasmuch as he or she moves along the path toward eschatological hope, can (and ought to) become a prolepsis of that hope in part by engaging in progressively greater practices of animal welfare. In doing so, humans can, in the words of Isaac, reveal "compassion...without measure" for all creatures "after the example of God."[73]

5
Breaking with Anthropocentrism: Genesis 1

In Chapter 3, I briefly explore various interpretations of the *imago Dei* and delineate arguments in favor of at least a functional dimension of it. In this chapter I revisit these arguments mainly for the sake of connecting humanity's bearing of the *imago* to the dietary allowances that God offers in Genesis 1:29–30. This task requires an inquiry into the context of the *imago* within the first chapter of Genesis. More specifically, it includes an examination of the particular God (Elohim) whose image humanity bears. An exegetical consideration of verses 29 and 30 (but especially verse 29) in conjunction with this examination yields an in-text interpretation of the content of the *imago*. Finally, comparing this interpretation of the original content of the *imago* with the re-creation narrative of Genesis 9:1–3, I argue that the nature of the image of God shifts in such a manner that its functional dimension is difficult to trace back to Elohim. In fact, the functional reign of humanity as depicted in Genesis 9 aligns more easily with the *imago* Marduk – the violent Babylonian deity of the *Enuma Elish* – than the *imago* Elohim.

Bearing the image of a *particular* God: Elohim versus Marduk

Terrance Fretheim laments that, regarding the doctrine of the *imago Dei*, there has been an "almost exclusive focus" on the terms "image" and "likeness," while the question of the God in whose image humanity is made is largely ignored.[1] My aim here is to establish more thoroughly what the functional role of the *imago* ought to look like. Per Fretheim's comment, I examine the God in whose image humanity is made.

However, this endeavor raises a problem. I am in sympathy with Janell Johnson's concern that while an understanding of the image of God is imperative for Christian life, the doctrine itself is based on a God who is presented in variegated manners throughout the Bible. In short, the character of God is difficult to delineate.[2] Thus, subscribing to a functional view of the image of God presents a challenge for theologians and biblical scholars alike. Since I am here concerned with Genesis 1 (and later Genesis 9 in relation to Genesis 1), my focus is on the Priestly author's depiction of God (Elohim) in the first creation narrative.[3]

Israel's creation myths were not written in a vacuum. The authors and redactors drew upon a milieu of cosmogonical images and themes of the ancient Near East and, in doing so, disputed many of the claims evident in other creation myths. Bill Arnold argues that the author of Genesis 1 "was familiar with Egyptian and Mesopotamian cosmogonies and intended to present an alternative worldview."[4] However, as James McKeown writes, "The theological teaching of Genesis is fundamentally different from anything else that has been discovered."[5] Thus, while there are thematic similarities between Genesis and other cosmogonies of the ancient Near East, the narrative of Genesis is far from derivative. It is in fact its uniqueness that helps shed light on the theological import of Genesis 1. When it is compared with competing cosmogonies, the areas of stark contrast highlight poignant theological emphases made by the Priestly writer.[6]

One such competing cosmogony is the Babylonian myth of the *Enuma Elish* (examined briefly in Chapter 3). It depicts a world of many gods, all the offspring of Apsu and Tiamat. The gods are too loud for Apsu, who plots to kill them all. This plot is thwarted when the younger gods learn of it and kill Apsu first. When Tiamat learns of Apsu's death and is again reminded of the noise made by the younger gods, she goes to battle against them. A younger Babylonian god, Marduk, is enlisted to battle Tiamat. Marduk defeats her and uses her body to create the world. After Marduk's victory, he is crowned king of the gods. As one of his first acts, he kills Kingu, one of the gods that fought with Tiamat, and uses his blood to create humans:

> Blood I will mass and cause bones to be. I will establish a savage, "man" shall be his name. Truly, savage-man I will create. He shall be charged with the service of the gods that they may be at ease![7]

This depiction of the creation of the cosmos and humanity is quite different in tone from Genesis 1. David Cotter, in his comparison of the two accounts, highlights a number of disparities.[8] The gods of the *Elish* are derivative (that is, they have an origin either in other gods or in the formless chaos), while Elohim is not. Marduk engages in warfare for the purpose of defeating Tiamat. Elohim has no rival and therefore engages in no combat. In the *Elish*, the heavenly lights are deities. In Genesis, they are lights that reveal the passage of time. Marduk makes humans out of the corpse of a rebellious enemy and enslaves them. Elohim creates humanity in his image and grants it dominion.

The theological contrast is sharp.[9] Elohim's rule is kenotic and other-affirming as opposed to exploitative and enslaving. This point is further confirmed by an investigation into whether or not Genesis 1 presents Elohim as creating in the wake of a victory over chaos (classically referred to as *Chaoskampf*, or "combat myth"). To explore this issue, I turn to the work of J. Richard Middleton.[10]

As already noted, in the *Enuma Elish* Marduk's act of creation of the cosmos follows upon the heels of a grand war among the gods. Hence, this Babylonian myth envisions creation via *Chaoskampf*.[11] In this model, the cosmos ultimately burgeons out of violence and death. The world itself is built from a divine corpse! While there are themes of combat with chaos in the Hebrew Scriptures,[12] Middleton notes,

> As with God's battle with the mythological waters, most of the references to God's defeat of these various monsters are not associated with creation, but rather describe God's historical judgment on foreign military or political powers.[13]

Because God's victories over chaos tend to occur within the context of an already existing creation, Middleton notes, "God's relationship to the world predates the origin of violence, which is portrayed as beginning with human disobedience in Gen 3."[14]

The lack of violence in Genesis 1 is also noted by Bill Arnold:

> "The most prominent literary feature in Gen 1 is its recurring formulaic structure and symmetry.... Such literary symmetry mirrors the balance and order of the created cosmos itself. Rhetoric imitates reality, as nothing is left to chance. Creation by God's word marches forward inexorably, encountering no resistance whatsoever, as plants, animals, and finally humans are created according to the will and design of that divine word."[15]

For Arnold, this feature of the Priestly cosmogony entails an implicit rejection of neighboring cosmogonies. He writes, "[The text] contains no theomachy, or cosmic conflict among the gods, or victory enthronement motif."[16]

There is no violent creation in Genesis 1.[17] In fact, even those creatures that typically symbolize the necessity for *Chaoskampf* (for example, the *tanninim*, or "dragons") are, according to Middleton, "part of God's peaceable kingdom."[18] God's act of creation is an act of sovereignty that includes other creatures in the creative process. It requires no violence. Whereas Marduk creates by conquering all other powers, Elohim creates by enabling other powers and giving them their own space to be.[19] Ultimately, Middleton states that this view of God as a nonviolent creator and loving enabler of the other develops "significantly different ethical implications for humanity made in God's image."[20]

It is these ethical implications that constitute the next step in this chapter. What might bearing the image of Elohim look like vis-à-vis nonhuman animals? Even if the only piece of information readers had to answer this question was the comparison of Marduk and Elohim, that still might be sufficient to argue for nonviolence. However, there is another piece of critical information that supports all the more the position of nonviolence: the verse that immediately follows the *imago* pronouncement and creative act of Genesis 1:26–28.

Reflecting Elohim to nonhuman animals: Genesis 1:26–29

Bill Arnold reads Genesis 1 as climaxing in the creation of humanity. While humans are a "subset of living creatures,"[21] their creation is nonetheless "distinguished by a different kind of divine speech."[22] That is, whereas God said previously, "let the waters bring forth" and "let the earth bring forth" with regard to the creation of nonhuman life, the creation of humanity begins with a divine reflection: "Let us make humankind in our image, according to our likeness."[23]

However, the uniqueness of the human is not simply (or primarily) a matter of status.[24] Arnold maintains that the *imago Dei*, when read in the sociohistorical context of the Priestly author, maintains that "humans are created to function as the divine image through the exercise of 'dominion' and 'rule'."[25] In Arnold's view, it is this function that is the "motivation behind God's creation of humans in his image."[26]

This functional interpretation, examined and defended in Chapter 3, finds earlier roots in the work of Gerhard von Rad, who writes, "The text speaks less of the nature of God's image than of its purpose. There is less said about the gift itself than about the task. This then is sketched most explicitly: domination of the world, especially over the animals."[27] Von Rad evades the question of the content of the *imago* and emphasizes rather the command that accompanies it. Similarly, while he avoids defining the exact nature of the image of God, Kenneth Matthews writes that the consequence of the *imago* is human dominion.[28] Thus, while God has created the various forms of life that preceded humans with capacities matching the domains of their particular existences (that is, water, sky, and land), God creates human beings with the capacities necessary for a particular function with regard to all of these domains.[29]

In light of this assertion, it is worth noting that Genesis provides the reader with further explication as to how one ought to understand the human dominion over the nonhuman creation that derives from bearing the image of Elohim. Many biblical scholars and theologians, when delineating the meaning of "image" with reference to Genesis 1, unfortunately focus solely on Genesis 1:26–28. But if one reads further, the text states:

> God said, "See, I have given you every plant yielding seed that is upon the face of all the earth, and every tree with seed in its fruit; you shall have them for food. And to every beast of the earth, and to every bird of the air, and to everything that creeps on the earth, everything that has the breath of life, I have given every green plant for food." And it was so.[30]

The significance of verses 29 and 30 is that they offer an *exposition on the nature of human dominion.* Claus Westermann notes that the Priestly writer's intention in connecting the *imago* to dominion over the animals "cannot mean killing them for food" in light of Genesis 1:29.[31] However, Westermann does not necessarily maintain that killing for food is therefore prohibited. Rather, it is simply not a dimension of dominion.[32]

Likewise, von Rad writes:

> For nourishment, man is given every kind of vegetable food; the animals are given only the herb of the field. That is the only suggestion of the paradisiacal peace in the creation as it came God-willed from God's hand. Thus, on the other hand, our report of creation places man in striking proximity to the animals. Just as he was created with them on the same day, so he is referred with them to the same table for his bodily needs. Killing and slaughtering did not come into the world, therefore, by God's design and command. Here too the text speaks not only of prehistoric things but of declarations of faith, without which the testimony of faith in creation would not be complete. No shedding of blood within the animal kingdom, and

no murderous action by man! This word of God, therefore, means a significant limitation in the human right of dominion.[33]

This claim – that Genesis 1 presents human dominion over nonhuman animals as limited to the extent that the latter are not to be used as food – is immensely significant, given that the language of dominion bears a history of justification for animal abuses.[34] It does indeed suggest that "killing and slaughtering did not come into the world, therefore, by God's design and command." For Westermann, the dietary allowances of Genesis 1:29–30 are consistent with the dominion given to humanity in verse 28; for "a dominion in which the master merely enjoys the profits coming from his subjects is unthinkable in the Old Testament."[35]

The significance of these verses (particularly verse 29) for human dominion notwithstanding, many theologians and biblical scholars ignore them altogether. Douglas John Hall, whose work is instrumental in understanding the *imago* as loving dominion, never cites either verse.[36] Likewise, Middleton posits that the *imago* provides an ethical framework through which one can rethink human engagement of creation. Still, he does not explore this link between a restricted diet and the *imago*. He does mention Genesis 1:29 but only in reference to the implications for cultivation of the earth.[37] Walter Brueggemann, in his introductory text to the Hebrew Scriptures, also negates any mention of verses 29 and 30.[38]

These omissions may be innocuous enough, given the limited (or extremely broad) focus of the authors. However, verses 29 and 30 are also frequently sidestepped or altogether ignored in commentaries on Genesis. Thus, regarding these verses, Westermann notes the lack of scholarly concern in the twentieth century: "None of the commentaries accessible to me asks the question, 'What is the tradition behind vv. 29–30 all about?'"[39]

For example, Russell Reno, in his contribution to Brazos's theological commentaries on Scripture, offers no theological significance whatsoever to the verses.[40] Similarly, Arnold completely bypasses verses 29 and 30 in his exposition on Genesis.[41] Cotter also avoids them, with the sole exception of noting their place in an outline of Genesis 1.[42] W. Sibley Towner completely skips over them in his commentary on Genesis 1.[43] McKeown also largely overlooks them, especially in his commentary.[44] In his theological reflections, however, he notes that verse 29 highlights the theme of "seed" in primeval history.[45] More significantly, he notes that the nature of humanity's rule – that of harmony – is "underlined by the indication that the animals are not a source of food at this stage, but they and the human beings eat green plants and the produce of the trees (1:29)."[46] No further theological (or ethical) reflection is offered; this brief explanation exhausts his engagement with the passage.

These omissions are particularly glaring in the face of an exploration of the syntax of verse 29. Barry Bandstra argues that the Hebrew הִנֵּה (*hinnêh*, rendered as "see" in the NRSV and as "behold" in the ESV) in the phrase "God said, 'See, I have given you every plant...'" suggests "something unexpected or new or *noteworthy in relation to the context of situation or in relation to the prior text*."[47] Furthermore, "the constituent that follows הִנֵּה typically represents a break with [what] went before, or is an unexpected consequence of what went before." Bandstra continues by arguing that הִנֵּה followed by נָתַתִּי (*natatiy*, "I have given"), "is taken as a significant development and new moment in the course of creation."[48] In other words, the syntax of verse 29 renders it an important and novel commentary on the preceding content – in this case the dominion of humanity as *imago Dei*.[49]

This syntactical observation makes biblical scholars' frequent overlooking of verse 29 particularly troubling. Arnold's omission is all the more perplexing because elsewhere in his text he echoes Bandstra's position that the syntax of הִנֵּה in verse 29 "marks significant benchmarks" in divine speech.[50] It is odd that a signification recognized as important should be completely overlooked by the one who recognizes it.

There are exceptions to the general failure to engage the dietary verses of Genesis 1. In light of these verses, Fretheim notes that the "killing of animals is a post-sin reality."[51] However, Fretheim does not link these verses to the *imago*. Walter Brueggemann, while excluding the verses from his introductory text, connects verse 29 explicitly to the *imago* in his commentary on Genesis. Even so, he does not explore its significance for the doctrine.[52] Similarly, the introductory text, coauthored by Bruce C. Birch, Brueggemann, Fretheim, and David L. Petersen, makes a clear connection between Genesis 1:29 and the *imago*: "It is God as sovereign Creator whose image we bear in our humanity and whose dominion we exercise as representatives of divine rule (Gen 1:26–29)."[53] This reference appears to suggest that the dietary allowances offered in verse 29 somehow capture a dimension of bearing the image of God. However, as in other cases, the authors do not explore this point at all. Furthermore, this reference exhausts the appearances of verses 29 and 30 in the work.

In each of the above cases, the authors mention Genesis 1:29 in passing but do not offer any significant contribution to its meaning in relation to human dominion. In other cases, authors' engagement with these verses leaves the reader confused as to their import. For example, regarding both verses 29 and 30, Nahum Sarna writes,

> God makes provision for the substance of man and beast – a reminder that man is still a creature totally dependent on the benevolence of God. The narrative presupposes a pristine state of vegetarianism. Isaiah's vision of the ideal future in 11:7 and 62:25 sees the carnivorous animals becoming herbivorous.[54]

Sarna notes the presupposition of the text and traces it forward to the eschatological vision of Isaiah. Yet he makes no claims concerning the ethical import of this presupposition. Furthermore, he offers a positive reading of God's eventual allowance for humans to eat meat in Genesis 9:1–3: "Man's power over the animal kingdom is *confirmed and enhanced*."[55] I engage Chapter 9 in detail below. Here, it suffices to note that while Saran recognizes the idyllic vision of both the Priestly author and Isaiah, he seems to suggest that dominion is "enhanced" (better?) in the absence of that vision![56]

Matthews also addresses Genesis 1:29–30 in his commentary. However, he focuses on God's extensive concern for humanity and the post-flood permission to consume meat.[57] Such a reading does not give full weight to the theological import of the passages – in fact, it gives little to no weight to them.

What is the significance of this lack of serious engagement with Genesis 1:29–30? Offering only speculation here, I might suggest that the passages constitute a theological and scientific embarrassment for modern readers. But to properly answer this question is not my intent in this chapter. Rather, I aim to argue that verse 29 explicates the nature of the dominion implied in the *imago*. This explication is naturally animal-friendly, for it suggests that dominion is more the other-affirming reign of Elohim than the other-dominating reign of Marduk. There is, after all, no reason why the Priestly writer had to portray the original creation as vegetarian. Why he did so strikes at the heart of Elohim's nature as a nonviolent creator. It therefore also offers a significant insight into how humanity ought to bear the image of that creator.

In my view, Westermann has it right when he proposes a purpose behind verses 29 and 30. He is here worth quoting at length:

> We can never demonstrate that there was a period when neither humans nor animals ate meat. Nevertheless the primeval statement in vv. 29ff. is talking about reality. There are two aspects to the

reality described: the first concerns the very existence of animals and humans. These words, which are in accordance with one of the traditions of humankind, express an awareness of a period in the history of humans and animals which was different from the present. We can say that this tradition is aware that both animals and humans have undergone a process of development up to the present state even though there are no guidelines at our disposal to study the process carefully…. The other aspect is concerned with the understanding of the nature of their existence. The human being in the world is acutely sensitive to a lack, to something wrong or contradictory; the killing of a living being touches the very existence of living beings. Such experience is linked with an awareness that the origin of all this must lie elsewhere, in a primeval period which is beyond the present. This is the source of the motif that P has taken up in Gen 1:29–30. And so it becomes clear how this motif of primeval time finds its counterpart in the motif of end time. There are a number of texts which speak of peace between the animals, Is 11:2–9; 65:25…. Both factors are at work here: the lived experience of destruction and contradiction, and an awareness of the future that has grown up out of the history of God's people, above all out of prophecy.[58]

This passage suggests that the tradition behind the dietary allowances of verses 29 and 30 is not one that depicts a historical moment of the world that is available to humans by means of an academic inquiry into the past. Rather, the depiction is one of faith in Elohim, one in which humans cannot bear assigning the origins of the harshness of nature's predatory existence to the nonviolent Creator.[59]

Richard Bauckham also addresses verses 29–30, stating that in the first creation narrative

neither humans nor animals are carnivorous. So the human dominion over other living creatures involves no conflict. Its exercise ensures that there is no competition for living space or resources. All is peaceable.[60]

In a manner similar to Westermann, Bauckham argues that given current scientific knowledge one can confidently assert that the nonviolent and completed creation of Genesis 1 never actually existed in history. However, because the creation narrative of Genesis 1 flows into the rest of scripture (and especially Genesis 2–3), the image of a finished and Edenic creation appears more a mythic (and for Bauckham, eschatological) hope than a historical reality. That is, it presents not the historical picture of a completed creation but rather the eschatological hope of creation's destiny. Says Bauckham,

> The way the biblical narrative itself continues is in considerable tension with this picture of a creation already completed in the beginning. Things can go wrong and very soon do. In the light of the whole biblical narrative, the finished character of creation in Genesis 1 takes on a proleptic character, anticipating the new creation with which the narrative ends in Revelation 21–22. Only then will creation, rescued from corruption, enter into God's rest. (Heb. 4:1–11)[61]

One more interpretation of verse 29 is worth noting. It maintains that the verse does not preclude the consumption of meat. Westermann writes, "An assignment or conveyance does not imply any prohibition; it is an action of the creator who is making provision for his creatures."[62] Similarly, Wenham claims that there is evidence enough to deny that the original creation was strictly herbivorous. Like Westermann, he notes the lack of a strict mandate *not* to eat meat in Genesis 1–2 and that after Adam and Eve's transgression, God made garments out of "skins" to cover their nakedness.[63]

While these arguments bear some weight, they are, in my view, overpowered by the parallel of the re-creation narrative after the flood in Genesis 9. Arnold notes, "The new, post-diluvian cosmic order begins as the old has done, reverting essentially to a pre-creation state."[64] However, this new state of creation proceeds differently. The text states:

> God blessed Noah and his sons, and said to them, "Be fruitful and multiply, and fill the earth. The fear and dread of you shall rest on every animal of the earth, and on every bird of the air, on everything that creeps on the ground, and on all the fish of the sea; into your hand they are delivered. Every moving thing that lives shall be food for you; and just as I gave you the green plants, I give you everything."[65]

Here, the dietary revision is explicit. Says Arnold, "The new order is not altogether the same as the old, since it also involves an alteration of the food chain."[66] Thus, while it may be true that there exist ambiguities concerning the peace between humans and animals in reference to "garments of flesh" (not to mention Abel's sacrifice to God), there is at the very least a clear strand of narrative that presents the original diet of humans as not including meat.[67] As Matthews writes, "God did not expressly prohibit the eating of meat in the initial stipulation at creation, but by inference 9:3's provision for flesh is used as a dividing mark between the antediluvian and postdiluvian periods."[68]

From dominion to fear: Genesis 1:28–29 and Genesis 9:1–3

The narrative development regarding dietary allowances in the Priestly strand from Genesis 1 to 9 bears significance for an animal-friendly hermeneutic. Whereas the original *imago* is linked to a dominion that includes neither the right nor permission to kill for food, the revised menu for postdiluvian humanity is linked to "fear and dread." There is, in fact, no mention of dominion in Genesis 9. It is thus odd that Arnold links dominion to this new relationship between humanity and animals: "The blessing of God declares that God is favorably disposed toward Noah and his family, and expresses God's will that they represent him on earth by exercising dominion."[69] Better is McKeown's acknowledgment that a "sinister" shift is afoot in this passage, one that grinds against humanity's original dominion:

As in the previous blessing, this pronouncement focuses on fertility and authority, but with significant differences. While the exercise of dominion is prominent in both pronouncements, the rhetoric of the blessing on Noah and his sons creates a more sinister atmosphere. Humankind originally exercised authority in the harmonious context of the garden of Eden. Now, however, postflood humanity will exercise dominion that will lead to "fear and dread" rather than to harmony. The language of 9:2 in contrast to 1:28 holds the tension between the benevolent Creator with his willingness to bless all his creatures, on the one hand, and the effect of human rebellion with its power to sour relationships, on the other.[70]

While humanity still bears the *imago* in some manner,[71] something has shifted in the relation between human beings and nonhuman animals. This "sinister" shift warrants a clearer delineation of the contrast between the blessing passages, one that is evident in Table 5.1.

While Noah and his family receive God's blessing, they are given no command to subdue the earth. Nor is there is any mention of dominion over the animals. Rather, the original rule of humanity is now depicted with the terms *mowra'* ("fear") and *chath* ("dread").[72] The Hebrew *mowra'* can denote reverence and awe, but it frequently bears a tone of war, of terrible awe.[73] The term is used to recount the fear of the Egyptians at the

Table 5.1   **Comparison of God's blessing in Genesis 1 and Genesis 9**

Genesis 1:28–29	Genesis 9:1–3
God blessed them [man and woman], and God said to them, "Be fruitful and multiply, and fill the earth and subdue it; and have dominion over	God blessed Noah and his sons, and said to them, "Be fruitful and multiply, and fill the earth.
	The fear and dread of you shall rest on
the fish of the sea and over the birds of the air and over every living thing that moves upon the earth."	every animal of the earth, and on every bird of the air, on everything that creeps on the ground, and on all the fish of the sea; into your hand they are delivered. Every moving thing that lives shall be food for you;
God said, "See, I have given you every plant yielding seed that is upon the face of all the earth, and every tree with seed in its fruit; you shall have them for food."	and just as I gave you the green plants,
	I give you everything."

plagues, a fear that will also fall upon the Canaanites when Israel routes them in war.[74] *Chath* is infrequently used in the Hebrew Scriptures. Yet it bears a consistently negative connotation. It suggests a notion of brokenness and cowering.[75] It is better not to have *chath*, evident in God's praise of the leviathan's lack of it in Job.[76]

It is true that, like *mowra'* and *chath*, the Hebrew terms *radah* ("rule," "have dominion") and *kabash* ("subdue") that appear in Genesis 1 also frequently bear violent or warlike connotations[77] and depict scenarios involving slavery.[78] Thus, their use raises an objection to viewing the depiction of the *imago Dei* in Genesis 1 as the loving and caring function of humanity for the nonhuman creation in juxtaposition to the reign of "fear and dread" depicted in Genesis 9. However, this objection fails for two reasons.[79]

First, as I note in Chapter 3, the syntax of Genesis 1:26 (which mentions *radah* and connects to verse 28, where *kabash* and *radah* are both used) suggests that the *waw* conjunction (often translated as "and let") is better understood as "so that" in the logical flow of the passage.[80] Thus, the development of the narrative logically links the image and likeness of God as the foundation for the *kabash* and *radah* over the created order. Towner argues,

This syntactical understanding trumps the etymological background of the words *radah*, and, by analogy, *kabash*, and suggests that in the Priestly account of the human vocation, meanings consistent with the Creator's own strong, universal, and loving "dominion" are intended.[81]

This view is also held by Fretheim, who claims that the "have dominion" in Genesis 1:28 "must be understood in terms of care-giving, even nurturing, not exploitation."[82]

Second, while *radah* does carry connotations of warfare and slavery, it is frequently used in a manner that is modified by a negative adjective. That is, on occasion those who rule are warned not to rule "ruthlessly" (Hebrew *perek*).[83] The addition of this adjective suggests that the connotation of *radah* itself is not *necessarily* negative. Indeed, in 1 Kings 4:24, the rule (*radah*) of Solomon results in peace. Thus Middleton rightly maintains that the meaning of both *radah* and *kabash* does not necessarily denote the violent images evoked elsewhere in Scripture.[84] This brief look into the nuances of *radah* reveals that there is a particular way in which ruling should occur.[85]

The main point to be made, then, is that the original *radah* of humanity, which the Priestly author syntactically links to the *imago Dei*, was a dominion of peace that reflected the nonviolent Creator, Elohim.[86] Thus, Towner concludes, "The picture presented need not be understood as one of rape and pillage, of power and lordship, but one of husbandry and nurture."[87] Cotter also offers a positive assessment:

> As God is to the entire universe – the One who creates a good, blessed, nonviolent place where life is possible and order reigns – so Humanity is to be to the world. We live up to this responsibility when we make the world good, live in just nonviolence, and render the blessed life possible here.[88]

The nonviolence of Elohim extends to the relationship between humans and animals as the former were not even permitted to eat the latter. Only in the postdiluvian world did humans receive such permission. In this case, the eating of flesh is syntactically tied to "fear and dread," not the peaceful *radah* that flows out of the *imago*. This exegetical evidence leads von Rad to write in reference to Genesis 9, "The relationship of man to the animals no longer resembles that which was decreed in ch. 1. The animal world lives in fear and terror of man."[89] Cotter describes this new dietary allowance by stating, "God gives humanity an outlet for its violence."[90]

In line with Cotter's point, I contend that violence is the key to understanding the shift in the text. For whatever reason, God permits violence where – at least according to the Priestly narrative – it was not permitted before.[91] Reno offers an anthropocentric reading of this shift:

> The scope and conditions of human dominion over the animals changes. In the first creation, God gives animals into the care of human beings, and plants as food. Now, God gives the animals as well for food.... There is both a price and a condition for this new bequest. The animals will fear humans, and thus they will now be very difficult to find, domesticate, and put into the service of humanity.[92]

Similarly, Matthews writes,

> Since 1:28 forms the background to the blessing (9:1), it is striking that the charge to "subdue" and "rule" (1:28b) is absent. This admits that the new circumstances of the sin-burdened world have altered this aspect of the Adamic blessing, which now will be difficult to accomplish in the hostile environs of the new world.[93]

Matthews goes on to interpret "fear and dread" in favor of human well-being. That is, these new facets of nonhuman existence "ensure that animal life will not be a threat to the human family."[94]

An anthropocentric interpretation is also offered by Sarna, who, as already noted, considers God's allowance in Genesis 9 an enhancement of humanity's God-given power in the world. In addition to this claim, Sarna describes Genesis 9 in juxtaposition to the Gilgamesh epic, noting that whereas in the latter the survivors "are granted immortality and removed from human society," in the former the characters "are not to withdraw from the world but to be fertile and to utilize the resources of nature for humanity's benefit."[95] Positively, Sarna notes the lack of escapism in the Priestly writer. Negatively – at least with regard to an animal-friendly hermeneutic – nature is reduced to a collection of resources for human use. Again, the downside of "fear and dread" is not the terror or death of animals but rather the complication for humans reaping the resources of the world.

In his interpretation of the term "fear", B. K. Waltke's anthropocentrism takes bold steps outside the text:

> This military term seems to be stronger than to "rule" in 1:28 and implies that the interaction between humans and animals will not

be peaceful.... It was God's intention that human beings voluntarily submit to him and animals to them (see Isa. 11:6–8). But both humans and animals in hubris transgressed their assigned roles. Apparently before the Flood, when all flesh corrupted its behavior (see 6:12), animals got out of control, having no fear of human beings. Despite human sin, God now confirms and enhances human dominion over animals.[96]

It is true that Genesis 6 states that "the earth was corrupt" and "filled with violence" and that "all flesh had corrupted its ways upon the earth."[97] However, the claim that this violence constitutes a violation of the animals' role of submission before humanity goes further than the text warrants.[98] In fact, I would argue that a better reading, given my discussion of Genesis 1 and a functional reading of the *imago*, is that the violence of all flesh traces itself to humanity's failure to represent Elohim – the God of nonviolent creation – to the earth and its nonhuman inhabitants. It is for this reason that Noah, who is righteous, elicits a nonviolent living arrangement among the animals on the ark. As Towner notes, "The ark is a kind of floating garden of Eden where animals and human beings live together in harmony."[99] When human beings properly represent Elohim, as Noah did, the *radah* of peace reigns in creation.[100]

The above readings recognize the dietary shift that occurs between Genesis 1:28–29 and Genesis 9:1–3. They also tend to acknowledge some negative nature of this shift. However, they suggest an anthropocentric foundation to it, claiming that the primary dimension of its negativity is the difficulty in human utilization of nonhuman resources. It is true that the text bears a strong sense of functional anthropocentrism (in which humanity bears a central role in the functioning and development of the cosmos); yet it is much more difficult to establish a clear value-based anthropocentrism (in which humanity is the only creature of intrinsic value) in the narrative. Thus, I maintain that these value-based anthropocentric interpretations overstep the boundaries of the narrative to claim that the negative side of "fear and dread" is encapsulated primarily in humanity's difficulty in utilizing animals efficiently. Such a reading ignores the exegetical evidence in Genesis 1 that humanity's dominion reflects Elohim's nonviolent nature to and for nonhuman animals.

The intrusion of the *imago* Marduk

What is one to conclude from the above exploration into Genesis 1:26–29 and 9:1–3? I already acknowledged in the Introduction that my theological extrapolations are my own, influenced by my personal narrative. That said, given certain key dimensions of my exegetical analysis, I think a *possible* and *valid* reading of the narrative presented in these Priestly texts is that God accommodates human violence by adjusting the "original plan" for creation – specifically, the functional role entailed by humanity's bearing the (nonviolent) divine image – and permitting the human creature a dark place within the nonhuman world. Indeed, human beings still bear the *imago* Elohim,[101] but they function in that capacity as the *imago* Marduk.[102] The *radah* of Elohim's empowering peace becomes the savagery of Marduk's enslaving warmongering, which elicits "fear and dread."[103] Norman Habel captures this reading when he writes:

> Humans are now transformed into beings that terrify the rest of the animal world.... Clearly, this tradition reflects an extreme reversal of the peaceful memory of Eden and the prophetic dream of lions, lambs and humans dwelling in harmony.[104]

Such a reading of the narrative is justified in light of the following exegetical observations:

1. Elohim does not create out of violence but rather by peaceful fiats that empower free creatures to be themselves within the various habitats of the world.
2. Elohim creates human beings to be the *imago Dei*, which at least in part entails a role of the human creature (dominion) vis-à-vis nonhuman animals.
3. Humanity's dominion is couched within dietary allowances (seed-bearing trees and plants) that, especially when compared to the postdiluvian blessing, imply dietary restrictions (humans cannot eat animals).
4. This form of dominion is consistent with the particular God (Elohim, as opposed to Marduk) whose image humanity bears. That is, the other-affirming nonviolence implied by the *imago* for humanity in relation to the animals is mirrored by the nonviolence evident in God's original acts of creation.
5. The postdiluvian permission to eat animals and the "fear and dread" that this permission elicits highlights a shift from the original dominion of humanity to a new form of reign, one that is inferior.

These five points suggest that humanity's new position in relation to nonhuman animals reflects more the violent reign of Marduk than the benevolent creation of Elohim.[105] Humanity effectively becomes the *imago* Marduk – creatures that evoke fear and dread from the animals as opposed to ones that rule as a representative of Elohim. They are enslavers instead of shepherds; heralds of death as opposed to protectors of life.

Moreover, theologically speaking, the original telos of nonhuman animals, at least according to the Priestly strand of Genesis, was not the satisfaction of humans, either for taste or nutrition. In fact, what nonhuman animals are *for humans* is not clearly delineated in Genesis 1. However, that human beings are to be *for animals* in the form of loving dominion is. That humans are no longer *for animals* in this way is further intensified today in our Cartesian reduction of nonhuman animals to commodities for human consumption.

To summarize my contention: the dietary shift between Genesis 1:29 and Genesis 9:2 entails nothing less than a shift in the nature of the *imago Dei* in which humans function no longer as coregents of the nonviolent Elohim but rather as the violent Marduk in his quest for power. The significance of this reading for today is that most humans – so I would wager – still want to encounter the benevolent Elohim in their search for God. They want God to provide for them, to free them, to give them a space to be. From the standpoint of Christian theology, they accept that God the Son died for them. They are grateful for this image of God. But many who want to encounter this God do not seek to reflect this God to animals. They do not provide for animals; they view them as resources for provision. They do not free animals; they trap them for human benefit. They do not give them space; they deny them room to move their limbs for the sake of maximizing monetary gain. Not only will they not die for them (in most cases); they will not even allow the death of Christ to have redemptive value for them.

In all of these ways, humanity continues to search for the face of Elohim while defending the "right" to reflect the *imago* Marduk. Humans cry out for love and mercy from God but joyfully cause fear and dread in animals. In light of my exegetical explorations into Genesis 1:26–29 and Genesis 9:1–3, I argue that human beings ought to strive (as suggested in Chapter 3) to be to nonhuman animals that which they hope God will be to them. They must be willing to pray the dangerous prayer: "Lord, treat us as we treat animals."

Concerning scientific validity

One further point requires a brief exploration in light of my animal-friendly reading of Genesis 1: the question of its scientific validity. It is surely problematic to argue that Genesis 1 represents an actual historical state in which predation is absent among all creatures. The history of biological existence renders such a claim untenable.

Equally problematic, however, is the position taken by David Clough, who maintains that a Darwinian reading of Genesis 1 need not elicit a rejection or even critical retrieval of the text. He argues that the parameters of such a reading are evident in the text itself.[106] I disagree. It is exegetically problematic to overlay the parameters of evolutionary biology onto Genesis 1 without the acknowledgement of critical retrieval. It is true that Genesis and evolution operate under a similar claim – namely, that the cosmos is ordered. But the stark difference is the *kind of order* Genesis presents to the reader, which stands in absolute contradiction to the order of evolutionary biology. The lack of predation evident in verses 29 and 30 (compared to 9:1–3) demands the acknowledgment that the Priestly account of creation (and the origins of predation) is essentially different from Darwinian accounts. This difference, at its core, is not a *historical* difference but a *theological* one. The peaceful God of Genesis 1 cannot be the source of a world as violent as that envisioned in Darwinian evolution.

It seems, then, that modern readers of Genesis are at an impasse. On the one hand, the primeval vision of Genesis 1 does not concur with any stage of cosmic history, from the big bang to its present "groaning." On the other hand, the Priestly cosmogony refuses to lay at the feet of the divine designer the logistics of a predatory world. While this apparent impasse requires much closer examination before anything close to a resolution of its tension can be offered, I concur with Bauckham's notion that Genesis 1 represents an eschatological hope as opposed to an historical reality.[107] In Genesis 1, the reader is glimpsing the divine desire for the world. Such a view does not mandate the rejection of biological history, nor does it *necessarily* unhinge the Priestly writer's understanding of Elohim.[108]

Conclusion

If humans were created in the image of Marduk, perhaps anthropocentric/ utilitarian approaches to the nonhuman creation could be justified. Marduk creates through violence – by oppressing all forces that might challenge him. Marduk creates humans as slaves – utilizing those "lesser" creatures for his own benefit.

However, according to Genesis 1, humans are not created in the image of Marduk. They are created in the image of Elohim, the one who enables and respects alterity. Their dominion – as God originally intended it – is limited to the extent that they were not allotted animals for food. While it is true that the nature of this dominion shifted, God's original intention remains a haunting reminder that humans have all too easily embraced a violent interpretation of dominion while praying for God to bring them peace. Such is the irony of a Judeo-Christian anthropocentrism: it more often than not claims the God it refuses to image.

6

Breaking with Conservationism: Isaiah 11:1–9

In Chapter 5, I examine Genesis 1:26–29 in conjunction with Genesis 9:1–3. That endeavor yields a vision in which God endows humanity with the divine image for the sake of keeping the divine order of the cosmos. This order is, according to the mythos of Genesis 1, not the violent cycle of Darwinian evolution but rather a harmony that mirrors the nonviolent creative acts of Elohim. While God does accommodate humanity's propensity to bear the *imago* Marduk, such an accommodation is subpar in the face of the original divine intention.

In this chapter I turn my attention to what appears to be the eschatological realization of that intention, the peaceable kingdom portrayed in Isaiah 11:1–9. To establish the significance of this passage, I first place the pericope in its larger canonical context, chapters 1–12. This effort requires inquiries into themes of early Isaiah and the sociopolitical context behind the text. I then explore the pericope itself. This exploration entails an inquiry into the unity of verses 1–9, the significance of the attributes of the anointed king in verses 1–5, the question of whether the animals in verses 6–8 ought to be understood literally or metaphorically, and finally the significance of the content itself. With these exegetical examinations in place, I offer an animal-friendly reading of the pericope – one that goes against the traditional view of animals discussed in Chapter 1.

Isaiah 11:1–9 in its larger canonical context of chapters 1–12

Scholars divide the canonical form of Isaiah into three sections: chapters 1–39 ("First Isaiah"), attributed largely to Isaiah of Jerusalem in the eighth century; chapters 40 to the end include work from "Second

Isaiah" and "Third Isaiah," both written in later centuries during the Babylonian exile and the return of the remnant to Jerusalem under the Persian king Cyrus. Because the book has seen the work of multiple authors and redactors, some passages are difficult to place historically. In fact, some scholars suggest the final redaction of the first segment of Isaiah took no less than four hundred years to complete.[1] This historical difficulty applies to Isaiah 11:1–9. Scholars have debated where it fits into the chronology of the book and whether it should be attributed to Isaiah of Jerusalem.[2] However, many scholars suggest the reign of Ahaz, specifically the Syro-Ephraimite crisis, as the backdrop for chapters 7–12, placing chapter 11 firmly in the eighth century.[3] Ulrich Berges reads 1–12 as a literary unit, the end of which is signaled by the songs of thanksgiving in chapter 12.[4] Regarding chapter 11, he writes, "Both syntactically as well as thematically, chap. 11 is securely linked with the previous material as a substantiation of the positive results of Assyria's punishment for the people of God."[5]

Such a reading places chapter 11 in the historical context of Judah's political upheaval in the eighth century. Isaiah received his calling in the year that Uzziah, king of Judah, died (Isaiah 6:1), probably in the year 742 BCE.[6] Isaiah's work in Jerusalem stretched from about 750 to 700 BCE.[7] Uzziah's reign brought about an era of prosperity for the Southern Kingdom, for "he did what was right in the sight of the LORD."[8] However, at the time Isaiah received his call, the world was in a state of dramatic upheaval. He witnessed the death of Jeroboam II in 746 BCE, whose reign signified a time of expansion for the Northern Kingdom of Israel;[9] the fall to pride, physical decline, and death of Uzziah (742 BCE); and the rise of Tiglath-Peleser III as the king of Assyria in 745 BCE.[10] Thus, Isaiah's calling corresponded with a critical time in Judah's history.[11] With the rise of Tiglath-Peleser III, the landscape of politics in the ancient world shifted. Judah was vulnerable to a new superpower. In addition, the presence of Assyria caused problems among the smaller nations. In response to this major power that arose in the east, smaller nations formed coalitions, attempting a creative solution to Assyrian vassalage. When the northern kingdom paired with Syria to form such a coalition, Judah refused to partake in their actions. As a result, Rezin the king of Syria and Pekah the king of Ephraim laid siege to Jerusalem, an event referred to as the Syro-Ephraimite crisis.[12]

Whether or not the poem of Isaiah 11:1–9 was written in this context is less important to me than its placement by the final redactor. I assume this redactor was familiar with Judah's history and was thus aware of the contextual nuances entailed by his or her placement of the passage. Therefore, my consideration of these verses in the context of chapters 1–12 assumes a level of congruency based on the final redaction of the work. Here I follow the point made by Brevard Childs, who notes that even though there are certain problems with the unity of the passage and the date of its authorship,

> nevertheless, there is a conceptual unity to be found in vv. 1–9 within the present literary context of the book. The theme of a description in the original divine intent of creation appears in chapter 1 as a recurring leitmotif. The themes of the restoration of Zion (1:26), the eschatological assembly of the nations of the world at the sacred mountain (2:1–4), and the establishment of a righteous rule by a future messianic ruler (9:1ff.) are reiterated by means of intertextual reference throughout 11:1–9.... In sum, from the perspective of the present literary unity, both in terms of position and function within the larger book, vv. 1–9 must be treated as an integral unit.[13]

Furthermore, while the various source materials that make up chapter 11 and its surrounding material may be variegated, the final redactor arranges the material theologically. Says Childs:

> Chapter 11 has been editorially positioned to form the culmination of a theological direction that commenced at chapter 6, moved through the promise of a coming messianic ruler in chapter 7, and emerged in chapter 9 with the portrayal of a righteous messianic king upon the throne of David. Chapter 11 offers both a correction and an exposition of the messianic reign.[14]

Reading the text from the perspective of canonical unity is significant because, in my interpretation, three key themes that help shed light on 11:1–9 run through the first eleven chapters of Isaiah.

First, there is an oscillation between judgment and hope. Judah has turned away from YHWH's commands. This turning is epitomized by Isaiah's accusation against the people: "They do not defend the orphan, and the widow's cause does not come before them."[15] On account of this injustice, YHWH threatens Judah: "I will turn my hand against you."[16] Even so, Isaiah repeats the hope that Judah "shall be called the city of righteousness, the faithful city."[17] This pattern of judgment and hope continues through much of the early chapters of Isaiah.

The second theme, already adumbrated in the first, is that the root source of the divine judgment against Judah is social injustice. There is oppression against the disenfranchised (the "widows and orphans"). Greed and bribery have replaced justice.[18] The powerful take advantage of the weaker among them, "grinding the face of the poor."[19] Where there ought to be justice, there is instead violence.[20] This theme is summed up well in chapter 10:

> Ah, you who make iniquitous decrees, who write oppressive statutes, to turn aside the needy from justice and to rob the poor of my people of their right, that widows may be your spoil, and that you may make the orphans your prey [Hebrew, *shâlâl*].[21]

In the midst of this injustice, "everyone is brought low."[22] God humbles the proud. Justice will be all or it will be nothing – but one way or another, whether through Judah's embrace of the weak within its borders or divine retribution against the powerful, there will be equality. The people will prosper together as a just community or they will suffer together as an unjust one.

The third theme is royal failure. More specifically, kings continuously struggle against God's sovereignty and thereby challenge it. Aside from Judah's general state of injustice – which certainly reflects on its kings – two particular narratives highlight this theme. In the wake of the death of Uzziah – a king whose reign sustained autonomy for Judah – God calls Isaiah to comfort Ahaz, the son of Uzziah's successor, with the assurance that YHWH will deliver the people in the face of the imminent danger posed by Syria and Ephraim (the Northern Kingdom of Israel).[23] Ahaz – and with him the people of Judah – is not comforted by Isaiah's message. Rather than trust YHWH, he turns to Assyria for aid as the people of Judah "melt in fear" before the political upheavals at their doorstep.[24] At this point, Isaiah's words turn to judgment. Assyria, the very one Judah turned to for refuge in the place of YHWH, will rise against them – and that at YHWH's hand![25]

Isaiah refers to the king of Assyria as the "rod of [YHWH's] anger."[26] In Isaiah's radical monotheism, even the king of Assyria who conquers Israel is under the rule of YHWH. Says YHWH, "against a godless nation *I send him* [that is, the king of Assyria]."[27] However, the king, in his "haughty pride"[28] and insatiable quest for power, seeks more violence than YHWH intends. As with Ahaz, this passage presents another failure of a king to submit to YHWH's authority. This failure elicits consequence,[29] much as Ahaz's failure led to Judah's bleak future.[30]

The narratives of royal failure correspond to hopes for a righteous king. Whereas in chapter 7 (and 8) King Ahaz leads people into judgment by refusing the sovereignty of YHWH, chapter 9 depicts a king who will lead the people out of darkness into endless peace.[31] Similarly, whereas in chapter 10 the proud Assyrian king engages in extended violence against other nations, chapter 11 envisions a future Davidic king who will rely fully on YWHW and thereby herald a cosmic peace for the earth. The royal prophecies of chapters 9 and 11 thus contain strong parallels. Each includes the promise of a Davidic king who will reign in a righteousness implicitly juxtaposed with the failures of other kings.[32] Additionally, each carries strong connotations of the establishment of justice for all[33] and peace.[34]

Regarding the place of verses 1–9 in relation to what follows them, Isaiah 11:10 presents an international perspective in which Israel's banner becomes a symbol to which all nations flock. This vision "is narrowed down in vv. 11–16 to the return of the Diaspora Jews from the world of the nations."[35] Childs offers a similar division, writing, "The chapter is divided into two main units, vv. 1–9 and 11–16, with v. 10 forming a connecting bridge between the oracles."[36] Chapter 12 caps the material of the first eleven chapters with a song of thanksgiving.[37]

The content of Isaiah 11:1–9

Collectively, the three themes I delineate above provide a hermeneutical key for interpreting Isaiah's vision in chapter 11. Before applying these themes, it is pertinent to explore the passage itself. In its most basic structure, the pericope breaks down into two major headings: the coming of the righteous king (vv. 1–5) and the new world under the king's reign (vv. 6–9). There is debate concerning whether these two sections are the work of the same author/redactor – that is, whether they form a cohesive pericope. For example, Gene Tucker maintains that there is a lack of coherency between verses 1–5 and 6–8.[38] However, I contend that this position is problematic because not only is there coherency in the passage but this coherency is to be expected from the themes that precede it in the earlier chapters of Isaiah.

Isaiah 11:1–5

Verses 1–5 begin with a parallel between the "shoot" (*chôtêr*) coming from the "stump" (*geza'*) of Jesse and the "branch" (*nêtser*) coming from his "root" (*sheresh*). The term *geza'* is a peculiar one, occurring in only one other place in the Hebrew Scriptures – the book of Job – where the death of a human is juxtaposed with the apparent destruction of a tree. Says Job:

For there is hope for a tree, if it is cut down, that it will sprout again, and that its shoots will not cease. Though its root grows old in the earth, and its stump [*geza'*] dies in the ground.[39]

Job recognizes that even after the death of a stump, unlike a human death, life remains a possibility for the tree. In light of this passage, Walter Brueggemann suggests that the context of Isaiah 11 "is a deep failure of the Davidic dynasty, the one that had carried the hopes of Judah."[40] Yet this failure does not constitute the complete dissolution of the dynasty, as the root remains.[41] There is still hope for the Davidic dynasty to spring to life again.

In the face of royal failure, what the opening verses of chapter 11 depict is a promise of a future Davidic king.[42] Whereas the failed kings (most of all Ahaz) did not trust YHWH but relied on their own political savvy or other worldly powers, the positive qualities of this king are directly related to the divine *rûach* (spirit) that rests on him. This relation emphasizes the character of YHWH over the king.[43] The spirit endows the king with wisdom, understanding, prudence, and might.[44] It is furthermore the spirit of "knowledge and the fear of the LORD."[45] Isaiah places special emphasis on these two facets, repeating the phrase "the fear of the LORD" in the subsequent verse and "the knowledge of the LORD" at the close of the passage: "for the earth will be full of the knowledge of the LORD as the waters cover the sea."[46] The repetition of the "fear of the LORD" underscores its importance. This emphasis is appropriate, as in wisdom literature "the fear of the LORD" is the catalyst for wisdom.[47] The link between fear and wisdom is further solidified by the fact that 25 percent of all appearances of the Hebrew *yir'âh* ("fear") occur in the wisdom literature of Proverbs, always as part of the phrase "the fear of the LORD." The implication is that kings fail when they trust in their own understanding or in worldly powers. A proper king acknowledges that his power is derivative of YHWH's anointing spirit.[48] Just as breath gives life to the body, so YHWH's *rûach* ("spirit" or "breath") is the source of a king's reign. When a king embraces his dependency, it is wisdom. When he denies it, it is folly.

Furthermore, as with my discussion of the *imago* in Chapter 3, the anointing of the spirit points toward a particular task that both depends upon YHWH and is other-affirming. Thus, the king anointed with the spirit of YHWH will make judgments and decisions but by neither his own sight nor his own hearing: "He shall not judge by what his eyes see, or decide by what his ears hear."[49] The parallel of "judgment" and "decision" with "sight" and "hearing" juxtaposes sound judgment that arises from dependency on YHWH with judgment exercised via typical human methods.[50] It is thus in the king's *derivative* righteousness that he will perform his task, which is the establishment of justice:

> But with righteousness he shall judge the poor,
> and decide with equity for the meek of the earth.[51]

The king rejects the hoarding of power over and against the weak and the poor that prevailed in Israel according to Isaiah's critique in the previous chapters. Instead, the king's judgment is engaged for the sake of the disenfranchised: the "poor" and "meek of the earth." As Tucker states, "The ideal king exercises power to protect the weak."[52]

Furthermore, the king will bring low those who have raised themselves up at the expense of the disenfranchised. Thus the chiastic structure:

> He shall strike the earth (A)
> With the rod of his mouth (B)
> And with the breath of his lips (B¹)
> He shall kill the wicked (A¹)

Significantly, the violence the king executes is derivative of YHWH. This point is evident in the author's reuse of the Hebrew *rûach* in the phrase "with the breath (*rûach*) of his lips."[53] Furthermore, the violence entailed in the context of judgment is aimed at bringing about the peaceful kingdom under the righteous ruler.[54] If the parts of creation that do not adhere to the righteous reign of the king are removed, only those parts that are good and peaceful remain. In short, if the original creation was not a victory of chaos, subsequent acts of creation aimed at retrieving the original harmony of creation tend in this direction.

In verse 5 the king's attributes are depicted as garments of "righteousness" (*tsedeq*) and "faithfulness" (*'ĕmûnâh*). The latter Hebrew term appears most frequently in the Psalms; it is used otherwise only here in Isaiah. In Psalms the term refers almost exclusively to the faithfulness of YHWH.[55] Used thus, the massive concentration of *'ĕmûnâh* in Psalm 89, where it appears eight times (about a third of the term's total appearances in the Hebrew Scriptures) in connection to YHWH's covenant with David,[56] is perhaps most noteworthy. With this use in mind, Isaiah's words suggest that the Davidic covenantal faithfulness of YHWH is reciprocated by the Davidic king in that he works toward the task of justice that the covenant entails.

Tsedeq typically appears in the Hebrew Scriptures as a quality of YHWH.[57] However, in Isaiah 1–39 the term never occurs in this capacity.

Rather, Isaiah posits righteousness as the quality that YHWH seeks in both the righteous ruler and the created order.[58] Thus, this central characteristic of YHWH is poured into the king for the sake of the establishment of justice in and for the world.

Another fascinating – and quite animal-friendly – connection between 11:5 and the Psalms is found in Psalm 36:5–6, where the author exalts both YHWH's *'ĕmûnâh* and *tsĕdaqah* (the feminine form of *tsedeq*, which has the common root of צדק). This reference concludes with the phrase "You save animals and humans alike, O LORD."[59] At the risk of claiming more than is warranted, I note the connection between *tsĕdaqah* and *'ĕmûnâh* in Psalm 36:5–6a and the inclusion of animals in YHWH's salvific activity in 36:6b. This connection corresponds to the appearance of *tsedeq* and *'ĕmûnâh* in Isaiah 11:5, which is immediately followed by a picture of peace among the animals. It seems at least a plausible reading to claim that just as YHWH's righteousness and faithfulness are evident in his animal-inclusive work (Psalm 36:5–6), so also the king anointed with the spirit of YHWH and clothed in righteousness and faithfulness will draw into his reign of peace not only disenfranchised humans but also animals (Isaiah 11:5–8). The parallel plays quite well (see Table 6.1).

As already stated, I do not want to make too much of this connection between Isaiah 11 and Psalm 36. However, it does seem that the transition from righteousness and faithfulness to the inclusion of animals in salvific activity is not altogether foreign to other parts of scripture. Perhaps the connection between verses 1–5 and 6–8 is not all that incoherent – or unexpected – after all. At any rate, this connection between the Psalm 36 and Isaiah 11 provides some extra justification to the

Table 6.1 Righteousness, faithfulness, and the salvific inclusion of animals

Passage	Appearance of *'ĕmûnâh* and derivatives of *tsadaq*	Salvific Inclusion of Animals
Isaiah 11:5–6	Righteousness (*tsedeq*) shall be the belt around his waist, and faithfulness (*'ĕmûnâh*) the belt around his loins.	The wolf shall live with the lamb...
Psalm 36:5–6	Your steadfast love, O LORD, extends to the heavens, your faithfulness (*'ĕmûnâh*) to the clouds. Your righteousness (*tsĕdaqah*) is like the mighty mountains, your judgements are like the great deep;	you save humans and animals alike, O LORD.

claims that the verses 1–9 are a united pericope and that Isaiah intends the inclusion of nonhuman animals to be taken literally by the reader.

Isaiah 11:6–9

The movement of verses 6–8 depicts a world of safety and security. This image leads effortlessly into the final verse: "They will not hurt or destroy on all my holy mountain. For the earth will be full of the knowledge of the LORD as the water covers the sea."[60]

The opening verses (especially 6–7) of this section stir much controversy regarding whether the author/redactor intends the poetry to be taken literally or symbolically. In the mid-nineteenth century Joseph Alexander writes, "Most Christian writers, ancient and modern, with Aben Ezra and Maimonides among the Jews, explain the prophecy as wholly metaphorical, and descriptive of the peace to be enjoyed by God's people."[61] In the mid-twentieth century, Edward Kissane places Isaiah's peaceable vision under the heading "The Citizens of Zion," writing, "All classes will live together in harmony, without injustice or violence."[62] He goes on:

> This idyllic picture must not be understood quite literally as meaning that the character and habits of animals will be changed. It is clear from verse 9 that it is meant as a symbolic description of peace which reigns among the inhabitants of Sion. As the preceding strophe dealt with the relations between the ruler and his people, so this deals with the relations of the people with one another.[63]

John Goldingay also casts his lot with metaphorical interpreters. He states,

> Context suggests that the talk of harmony in the animal world is a metaphor for harmony in the human world. The strong and powerful live together with the weak and powerless because the latter can believe that the former are no longer seeking to devour them.[64]

Certainly not all interpreters of Isaiah read verses 6–8 symbolically. As early as the second century, Irenaeus and other thinkers argued that the passage ought to be understood literally.[65] This literal reading has a voice in modern scholarship as well. W. E. Vine maintains, in a rather theologically weighted assessment, that Isaiah's vision of peace depicts "millennial conditions."[66] Thus, "*Verses 6 to 9* are not to be regarded as symbolic. The actual fulfillment of the conditions in the animal world will be the natural outcome of the presence and authority of Christ."[67]

Hans Wildberger argues for the unity of verses 1–9 under the authorship of Isaiah. He accepts that Isaiah is emphasizing human relations. However, he maintains that Isaiah is "using a way of thinking which employs traditions that were already available to him."[68] This tradition includes the "motif about peace among the animals," which was "a concept known by everyone at that time."[69] Thus, Wildberger, denying an allegorical reading of the text, adds two primary reasons for a literal reading: first, that unidentified allegory is not Isaiah's typical fashion of writing; and second, astutely, that "If the text were meant to be interpreted allegorically, it would be radically different than it is – it would speak *only* of animals and not of the children."[70]

Gary Smith also defends the plausibility of a literal reading of verses 6–8:

> One might interpret these animals metaphorically (Ezek 22:27 calls Judah's officials wolves and Ezek 34:6 calls the people sheep) though later prophets also seem to understand the ideal that God will restore the paradise of Eden once again at the end of time (cf. Ezek 34:25; 36:35).[71]

Smith also rejects the arguments against literalism based on the biological impossibility of vegetarian predators:

> One should not be concerned with trying to explain the biology of how lions can survive by eating straw or how it is possible for there to be such dramatic changes in the animal behavior of vicious wild beasts. The prophet draws a picture of how God will transform the world. The picture communicates the beauty of his revolutionary transformational power, no matter how one interprets the scene (literally or metaphorically).[72]

These literal interpretations notwithstanding, in my view the argument for symbolism suffers a fatal flaw. Isaiah does not use symbolism without defining it for his audience.[73] Consider his uses of nonhuman symbols in the first ten chapters. Isaiah analogously contrasts Israel, who does not know God, with an ox who knows its owner.[74] Later he indicts Israel with the following simile: "You shall be like an oak whose leaf withers, and like a garden without water."[75] In chapter 5 Isaiah utilizes the imagery of a vineyard in order to develop an analogy of Israel's disobedience. As the analogy takes shape, Isaiah leaves no doubt about the symbolism: "For the vineyard of the LORD of hosts is the house of Israel."[76]

Isaiah's symbolism is especially obvious when he uses nonhuman images to depict nations – a point doubly problematic with regard to chapter 11 since the most common argument is that the animals there represent various peoples. He states that the roaring of Assyria is "like a lion."[77] Later, God threatens Judah with "the mighty flood waters of the River, the king of Assyria and all his glory."[78] Again, Isaiah clearly defines his nonhuman symbolism for his audience. In chapter 10 Isaiah uses simile to explicate God's sovereignty:

> My hand has found, like a nest, the wealth of the peoples; and as one fathers eggs that have been forsaken, so I have fathered all the earth, and there was none that moved a wing, or opened its mouth, or chirped.[79]

Lastly, with reference to the cedars of Lebanon, Isaiah uses the imagery of trees to express national identity but still clearly equates that identity with Lebanon.[80]

In all of these cases, Isaiah's nonhuman symbolism is clearly and specifically defined. Thus it is inaccurate to argue, as Goldingay does, that Isaiah 11 is metaphorical based on the claim that "the book opened by using animals to stand for human beings (1:3) – also in connection with the question of knowledge, as here [in Isaiah 11]."[81] As already noted, Isaiah clearly connects the image of the ox in 1:3 with Israel's lack of knowledge. No such connection exists in 11:6–8.

Not only does Isaiah clearly connect his symbols to a specific meaning in all the above examples, but also, to my knowledge, nowhere does Isaiah use nonhumans as symbols without clearly and specifically defining what they symbolize. If then there is no precedent for Isaiah's use of animal symbolism without obvious definitions of the meaning of the symbols, why should the animals in chapter 11, whom Isaiah does not remotely suggest represent something else, be anything other than the literal animals? Much better is an acknowledgment that Isaiah's tendency to define nonhuman symbolism in conjunction with the lack of such definition in chapter 11 suggests that he intends the animals therein to be understood literally.

However, another debated question arises at this point: even if the animal imagery is taken literally, what is the author/redactor actually depicting? Tucker, for example, suggests the heart of the symbolism is the contrast between wild and domestic animals.[82] He maintains that Isaiah's central aim is to depict a world that is safe for humans and fully conducive to human well-being. That is, wild animals will not harm domestic animals, yielding the intended result that domestic animals may reach maximal efficiency in their fruitfulness to humanity.[83]

I fully acknowledge the validity of the distinction between domestic and wild animals in verses 6–8, especially considering the image of a young child leading a herd to pasture without the potential danger of wild animals.[84] However, as Tucker's conclusion is partly predicated upon his assumption that verses 1–9 are not a coherent whole and thus verses 1–5 bear no relevance for verses 6–8, he therefore, in my view, misses a key parallel, identified below, that connects these sections. Tucker's assumption is at any rate problematic because, at the very least, the final redactor saw no problem with combining two separate source materials into a whole. If Tucker's assumption is set aside and the passage is viewed as a whole, there is a larger theme to the pericope that suggests interpreters need not consider domestication and wildness the primary division in Isaiah's animals.

The most basic distinction running through verses 1–9, I contend, is that between the powerful and the vulnerable. Specifically, the passage consistently presents those with power acting in a manner favorable toward those that are vulnerable. On this ground Joseph Blenkinsopp argues for the unity of the passage:

> The transition to peaceful coexistence in the animal world is not so abrupt; indeed those commentators who insist on making the following verses into a separate poem may be missing a subtle parallel between 3–5 and 6–8 consisting in the contrast between the strong and the weak in both the human and zoological realms.[85]

Indeed, such a parallel is quite visible in the text (see Table 6.2).

This parallel is all the more valid in the face of the three themes, discussed above, that run through the first eleven chapters of Isaiah. Israel's perpetual sin of injustice in not caring for the widow and the orphan depicts a nation in which the powerful are taking advantage of the vulnerable. It is in the face of this inequity that YHWH offers

Table 6.2 The thematic parallel of Isaiah 11:1–9

Verse	The Powerful	Favorable Action toward	The Vulnerable
11:4	The king	shall with righteousness judge	the poor
11:4	The king	shall in equity decide for	the meek of the earth
11:6	The wolf	shall live with	the lamb

judgments against his people. In fact, Isaiah at one point describes the relationship between powerful and vulnerable humans as that between predator and prey. The powerful of Israel structure the law in such a way that they "may make the orphans [their] prey" (Hebrew, *shâlâl*).[86] Along this line of thinking, Wildberger notes that the Hebrew '*anav* ("meek") in verse 4 suggests more a diminishment of power than economic status.[87] This reading only strengthens the link between verses 1–5 and 6–9. It is the common status of those preyed upon by the powerful and those creatures preyed upon by their strong predators that constitutes some form of consistent injustice. Unlike many eco-theologians today, Isaiah does not see fit to draw a sharp dividing line between the predatory relationship among humans and that among animals (or between humans and animals), the former being tragic and the latter being a beautifully ordered system. Rather, predation itself is presented as an injustice, one that will be overturned with the arrival of this righteous king. This overturning does not exclude peace within or among political communities, as verses 4–5 and 10–14 reveal, but neither is it limited to these dimensions.[88]

The theme of kings failing to do what is right in the eyes of YHWH suggests a nation in which just and righteous leadership is absent.[89] In the nineteenth century Franz Delitzsch recognized the movement of the humiliation of the house of David to its exaltation and perfection.[90] In a similar vein, Smith maintains that the messianic vision of 11:1–9 (and 9:1–7) stands in contrast to both Israelite failure (evident in Ahaz) and Assyrian arrogance.[91] This movement from royal failure to royal righteousness corresponds to the injustice of Israel: the state of unequal power and a resulting injustice and violence, on the one hand, and the state of equal power and the resulting peace, on the other. The contrast of the sweeping injustice that exists under failing kings with the justice that arises under the reign of the anointed king indicates the extremes of the pendulum swing from judgment to hope. Hope comes to its fullest form in the dramatic poem in chapter 11.

Israel and its kings (and Assyria's king) are judged because they are neither faithful nor righteous with regard to the covenant of justice that YHWH has established with them. The final hope, then, is a Davidic king par excellence, whose character is derivative of YHWH's character. This king will act as God intends a king to act – in a manner favorable toward the vulnerable. Israel's perpetual sin, social inequity, will be set right. Furthermore, as Israel becomes the covenantal nation that YHWH desires it to be, the whole earth is so set right as to herald the edenic peace of early Genesis.[92] The world Isaiah depicts is one in which the youngest of children will not be in harm's way even in the most harmful of places.[93]

Such a reading is conducive to that offered by Blenkinsopp, who notes that the connection between society and the cosmos is not uncommon in ancient Near Eastern thought:

> This splendid poem announces the emergence from David's family line of a ruler divinely endowed with all charismatic attributes required to fulfill the ideal, often proclaimed but rarely if ever realized, of bringing about a just order in which the poor and powerless can enjoy equal rights with the wealthy and powerful. At his coming, war and all manifestations of violence will be abolished…not only in human society but in the animal world as well. With the tradition of a future golden age, often in the form of an *apokatastasis* or restoration of the first creation, the political order and the order of creation as a whole can be and sometimes are connected and interdependent…. It is therefore by no means necessary to follow those exegetes who argue for a conflation of two distinct poems (1–5, 6–9), a hypothesis that has little to commend it.[94]

Collectively, these points suggest that the passage holds up as a cohesive unit and that the hope for justice and peace in the human realm is properly mirrored in the hope for justice and peace in the nonhuman realm. Thus, Wildberger can acknowledge, on the one hand,

> With the reference to the [faithfulness] of the Messiah, vv. 1–5 draw to a very acceptable conclusion. With v. 6, a new theme is introduced: the peaceful coexistence of animal with animal and animal with human. There is no more mention of the Messiah at this point.[95]

On the other hand, he recognizes that there is a connection: "Where a legitimate king is in charge, as the representative of the deity and/or as the guarantor of world order in the righteousness appropriate to his office, the world can recover from its wretchedness."[96]

Still, more can be said. I contend that in verses 6 and 7 smaller parallelisms appear within a larger chiasm. The basic structure of the parallel remains the powerful acting favorably toward the vulnerable. However, it here takes a more specific form: a predator shall act in a manner of peace that is uncharacteristic of its *current expected* nature (but perhaps, as with the king who serves the disenfranchised, *more* in line with the divine intention for them) and that benefits a form of prey. The wolf (predator)

Table 6.3   Proposed chiastic structure of Isaiah 11: 6–8a

(A)	The wolf	shall live	with the lamb
(B)	The leopard	shall lie down	with the kid
(C)	The lion	and the calf	will get fattened (*mĕriy'*) together[97]
(D)		And a little child shall lead them	
(C¹)	The cow	and the bear	shall graze[98]
(B¹)	[The cow's young]	[and the bear's young]	shall lie down together
(A¹)	The lion	will eat straw	like the ox

lives with (uncharacteristically benefiting) the lamb (the prey). These parallels are fairly clear. Admittedly less clear is my proposed chiasm (see Table 6.3).

According to this chiastic organization, the central (therefore pivotal) phrase in these verses is "and a little child shall lead them." The emphasis on children continues in the parallelisms of verse 8:

> The nursing child (A)
> shall play over the hole of the asp (B)
> and the weaned child (A¹)
> shall put its hand on the adder's den (B¹)

If this chiastic reading of verses 6–8a is valid, the pivotal placement of the human in the peace of a nonhuman world suggests not only that the world will be safe for humans but that humanity *leads the nonhuman world into that safety*. That is, there is a role of *eschatological steward- ship* for humans: the responsibility to work toward peace in the human realm that peace may also reign in the cosmos.

It is here that I quarrel somewhat with Tucker's claim that the main point of verses 6–8 is that the world will be peaceful for human utiliza- tion of animals. Tucker seems to maintain that the peaceful kingdom applies only to relations among nonhumans – and this for human benefit.[99] Why are the wild animals the only carnivores that turn to herbivores? Why not humans as well? Does the "little child lead" all the animals to the slaughter? If so, why does the poem conclude with the claim, "They will not hurt nor destroy in all my holy mountain"?[100] Surely the end of destruction does not include the promulgation of suffering and death for nonhumans. As Smith states, "This fundamental change in the nature of animals omits mention of the change in the nature of mankind, but the emphasis on righteousness and the end of evil requires a radical change in man's behavior too."[101]

It seems more appropriate, in line with Smith's claim, to understand humanity's role in terms of facilitating peace – a favorable reading in light of the Priestly depiction of the *imago Dei*. Humanity's role is pivotal with regard to the peace of creation. As Brueggemann states, "The distortion of human relationships is at the root of all distortions in creation."[102] Likewise, when the righteous and faithful king, anointed with the spirit of YHWH, establishes peace in the human realm, the nonhuman realm will also benefit from this peace ("you save humans and animals alike"). The *imago* of Genesis 1 becomes an eschatological stewardship. The peaceable world hinted at in the first creation narrative becomes the prophetic vision of an eschatological hope.[103] In the words of Richard Bauckham:

> In the light of the eschatological consummation, the human dominion, as Genesis 1 envisages it, becomes the hope for the peaceable kingdom depicted in Isaiah (Isa. 11:1–9; 65:25), in which, under the rule of the Messiah, the wild animals will live harmoniously with the domestic animals, the carnivorous will become herbivorous, and the most vulnerable of humans, the small child, may play without danger from the once deadly creeping things. This is an ecotopia that is both impossible to realize short of the new creation but also an invitation to practice nonviolent, caring dominion to whatever extent might be possible in the meantime.[104]

The final verse constitutes the culmination of the hope presented. It also reveals the connection between the world of peace and the foundation for that peace. There will be neither harm nor destruction on YHWH's "holy mountain" *because* (Hebrew, *kiy*) "the earth will be full of the knowledge of the Lord as the waters cover the sea."[105] The causal relationship denoted by the particle *kiy* strikes against readings that reduce the peace of the king's reign to Jerusalem (the "holy mountain"). If that peace derives from the knowledge of YHWH, which is an important characteristic of the anointed king, then the claim that the knowledge of YHWH fills the entire earth suggests that the entire earth shares the means to create peace. While it is true that it is not until later chapters that the promise of peace becomes *clearly* holistic regarding the nations[106] – for instance, in chapter 56 – it is implied in chapter 11. Hence, it is not only Zion but the entire world that benefits from the righteous ruler.[107]

Toward an animal-friendly reading of Isaiah 11:1–9

Here I move from an exegetical study of the text itself to a synthesis and application of it. This move will transition more smoothly if I begin by clearly reiterating the claims that my above exploration yields. There are seven:

1. Whether or not Isaiah 11:1–9 is a literary unit or its author is Isaiah of Jerusalem or a later source tradition, the final redactor responsible for the canonical form of the pericope uses the passage to epitomize themes from Isaiah's prophecies.
2. These themes include the oscillation between judgment and hope, the systemic injustice in Israel, and the failure of royalty vis-à-vis YHWH's commands and sovereignty.
3. These themes come to a climax in Isaiah 11:1–9, corresponding to a cosmically inclusive hope that entails a righteous and faithful king, anointed by the spirit of YHWH, setting right the injustices of Israel.
4. The king's covenantal faithfulness establishes a paradigm in which the powerful act in a manner favorable toward – as opposed to exploitative of – the vulnerable. This paradigm connects verses 1–5 and 6–9 in that the anointed king's actions are paralleled in the actions of predators toward their prey.
5. The peace that Isaiah envisions in the animal world ought to be read literally. Indeed, a metaphorical reading would belie Isaiah's style with regard to nonhuman symbolism, a style that entails an explicit connection between the symbol and that which it is symbolizes.
6. The peace that Isaiah envisions in the animal world is best understood as the dissolution of the violent distinction between the powerful and the vulnerable in which all creation, both human (in the relation between the king and the weak) and nonhuman (in the relation between predator and prey), benefits from the reign of the anointed king. Such a reading opposes the anthropocentric claim that humans will no longer face hardships in utilizing domesticated animals for their benefit.
7. The chiastic structure of Isaiah 11:6–8a places the phrase "and a little child shall lead them" as the center of the edenic/eschatological peace in the nonhuman world.

Based on these points, I suggest that Isaiah's vision provides a scriptural example of an alternative to the dominant tradition. YHWH is concerned about justice not simply in the human realm. Rather, the divine concern encompasses all the victims of the cosmos. Thus, when humans, following the righteous reign of the king, bear the anointing of YHWH's *rûach* and embrace the resulting righteousness and faithfulness, they also widen their concern to include the entire creation. In this manner, a "little child" leads creation as a herald of eschatological peace.

However, the image in verses 6–8 are not a picture of a utopian cosmos built upon the effort of humans. Rather, it is derivative of YHWH and the anointed Davidic king. Even so, the poem as a whole suggests that the eschatological telos of humanity is a state of peace *with animals*. For this reason, just as humans ought not to be satisfied with social injustice simply because it seems an inevitable outcome of human interaction this side of the eschaton, so also should humans not be satisfied with causing animals harm for human benefit simply because nature is structured in such a way that harm is ultimately unavoidable.

Humans bear a role as eschatological stewards. Such is, holistically speaking, the transformation of the *imago Dei* in Isaiah's vision. Eschatological stewardship does not mean constructing the kingdom; rather, it entails heralding the future peace of the cosmos. The phrase "and a little child shall lead them" may indeed image both a pastoral setting and a leadership role in cosmic peace. At any rate, the ultimate desire of YHWH is that the divine mountain should see neither harm nor death. Humans aware of this desire bear the responsibility to be faithful to it to whatever extent they can within the confines of a disordered world. While the exact application of this principle to particular practices in modern times requires further exploration, that the principle itself finds justification in scripture is enough to warrant such explorations within Christian (and Jewish) communities.

7
The Sacramentality of the Cosmos

In this chapter I explore representations out of the wealth of recent material written on the sacramentality of the cosmos and adjudicate its significance in relation to the place of nonhuman animals in Christian theology and ethics. In particular, I consider whether this retrieved strand of Christian thought breaks from the dominant tradition and, if so, to what extent. This consideration will require an in-depth search into Orthodox theology, as Eastern Christianity has best maintained the affirmation of cosmic sacramentality. However, while such an affirmation has been somewhat wanting in the West, I do not want to ignore the recent developments in Roman Catholicism that have retrieved it. Thus, what follows examines the concept of cosmic sacramentality in general, with attention to both Eastern and Western theologians.

My explorations into both Catholic and Orthodox thought emphasize two points: the manner in which the world is understood to be a sacrament and the priestly vocation this understanding conveys upon human beings. I begin by considering the development of the notion that the cosmos is a sacrament, including its fading and recovery in the West. This consideration leads into the retrieval of cosmic sacramentality in the work of two Catholic theologians, Kevin Irwin and Denis Edwards. Next, I consider the diversity of views on cosmic sacramentality within Orthodox theology, examining the nuanced position of different theologians with regard to the issue. With these considerations in place, I evaluate the extent to which the more common themes of the position affirm or break with the dominant tradition. Lastly, I suggest how the notion of the cosmos as sacrament might be retrieved in such a way as to remain consistent with its fundamental tenets while at once providing a stark alternative to Aquinas's theological ethics of nonhuman animals.

The world as primordial sacrament in Roman Catholicism

In his seminal work on the development of the sacraments, Joseph Martos traces how the notion of *sacramentum* (a Latin translation of the Greek *mysterion*) developed over hundreds of years, within a matrix of religious, philosophical, and political influences, into the notion of sacraments as referring to seven specific sacred rites in the Roman Catholic Church.[1] This process of development was largely elicited by periods of both external persecution (out of which the Donatist controversy arose) and internal debate.

In the first few centuries of Christian thought, Augustine and other theologians posited a broad and open-ended understanding of sacraments.[2] Anything could become a sacrament for the human being. However, on account of contextual concerns, this view, which thrived in the East – notably in the work of Maximus the Confessor – was truncated in the West. This truncation reached an apex with scholasticism.

In the wake of Peter Lombard, the sacraments were limited to seven. Those following the work of Thomas Aquinas systematized his appropriation of Aristotelian philosophy, which led to a critical analysis of what made a sacramental rite (the *sacramentum tantum*) valid and how a valid sacrament efficaciously resulted in a sacramental character (the *sacramentum et res*) and finally to the guarantee that the sacramental character inherent in a valid sacrament enabled the recipient to receive grace (the *res tantum*).[3] The sacramental characters were parsed according to the type of recipient (for example, the power received in ordination as opposed to the cleansing received in baptism). Mystery flirted with the line of concise calculation. Sacraments functioned *ex opere operato* ("by the work worked"), provided that the matter and form were properly observed.[4] The earlier broadness and openness of sacramental thought narrowed to a closely defined focus. The sacraments were even more severely truncated in Western Protestant thought, being reduced in most circles to two.[5]

Both Catholic and Protestant theologians have since retrieved a wider understanding of the sacraments.[6] For Catholicism, conciliar and postconciliar theologians have revisited the (necessarily) reactionary development of the sacraments that led to the myopic view of scholasticism. Such inquiries have elicited broader categories of sacramental thought. Two such categories – both attempting to express a foundational sacrament out of which all other sacraments (formal and informal) burgeon – are especially worthy of note: Christ as the primordial sacrament and the Church as sacrament.[7] These views were championed by Edward Schillebeeckx and Karl Rahner, respectively.[8] Kevin Irwin claims that both theologians provided "a lasting legacy in the revival of emphasizing that sacraments are *actions* not things and *events of salvation* not simply occasions when grace is conferred."[9] This legacy aside, Irwin maintains that these perspectives are limited. He argues that Catholic theology requires a new paradigm in which the sacramentality of the world receives primacy. From this paradigm, Irwin writes,

> Sacraments can be understood to mirror a much wider sacramental vision of all of reality and the celebration of sacrament can come to be appreciated as the things which humans need in order for them to appreciate and interpret the world in which they live.[10]

The sacramentality of the cosmos

Irwin maintains that though a "positive theology of creation and sacramentality" is still to be recovered, it is nonetheless "characteristic of the Catholic tradition."[11] He argues that even when the number of sacraments was limited to seven, the acknowledgement of *sacramentals* (that is, the physical materials used in liturgical rites) witnessed to a wide view of creation's role in humanity's encounter with the divine.[12] Still, Irwin suggests, "The Tridentine and post-Reformation emphasis on the number, origin, and efficaciousness of the seven sacraments may well have eclipsed the principle of sacramentality on which they were based."[13]

To recover the broader sacramentality of the Catholic tradition, Irwin argues for a paradigm of sacramentality in which the world witnesses to God's presence.[14] From this paradigm, both liturgy and specific sacraments, dependent upon sacramentality, express the blurring between the secular and profane in which "all that is of God is incarnated among us."[15] In this sense, the liturgy differs in degree – not essence – from the sacramentality of the world itself. Thus, sacramentality is "the key that unlocks and unleashes the depth and value of any liturgy and all sacramental celebrations."[16]

For Irwin, sacramentality provides a primary place for the nonhuman creation in the economy of salvation. This view renders

> creation the ground of theology, both natural and revealed, and would order a study of sacraments as based on how the God of creation and redemption is incarnated in the world and therefore discovered in the world and in all of human life.[17]

In other words, sacramentality "comes first; rituals of liturgy and sacraments derive from it."[18] Furthermore, the liturgy serves to "deepen our experience of God in this world."[19] In the liturgy one learns how to see the world properly; that is, to see it as a sacrament.[20]

Thus, the world is both before and after the liturgy. It is before because the sacramentality of the world precedes our heightened encounter with the divine in the liturgy (of which sacraments are a part). It is after because our heightened encounter with the divine turns us to see the sacramentality of the world in the encounter itself.[21] For Irwin, this emphasis on the world constitutes a "sacramental world view." In such a view,

> The world in which we live is interdependent – all that dwell in it are part of God's plan for us all. It is also a locus where God is revealed, disclosed, and experienced. This means the world, humans and all creatures great and small, are all signs of God among us.[22]

At its root, then, sacramentality means that

> Jesus, the church and the seven sacraments are best appreciated as particular and privileged expressions of a sacramental world in which God has revealed and continues to reveal God's very self through the material of human existence, set within the world as itself regarded as sacramental.[23]

This definition suggests that the experience of the sacramental world is limited to humanity. That is, the world is a sacrament *for humanity*. This point is further solidified in Irwin's claim that the sacramental liturgy "articulates our belief that we worship God through the *things* of this world."[24]

In sum, the sacramentality of the world entails that all *things* can become a sacrament *for humanity* inasmuch as they participate in God's self-disclosure to humans. This view renders the formal sacraments subsequent to the revelatory potential of the nonhuman creation at large. However, in my understanding it does little to stymie the anthropocentrism of the dominant tradition. This claim is further evident in the priestly vocation of human beings.

The priestly vocation of human beings

The notion of the priestly role of humanity vis-à-vis the cosmos, while most prominently represented in Orthodox theology, has also been taken up by modern Catholic theologians. Such a view is evident in Denis Edwards's understanding of the Eucharist. For Edwards, the Eucharist expresses the common plight of the entire cosmos: "Eating and drinking bread and wine together remind us of our grounding in the whole inter-connected pattern of fleshly life, of hunger and thirst, nourishment and refreshment."[25] Furthermore, the elements of bread and wine challenge the participants ethically. "They raise questions about the ecological, economic and political realities they represent. The way we grow and process our food and drink can come at an unbearable cost to other human beings and to other creatures of our planet."[26] Thus understood, the celebration of the Eucharist is a cosmic event with ethical ramifica-tions for its participants. "When we come to the Eucharist we bring the creatures of the earth with us. We remember the God who loves each one of them. We grieve for the damage done to them. We feel with them. We hope for their future in God. We commit ourselves to their well-being."[27]

This commitment is quite in line with the notion of priesthood. It furthermore seems to offer a break with anthropocentrism inasmuch as participation in the formal sacraments raises an awareness of the "unbearable cost ... to other creatures of our planet" and also invites us to "grieve for the damage done to" animals and "commit ourselves for their well-being." However, for Edwards there is an ambiguity regarding whether this priesthood recognizes the *intrinsic* value of the nonhuman creation or is ultimately anthropocentric. The human cares for the world as a steward. However, the culmination of this human role is the action of "lifting up of the whole creation to God."[28] The human priest is the one who, as opposed to other creatures, can remember. This ability enables humanity to remember the source of the gifts of the cosmos and, as priest, to lift those gifts back to God in reverential use.[29] This instrumental understanding is also evident in Irwin's thought: "To use creation in liturgy is to show reverence for creation through, with, and in which the incarnate God is disclosed and discovered."[30] In lifting the gifts of creation back to God – that is, in using the creation sacramentally – humanity transforms the created order into a source of divine self-disclosure *for humanity*. This reverential use before God "is meant to be played out around the planet continually by every human being."[31]

Thus, both Edwards and Irwin maintain some understanding of a priestly vocation of humanity in relation to the cosmos. This vocation entails using creation in a reverential manner. Edwards claims that the ethics that derives from this view is "clear."[32] I disagree.

What uses qualify as reverential? Can an animal be killed for the sake of a human desire (as opposed to need)? Can hunting for sport be reverential? What about using cosmetics tested on animals? Again, what of eating meat when it is not vitally necessary to do so? Can these actions be termed "reverential" simply because humans are thankful to God that they can cause unnecessary harm to animals? If so, how can such a relationship between humans and animals be a "kinship of creation"?

Similar questions arise from Irwin's retrieval of the sacramentality of the world with regard to ecological concern. He maintains both that the creation will share in God's redemptive action as a *community* and that the earth is full of "resources."[33] Is such a relationship really indicative of "community"? What sort of community is it when some members of the community justify using other members as resources – even to cause suffering and death – as long as such use is "sacramental"?[34] Is there not a "real" community within that larger web of life in which *persons* use *things* reverentially? At any rate, I maintain that the ethical implications of natural priesthood are far from clear.

The sacramental cosmos in Orthodox theology

While western theology, both Catholic and Protestant, has tended toward the truncation of sacramental theology, Orthodox thought has more consistently maintained a broader notion of sacramentality. It developed the insights found in both Augustine and Irenaeus as they defended the goodness of the entire creation against Gnostic and Manichean degradations of it. Orthodox theologians have followed the lead of many early Christians, for whom the cosmos was ripe with expressions of the divine.[35] They furthermore emphasize the priestly role of human beings, who are typically envisioned as bearing a responsibility in recognizing the sacramentality of the cosmos and facilitating its use as a means of communion with God.

Foundations in Maximus the Confessor

In the Orthodox tradition, an emphasis on both the sacramental nature of the cosmos and the priestly vocation of human beings has maintained a solid standing in the thought of the theologian Maximus the Confessor, among others. Representation of this strand of thought has intensified in modern Orthodox theology. Many have sought to recover Maximus as a voice to speak to ecological issues.

Radu Bordeianu engages Maximus in order to respond to the dual critique that Christianity has contributed to the ecological disposition of the current age and has very limited potential to provide sources to address this disposition.[36] He draws on Maximus's understanding that each part of the created order is infused with the imprint of the divine, inasmuch as God creates each part with a telos toward which God intends them to move. This movement is not simply a matter of nature playing itself out according to natural laws. Rather, it is facilitated by human beings, whom God calls to direct creation toward its proper end. In this sense, with regard to the original creation Bordeianu states, "The movement of Adam determines the direction in which the rest of creation moves."[37] Thus, the sin of human beings engenders a cosmic distortion in which the various dimensions of the nonhuman cosmos are directed, through human fault, toward something other than the divine intention for them.[38]

God calls and empowers human beings to discover and nurture the divine imprint in creation. This call constitutes part of the telos of humanity. Humanity's role vis-à-vis creation entails working to align the present conditions of all life occupying the cosmos with God's ultimate desire for the entire creation.[39] This role is priestly because the divinely intended destiny for all creation is participation in the divine – that is, deification. Humanity is to guide the creation toward union with the divine.

For Maximus, the human creature is well equipped for this task because he or she is a microcosm of the universe. By this, Maximus intimates that humans are the union of the spiritual and the corporeal dimensions of creation. They are thus a microcosm of all things in the cosmos – matter, energy, spirit. As spiritual, humans are able to give expression to the corporeal creation's silent praise. In doing so, they facilitate the reunion of five divisions in creation. These divisions are: "uncreated and created, intelligible and sensible, heaven and earth, paradise and the inhabited world, male and female."[40] Says Bordeianu, "Maximus affirms that, as both microcosm and priest of creation, Adam was called to mediate and overcome these divisions."[41]

In Bordeianu's estimation, Maximus's theocentric worldview entreats humanity to respect creation properly by offering it back to God through sacramental engagement of it. Thus the role of humanity as priest of creation tends toward reverential use of creation. Says Bordeianu, "Our attitude toward creation should be as towards the Eucharist, to which we show much attention and care, so that no miniscule crumb will fall and be trampled upon or wasted."[42]

The sacramentality of the cosmos

Maximus provides a historical venue through which to develop the sacramentality of the world in modern times. Many modern theologians have contributed to this development. One such theologian is Alexander Schmemann,[43] who provides a view of sacramentality from the liturgical perspective of the Orthodox Church. He laments theologies that have sought to isolate the *esse* (the substantial essence) of the sacrament from its liturgical context.[44] For Schmemann, this divorce is devastating for sacramental theology, as the sacraments have meaning only within the liturgy of the Church.[45]

Schmemann also argues that the liturgy must not be separated from the sacredness of the entire creation. Christ has revealed the sacramentality of the whole cosmos.[46] The place of human beings in the cosmic order is to serve as priests of creation by realizing that which the created order ultimately is: *the sacrament of humanity's communion with God*.[47] In this sense, the formally recognized sacraments (for example, the Eucharist) are not divided from the "profane," nonsacramental things of life. Rather, in the Eucharist matter is manifested in its truest reality: the gift of divine self-communication.[48] This outlook, maintains Schmemann, is biblical: "In the Bible the good that man eats, the world of which he must partake in order to live, is given to him by God, and it is given as *communion with God*."[49] Thus the world as sacrament is a gift from God to humanity meant to facilitate humanity's relationship with God. In this sense, the Fall is for Schmemann not an ontological distortion or an idolatrous romanticizing of nature but rather a rendering of the world by humanity to be *merely* the world, divorced from its sacramental character.[50] Human beings use the world but not reverently and, thus, not as communion with God. They grasp the world for themselves, ignoring its sacramentally relational character.

Another modern Orthodox theologian who has expanded the view of the world as sacrament is Dumitru Staniloae.[51] In the second volume of *The Experience of God*, Staniloae, writing from a Romanian (and communist) context, explores the notion of deification with regard to the created order (both humanity and the cosmos). His view is vividly (and admittedly) anthropocentric, thus providing a contrast to those ecological views that jettison the centrality of the human creature. Staniloae states, "Nature itself proves itself to have been made for the sake of consciousness, not consciousness for the sake of nature."[52]

For Staniloae, the nonhuman physical world is created by God as a gift for humanity. It is meant to serve as a space and means for the divine-human dialogue (and thus divine-human communion).[53] Nature, for Staniloae, is "an object or…succession of objects." Furthermore, "God creates this ensemble of objects…for the sake of a dialogue with humans. Otherwise, their creation would have no point."[54] When humans view the nonhuman creation as an object meant sacramentally to facilitate communion with God and use it in accord with this view, they offer the corporeal world back to God as a reciprocal gift now stamped with the imprint of human work.[55] God aids humanity to this end. In this synergistic process, the "rationality" detectable in all nature is moved forward toward an eschatological telos, which is communion between the cosmos – especially humanity – and the divine. In this sense, nature properly understood is both dynamic – in that it is directed toward that which it is presently not rather than sustained as what it is in its static laws[56] – and dependent upon a synergism between the divine will and human work.

While not explicitly referring to the world as sacrament in his seminal work *The Mystical Theology of the Eastern Church*, Vladimir Lossky certainly has the notion in his purview.[57] Though God created the world ex nihilo – and thus the world is not equated with the divine – nonetheless the entire cosmos is graced from the moment of creation and thus naturally tends toward a participation in God's triune life.[58] Thus, Lossky claims, "The Eastern tradition knows nothing of 'pure nature' to which grace is added as a supernatural gift. For it, there is no natural or 'normal' state, since grace is implied in the act of creation itself."[59] For Lossky, the creation makes possible the Church, and the Church in turn becomes the transfiguration of the created order.[60] The first Church is "the Church of Paradise."[61] The human creature, as priest, bears the vocation to bridge the division between Paradise and the cosmos so that the entire created order might become the Church and thereby fulfill its telos by sharing in God's life.[62]

Also drawing on Maximus's theology, Kallistos Ware affirms that God is present in the entire cosmos, even explicitly referring to his view as panentheism. "As creator...God is always at the heart of each thing, maintaining its being.... As Christians we affirm not pantheism but 'panentheism'. God is *in* all things yet also *beyond* and *above* all things."[63] The entire cosmos is good and witnesses to the divine.[64] In this sacred world, humans, as priests, have the "God-given task to reconcile and harmonize the noetic [that is, the spiritual/intellectual] and the material realms, to bring them to unity, to spiritualize the material, and to render manifest all the latent capacities of the created order."[65] For humanity, as a unique species, "is capable of seeing the world as God's gift, as a sacrament of God's presence and a means of communion with him."[66]

Summarizing many of the above notions, John Chryssavgis provides an overview of Orthodox contributions to ecological issues.[67] For Chryssavgis, multiple dimensions of theological thought – theology proper, christology, eschatology, anthropology, creation – form a foundation for viewing the world as sacrament. Ultimately, Chryssavgis affirms the view of Nikos Kazantzakis that, on account of its relationship with God, the nonhuman creation is of immeasurable value.[68]

The priestly vocation of human beings

As should already be evident, in Orthodox theology the notion that the world is a sacrament is consistently accompanied by the notion that all humans are priests of that sacrament. More often than not, this priestly role finds its foundation in humanity's bearing of the *imago Dei*. That is, the image of God provides humanity with a unique status and a crucial responsibility.[69] As already noted, for Maximus the human being is the microcosm of the cosmos and thus the creature in which the divisions in the created order – most often between the spiritual and physical – are joined. As such, humans are uniquely positioned to draw the physical cosmos into the spiritual realm.

These claims of Maximus have been taken up by many other contemporary Orthodox theologians. John Meyendorff links Maximus's interpretation of the image of God to his view of humanity's responsibility of uniting the five divisions in the cosmos.[70] Nonna Vernon Harrison also cites Maximus's five divisions in conjunction with the image of God. Drawing on this conjunction, Harrison states, "As human beings we are called with Christ to a cosmic priesthood whose task is to offer the world to God and bestow God's blessing on the world."[71]

For his part, Alexander Schmemann limits the effect that humanity can have as priest prior to the end of history itself. In the face of Christ's death, the world "lost its last chance to become the paradise God created it to be"; for "in that murder the world itself died."[72] Even so, there remains a role for humanity as priest in the world.[73] For at baptism, "Man is again king of creation."[74] The redeemed human being "knows what to do with" the world.[75] This action is realized in the Church, understood as *leitourgia* (the becoming of a true community), in which humanity departs from the world and enters into Christ's Eucharistic life and offers the world (as bread and wine) back to God in thanksgiving. Afterwards, Christians return to the world to live as Eucharist in it.[76] In this sense,

> The Church in its separation from "this world," on its journey to heaven, *remembers* the world, remembers all men, remembers the whole of creation, takes it in love to God. The Eucharist is the sacrament of cosmic remembrance: it is indeed a restoration of love as the very life of the world.[77]

In the liturgical life of the Church, the world is brought to its telos via humanity.[78] Furthermore, the liturgy turns humanity toward the world: "In Christ, life – life in all its totality – was returned to man, given again as a sacrament and communion, made Eucharist."[79]

Above, I noted Dumitru Staniloae's anthropocentric view, in which the world exists for humanity (that is, consciousness), not the other way around. However, there is a tension in Staniloae's thought. He states, "God created the world for the sake of humanity, and...his project was that the world be led towards the purpose of full communion with himself, in a special way that is by means of dialogue with humanity."[80] Thus, there appears to be some sense in which humans exist for the cosmos, for it is in humanity that the cosmos reaches its ultimate telos of divine communion. But for the cosmos, this communion is ultimately for the sake of the human-divine communion.[81] The cosmic-divine communion thus appears to lack an intrinsic integrity.

Staniloae maintains that humanity's "responsibility toward nature given by God appears today as a duty to use *resources* sparingly and not to disfigure nature through pollution."[82] For the gift of nature to humanity also entails a responsibility of the individual for other humans. Hence, nature serves as a means of communion not only with God but also with other humans.[83] Staniloae links this service of nature to the role of humanity as the image of God:

> Man is called to grow by exercising spiritual rule over the world, by transfiguring it, by exercising his capacity to see the world and make of it a medium transparent of the spiritual order that radiates from the person of the Word.[84]

Vladimir Lossky, engaging the work of both Dionysius and Maximus, claims, "The world, created in order that it might be deified, is dynamic, tending always toward its final end."[85] This end is union with God, which is in part predicated upon the role of humanity. Thus the process of cosmic deification is synergistic.[86] Drawing on Maximus's five divisions of creation, Lossky claims, "It was the divinely appointed function of the first man, according to Maximus, to unite in himself the whole of created being; and at the same time to reach his perfect union with God and thus grant the state of deification to the whole creation."[87] In this process humanity, in communion with God, engages in transforming "the whole earth into paradise."[88] This priestly role of the human being engenders a heart of compassion for all creatures.[89]

Regarding the place of humanity in creation, Kallistos Ware holds that "the human person forms the centre and crown of God's creation."[90] As such the human creature is "infinitely precious."[91] Humanity's role as royal priest is predicated upon the human's unique capacities. First, humanity can express gratitude to God for the gift of the world. Thus Ware states, "Man is not best defined as a 'logical' but as a 'eucharistic' animal."[92] Human beings are thus most unique, not in their capacity for rational thought, but because they are "capable of seeing the world as God's gift, as a sacrament of God's presence and a means of communion with him."[93]

Another unique human capability, one that enables the role of royal priest, is creativity, the ability to contribute to the process of creation. Ware is cautious to note that this transformative role must always be informed by the eucharistic role. That is, the role of humanity "is not to dominate and exploit nature, but to transfigure and hallow it."[94] In transforming nature, humanity gives it a voice of praise before God and offers it back to God with the stamp of human creativity.

Thus, humanity's role of priest involves transforming nature and offering it back to God in thankfulness. Even so, according to Ware, this priestly role was compromised by the human misuse of freedom.[95] At the heart of the Fall and original sin is, not an ontological shift in humanity, but a relational and dispositional shift.[96] For Ware,

> the "original sin" of man ... meant first and foremost that he no longer looked upon the world and other human beings in a eucharistic way, as a sacrament of communion with God. He ceased to regard them as a gift, to be offered back in thanksgiving to the Giver, and he began to treat them as his own possession, to be grasped, exploited and devoured.[97]

An evaluation of theologies of cosmic sacramentality

What can be said by way of summarizing the above examinations into both Catholic and Orthodox claims regarding the sacramentality of creation and the priestly vocation of humans? First, it must be acknowledged that there is not a clear uniformity on all matters concerning these positions. While Staniloae is admittedly anthropocentric, Ware and others seem much less so. Also, the framework within which theologians work varies. Schmemann emphasizes the sacramentality of creation from a liturgical outlook. Lossky and Staniloae stress the deification of the cosmos and the role of the human creature in the world at large.

Second, on account of the diversity in the field, it is difficult to assess the extent to which sacramental theology as a whole breaks with the dominant tradition I outline in Chapter 1. Even so, the majority of the writers I have surveyed here tend to maintain a strong anthropocentric leaning. Human beings, as priests, are commissioned to transform the world through reverential use. This transformation entails the world becoming a means of communion between God and humanity and among humans. In this sense, a theology of the sacramentality of the cosmos does blur – if not eradicate – the line between the profane and the sacred. However, the categories of "person" and "thing" – or "community" and "resource" – remain intact. Indeed, they are reinforced inasmuch as the created order is divided into intended recipients of the sacramental dimensions of the world and the things of the world intended to be sacraments for those recipients. In reality, there is little difference between this position and that proffered by Aquinas, who also recognized the revelatory nature of the nonhuman cosmos for humanity.

Third, the ethical ramifications of cosmic sacramentality and the cosmic priesthood of humanity seem vague with regard to nonhuman animals. On the one hand, humanity must respect the created order as a sacramental gift of God. Because the line between the profane and the sacred blurs so strongly in the face of cosmic sacramentality, the so-called "things of the world" should evoke the same level of respect as the elements of the Eucharist. On the other hand, this respect seemingly permits extensive use of the created order – indeed it was for this purpose that God created the cosmos. After all, the bread of the Eucharist is eaten. So also it seems that humans may cause animals to suffer and may kill them and that these actions may fall into the category of "reverential use." In such use, humanity lifts the nonhuman creation up to God as a return gift. As this reciprocal gift, the cosmos facilitates a gift exchange between God and humanity. This exchange is communion. God gave humanity the cosmos. Humanity offers it back to God in reverential use. Yet such a view relegates the entire created order to a resource for the divine-human drama. The limitations of reverential use thus seem geared toward the sustaining of the cosmos as a whole as opposed to concern for the well-being of individual animals.

Fourth, the main difference between the dominant tradition and at least the majority voice in Orthodox theology pertains not to anthropocentrism but rather to eschatology. Transfiguration is the destiny of the entire cosmos. Whereas Aquinas maintains that animal and plant life will cease to exist in the eschatological consummation of the world,

Orthodox writers acknowledge the sacramental necessity of these creatures in the world to come.[98] In Ware's estimation, even animals "in and through man...will share in immortality,"[99] though the exact nature of this sharing is far from clear. At any rate, this eschatological inclusion of the nonhuman creation does differ from that of Aquinas, mainly in the sense that Orthodox theologians include more than just the elements and unmixed bodies. This more inclusive eschaton bears, however, the same teleological purpose: service to the divine-human rapport.

At any rate, I do not see much divergence between the dominant tradition promulgated by Aquinas and many of the recent retrievals of the sacramentality of the cosmos with regard to actions toward nonhuman animals. I acknowledge that there is a difference between reverential slaughter and careless slaughter. But if the main concern is reverencing the sacramental cosmos because it is a sacrament *for humanity*, then the real difference pertains to the manner in which humanity slaughters – a point that can also be made from Aquinas's view. That humanity is justified in slaughtering, however, seems to be consistent with most claims that the cosmos is sacramental. This point notwithstanding, I do believe that *some* retrievals of this theological concept hold great potential in offering an alternative tradition. It is to this potential I now turn.

Sacramental reciprocity as an alternative tradition

Many of the positions regarding the sacramentality of the cosmos delineated above evoke numerous questions regarding the ethical treatment of nonhuman animals. Is reverential slaughter possible? What does cosmic sacramentality mean for individual creatures? What is the significance, if any, of the "silent praise" the created order offered God prior to humanity's existence? Is there an intrinsic integrity to the relationship between God and the nonhuman order or is that relationship wholly predicated upon human intervention?

Furthermore, what is one to make of the frequent expressions of kinship between humanity and creation found in the saints?[100] After all, Saint Ephrem, whom Lossky cites as an Orthodox authority, did not say that the humble person reverentially uses creation to achieve union with God. Rather, he said that the humble person tames the wild and that the merciful heart weeps for animals and reptiles and in doing so reveals the heart of God.[101] Furthermore, as noted in Chapter 4, many early and modern Christians depict an eschatological consummation that includes nonhuman animals and entails peace among them and between them and humans.

These thoughts, grounded in the Christian tradition, provide the foundation to claim that a unilateral view of cosmic sacramentality is insufficient. That is, a vision in which the nonhuman world is a sacrament *for humanity* and humans are, as priests, to use creation *for God* does not capture the communal images in which God, humanity, and creation participate together in eschatological communion. Thus it might be appropriate to consider another paradigm with the capacity to house this threefold community. I suggest a paradigm of sacramental reciprocity.

By this phrase I intimate that the nonhuman creation, including animals, is indeed sacramental in that in it is revealed to humans the glory and goodness of God. Animals do so both as a whole and as individuals. However, humans, as priests of the cosmos, are commissioned by God to reveal the glory and goodness of God *to nonhuman animals* as well. Such a reading is not altogether foreign to the theological claims made by those who advocate cosmic sacramentality, though it does contradict the ethical inferences of many of those claims.

If, as Schmemann states, the "Eucharist is the life of paradise,"[102] perhaps it is worth noting that the liturgical rite does not require the death of any animal. Humanity is once more, on account of Christ's cosmic sacrifice, turned to the fruit of the earth, which enables a new kind of peace. The Eucharist is thus either a restoration of the mythic peace of paradise or a witness to the future peace that will envelop the entire cosmic community in the eschaton.[103] If indeed humanity as priest is the proclamation of Christ's death "for the life of the world,"[104] for which death is "the enemy to be destroyed, not a 'mystery' to be explained,"[105] what can be said about killing animals for human pleasure (or even human need)?

Likewise, Staniloae maintains that "nature as a whole is destined for the glory in which men will share in the kingdom of heaven." He furthermore holds that "even now that glory is felt in the peace and the light that radiate from the person who is a saint."[106] He later defines the ultimate telos of all created reality as "full communion with God."[107] Although Staniloae does not develop this notion in great detail, instead emphasizing proper human use of the created order, here we find a hint that the experience of peace between the saint and nature witnesses to the future hope of the entire cosmos, which is communion with God.[108] In this sense, one can maintain that the nonhuman animal experiences a taste of divine communion in the encounter with the saint even as the saint sees the animal as a sacrament of God. The nonhuman animal receives the sacrament of divine presence *through* the saintly human according to the animal's capacity.[109] Indeed, such claims are consistent with Staniloae's depiction of the primordial state.[110] In this state, the cosmos knew a peace facilitated by the gentleness of humanity, which in turn derived from humanity's relation to God. "A great feeling of solidarity with all things granted him a peace with all things."[111]

Does such a view not suggest a sacramental reciprocity? Indeed, Staniloae affirms, "The entire world senses the fact that it is inserted within the spirit through the medium of the human body."[112] That is, humanity, as the microcosm of matter and spirit, introduces spirit to the material cosmos, even to the point that the nonhuman creation may, through the bodily existence of humanity, "come to have a share in the quality of being a subject."[113]

These quotes aside, Staniloae resists such claims in other passages. The point of the world's communion with God is for the sake of humanity:

> The world was created in order that man, with the aid of the supreme spirit, might raise the world up to a supreme spiritualization, and this to the end that human beings might encounter God within a world that had become fully spiritualized through their own union with God.[114]

Thus it appears that even ultimately speaking, nature exists "only as a framework."[115] Considering the eternal value of the world as such a framework, Staniloae maintains that the eternal relationship between humanity and God will always be mediated through the materiality of the world, albeit a world spiritualized and transparent.[116] The world is thus the final and eternal sacrament.

From his Catholic framework, Irwin maintains that in the liturgy Christians come to see the sacramentality of creation, which leads to a view not only of what the creation *is* (infused with divine presence) but also of what it is *not* (a place that humans are presently reverencing properly).[117] Thus the priestly role must have an ethical dimension:

> Actual celebrations for real people in specific communities are intended to be reminders for them of where God is (and always will be) as well as confront them about where God's presence is diminished because the very human ingenuity that enables liturgy and sacraments to occur is the very ingenuity that is needed to ameliorate injustice to persons and the whole created cosmos.[118]

Note that for Irwin, sacramentality means that justice is extended to the cosmos through the uniqueness of the human creature. In bringing justice to the nonhuman creation, are not humans a sacrament to it? Indeed, Irwin maintains that cosmic sacramentality entails that "humans and all creatures great and small, are all signs of God among us."[119] What does Irwin intend here with the word "us"? The human community? A cosmic community? Are humans only signs of God to each other? Why not also to the nonhuman cosmos, including animals? And if so, are humans really acting as sacraments of divine justice in causing suffering to animals by buying cosmetics tested on them or eating meat – let alone meat from factory farms! – for reasons of personal satisfaction as opposed to vital necessity?

Edwards provides a keen insight here. The Eucharist reminds us of the "unbearable cost to other human beings and to other creatures of our planet" incurred by our eating and drinking.[120] More than that, in the Eucharist "we remember the God who loves each one of them [the nonhuman creatures]. We grieve for the damage done to them. We feel with them. We hope for their future in God. We commit ourselves to their well-being."[121] Should not hoping for the future and committing to the well-being of animals entail witnessing to that future – in which God will secure their well-being – even in the present? Would not such a witness ultimately be to the deification of the cosmos and participation of all creatures in God's life? If so, then would not such a witness be sacramental *for the nonhuman animals?*

Much more could be said. My point comes down to this claim: If human beings are priests of creation, then this priesthood ought to draw them not only to see the cosmos as sacred but also to become the sacramental presence of God *to the cosmos*, particularly through actions that witness to the eschatological hope of communion among God, humans, and the nonhuman cosmos, including the animals. Such a view of priesthood is thoroughly consistent with my reading of a functional interpretation of the image of Elohim (the *particular* God of Genesis 1) and the eschatological stewardship entailed by both Genesis 1:29 and Isaiah 11:1–9.[122]

God is with and beyond the cosmos, with and beyond humanity. But more importantly, God is within the relationships of the world. God indwells in the fellow suffering of creatures. Indeed the groaning of the Spirit in those who do not know how to pray is indicative of the very groaning of the created order itself, both human and nonhuman.[123] A priest of creation then ought to be one who sees God's glory *in the cosmos* and reveals God's love *to the cosmos*. Such is the nature of sacramental reciprocity. Humanity receives the sacramental world. The world receives sacramental humanity. Each is *for* the other in a manner consistent with their natures.

In this sacramental exchange, the entire cosmos, human and nonhuman alike, experiences the burgeoning of salvation because it experiences communion with the divine within its own interrelatedness. God is irrevocably for the world. The world is for God. The nonhuman world is for humanity. Humanity is called to be for the nonhuman world. It is the very God of love that humans encounter through the sacramentality of the cosmos that animals ought to encounter through the sacramentality of humans. For humanity to benefit from the sacramentality of the cosmos without reciprocating this sacramentality for the cosmos is for humanity to be not creation's priest but a thief in its presence.

Conclusion

I have examined modern appropriations and retrievals of the sacramentality of the cosmos. While there are important nuances among the various Catholic and Orthodox voices in this area, a majority of those voices seem to maintain the anthropocentric leanings of Aquinas. The world is sacred. It is the eternal sacrament. It is included in the purview of God's eschatological redemption. However, it is these things *for the sake of humanity in relation to God*. Furthermore, the priesthood of humanity in relation to the cosmos that derives from cosmic sacramentality entails reverential use. This use does not seem to preclude causing suffering or death to individual animals. Nor does it, in most cases, explicitly express concern for the welfare of the individual creature for its own sake. In this sense, rather than a world of profane "things," theologians of cosmic sacramentality tend to envision a world of sacramental "things" – sacred things but things nonetheless. The nonhuman creation remains a network of resources for the well-being of the human community.

However, I contend that there is, within the framework of cosmic sacramentality and the priestly role of humanity, a space to offer a stark alternative to the dominant anthropocentrism of Christian history. This alternative entails a sacramental reciprocity in which humans learn to see the cosmos as a sacred expression of the divine and work to express God's eschatological vision of cosmic communion to the nonhuman creation. In doing so, the human and nonhuman creation become sacramental to one another and together move toward the eschatological communion for which God intends both.

8
Alternative Traditions and Interreligious Dialogue

Up to this point, I have explored the dominant tradition regarding Christianity and nonhuman animals and strands of tradition that either break from that tradition or contain a framework conducive to breaking from it. Here I want to highlight how alternative traditions open fresh possibilities for interreligious dialogue. To do so, I examine the basis for animal welfare in the works of Mohandas Karamchand Gandhi and Albert Schweitzer. For Gandhi, the principle of *ahimsa* (nonviolence) forms the foundation for extending moral concern to nonhuman animals. For Schweitzer, the principle of reverence for life does so. In what follows, I compare how these two principles function in the thought of Gandhi and Schweitzer with regard to their background and development, the different forms of life to which they apply, their ethical ramifications for human/ nonhuman relationships, and the limitations of their application.

Both Gandhi and Schweitzer maintain a functional form of anthropocentrism, in which human beings bear a unique responsibility in relation to the cosmos. Humans have distinctive capacities that render them able to witness against and to a certain extent overcome the violence of the world. These capacities make humans important for the world. However, their importance is not antithetical to the importance or intrinsic value of animals; rather, the former serves to ground the latter. The significance of this comparison for the present work is that it reveals how Schweitzer's rejection of anthropocentrism (in the form of the claim that only humans are intrinsically valuable) is what opens a common space to compare his thought with Gandhi's.

Mohandas Gandhi and *ahimsa*

Mohandas Gandhi (1869–1948), known as Mahatma, the "Great Soul," is renowned for his various applications of nonviolence, most notably in the liberation of India. This pursuit began in Gandhi's hometown of Porbandar, in the Gujarat district, an area in which Jainism and Vaishnava Hinduism were the two dominant influences. Renunciation and *ahimsa* are two vital pillars in these traditions.

Regarding Jainism and *ahimsa*, Ronald Huntington writes, "Jainism's all-encompassing ethical principle can be summarized as follows: Do your duty, and do it as humanely as you can – not just toward other Jains nor even all humankind, but toward the entire world."[1] In line with this cosmic ethic, one dimension of *ahimsa* is vegetarianism, a practice aimed at restraining human violence toward nonhuman animals. Thus, in Gandhi's cultural context vegetarianism is a foundational practice. He recalls, "The opposition to and abhorrence of meat-eating...were the traditions in which I was born and bred."[2] *Ahimsa* thus formed a cultural foundation for Gandhi's ethics.[3] It did so all the more because his parents, whom he admired greatly, fully accepted the practices it entailed.

Despite both cultural influence and family respect, Gandhi rebelled. As a youth, a friend convinced him that his childish fears derived from the cultural shackles of the Gujarat district, in particular, vegetarianism. This belief was common, evinced in a poem recited by schoolboys and recorded by Gandhi:

> Behold the mighty Englishman, He rules the Indian small
> Because being a meat-eater, He is five cubits tall.[4]

This view created a dilemma for Gandhi. The English were strong because they ate meat. Gandhi desired to free India. To match the strength of the occupying force, he had to commit to a different diet, denying the religious convictions instilled in him by his family and culture. Yielding to this logic, Gandhi ate meat for the good of India. However, guilt immediately followed: "A horrible night-mare haunted me. Every time I dropped off to sleep it would seem as though a live goat were bleating inside me, and I would jump up full of remorse."[5] Despite his remorse, Gandhi continued eating meat. Eventually, he abandoned the practice, not out of compassion for animals but out of guilt over deceiving his family.[6] His reverence for his parents grounded his ongoing commitment to vegetarianism. It took a crisis abroad before Gandhi accepted vegetarianism as his own, an indelible facet of *ahimsa*.

Having received an opportunity to study law in England, Gandhi decided to leave India. The temptation to eat meat resurfaced. A friend, using Jeremy Bentham's *Theory of Utility*, pressed Gandhi to the brink of rejecting his tradition. In exasperation, Gandhi admitted that meat eating was necessary but adamantly held to a vow made to his mother before departing for England.[7] This vow stayed his desires until, in a vegetarian restaurant in London, he stumbled upon Henry Salt's *A Plea for Vegetarianism*.

Gandhi believed that God had come to his rescue. This experience also transformed his practice of vegetarianism from a cultural and familial obligation to a personal truth and passion: "From the date of reading this book...the choice was now made in favour of vegetarianism, the spread of which henceforward became my mission."[8] He further studied writers on vegetarianism, expanding his rationale for the practice:

> Ethically they had arrived at the conclusion that man's supremacy over the lower animals meant not that the former should prey upon the latter, but that the higher should protect the lower, and that there should be mutual aid between the two as between man and man.[9]

Gandhi thus came to see a foundation for *ahimsa* in reason and ethics. He also noted its commonality in various religions.[10] As Florence Burgat notes,

> while the extension of non-violence to cover all living creatures capable of suffering (including insects, and even plants) is a contribution of Jain philosophy, Gandhi perceives it as a pillar of universal ethics, which must necessarily be incorporated in all religions once they are rid of everything that runs counter to conscience and reason, in other words, the moral sense and internal coherence of judgment.[11]

With new grounds for his passion, Gandhi began to explore further how *ahimsa* included nonhuman animals.

The boundaries of *ahimsa*

Gandhi is best known for his application of *ahimsa* to human relationships. Many of his writings and many secondary sources focus on this aspect of nonviolence. For this reason I mention it only briefly, summarizing Gandhi's view with three observations. First, perhaps most obvious, Gandhi believed freedom should be extended to all humans.[12] Second, he emphasized a reorientation of the Hindu caste system in order to improve the conditions for the poor and untouchables.[13] Third, he seeks to establish these two facets of *ahimsa* not through battle but rather through the nonviolent method of *satyagraha*, which entails redirecting "the focus of a fight from persons to principles."[14] The aim is to find the value of opposing positions in order to get to the truth behind them, all in the pursuit of peaceful cohabitation.[15] Gandhi greatly values even the lives of his enemies, those opposed to nonviolence and peace.[16] Thus, for Gandhi *all* humanity is included in the boundaries of *ahimsa*. Every life bears value, even the life of an enemy. Gandhi finds strong support for his view in Jesus's Sermon on the Mount, a text he praises.[17] The boundaries of *ahimsa* do not end with humanity, however. Gandhi also extends the principle to nonhuman animals.

Even so, scholarship on Gandhi and nonviolence largely overlooks the issue of animal welfare.[18] Many sources that do address it focus mainly, if not exclusively, on Gandhi's concessions that animals are lesser creatures than humans and thus, if necessary, may be killed for human benefit.[19] When scholars do discuss Gandhi's positive concern for animals, they truncate it, suggesting its importance is secondary.[20]

This truncation is in part due to the emphasis placed on *Hind Swaraj*. Gandhi's primary emphasis in this text is the establishment of a free India by way of nonviolent self-rule.[21] For this reason, he focuses primarily on nonviolent interaction between humans as the political pathway to freedom.[22] Outside Gandhi's famous *Hind Swaraj*, however, numerous texts emphasize the importance of extending *ahimsa* to nonhumans. As I explore a host of such passages in the following subsection, I focus on only one here.

In a letter to Asaf Ali, Gandhi addresses the issue of Muslim cow slaughter. He holds that the issue is a moral one, claiming, "I consider that God has not created lower forms of animal life for man to use them as he will. Man realises his highest station not by indulging but by abstinence. I have no right to destroy animal life if I can subsist healthily on vegetable life."[23] Closing the letter, he concludes, "If you accept the proposition that man is more man as he abstains more, you will have no difficulty in allowing that cow-slaughter is indefensible on moral grounds."[24] Hence, as Burgat claims, Gandhi's extension of *ahimsa* to animals is based on his "moral perception of man" and in this sense, was anthropocentric.[25] However, this anthropocentrism is functional as opposed to value-based. That is, it does not deny that animals have intrinsic value.

In Burgat's estimation, "the ability to suffer forms the foundation to *ahimsa*" in Gandhi's thought.[26] Gandhi thus extends the practice of *ahimsa* to all sentient creatures. The way humans interact with nonhuman animals should reflect compassion and love, not self-serving dominance. Gandhi's experimentation with vegetarianism leads him to extend practices of nonviolence to nonhuman animals.

The ethical ramifications of *ahimsa* for human/nonhuman relations

Gandhi maintains that *ahimsa* mandates bold action.[27] In this vein, he desires to change the way human beings interact with nonhuman animals. He urges members of the Band of Mercy, an organization that worked to prevent cruelty to animals, to practice vegetarianism in the name of consistency.[28] In addressing the All-Indian Humanitarian Conference, the *Tribune* reports that Gandhi "appealed to them, if they had any regard for him, to follow vegetarianism and to abstain from killing animals of any sort."[29] Ultimately, Gandhi claims that "anatomically, physiologically, economically and morally vegetarianism is far superior to meat-eating."[30] Hence, for Gandhi, meat eating is a violation of *ahimsa*. Thus, in the *Hind Swaraj* he writes, "We may observe that many Hindus partake of meat and are not, therefore, followers of Ahinsa."[31]

Refusing to eat nonhuman animals, however, does not exhaust the ethics of *ahimsa*. Use of these animals in scientific and medical experiments is another violation. Gandhi rejects the utilitarian justification for such practices:[32]

> There are three schools of humanitarians. One believes in replacing animal power by the use of any other. Another believes in treating animals as fellow-beings and making such use of them as a brotherly spirit will permit. The third will not make use of lower animals for man's selfish purpose but will employ instead one's power and that of fellow-beings to the extent that the latter give intelligent and willing use. I belong to the third school.[33]

Gandhi refuses to accept use of animals in medical experiments even when such uses clearly yield human benefit. In a letter to H. S. L. Polak, Gandhi discusses the possibility of engaging in methods of medical and scientific advancement. He concludes, "I would neither kill a frog, nor use one for dissecting, if it has been specially killed for the purpose of dissection."[34] On another occasion, a correspondent asked Gandhi to address the practice of shipping monkeys to America for experimentation. In his response, Gandhi disavows such actions despite their benefits for humanity: "It would be wrong to subject the lower creation to living death even if it could be proved that it contributed something to the alleviation of human suffering. Surely, it can never be an end in itself justifying adoption of inhumanities involved in vivisection."[35]

For Gandhi, humanity's greatness does not derive from the ability to utilize the "lower-creation" in whatever way that yields benefit. On the contrary, humanity's greatness rests in the ability to rise above nature's bloody competition and compassionately care for less powerful creatures.[36] Thus, in an interview with Captain Strunk, a member of Hitler's staff, Gandhi claims, "I have reasoned out the doctrine of the sword, I have worked out its possibilities and come to the conclusion that man's destiny is to replace the law of the jungle with the law of conscious love."[37]

While Gandhi concedes certain value to Western medical practices,[38] he is quick to add a limitation to imitating the methods of the West, calling all Indian practitioners to

> shun the irreligion of the Western scientists, which, in order to heal the body and in the name of science, subjects the lower animal kingdom to the hideous tortures which pass muster under the name of vivisection. Some will retort that there is warrant for vivisection in Ayurveda. If there is, I am sorry. No warrant even in the four Vedas can sanctify sacrilege.[39]

Here Gandhi argues that *ahimsa*, when properly interpreted as an ethical principle, surpasses even the authority of the Vedas. Hence, Gandhi challenges all forms of abuse to animals in the form of religious sacrifice:

> From the standpoint of ahimsa, it is not a yajna [i.e., worship or sacrifice] to sacrifice lower animals even with a view to serving humanity. It does not matter that animal sacrifice is supposed to find a place in the Vedas. It is enough for us that such sacrifice cannot stand the fundamental tests of Truth and Non-violence. I readily admit my incompetence in Vedic scholarship. But the incompetence, so far as this subject is concerned, does not worry me because, even if the practice of animal sacrifice be proved to have been a feature of Vedic society, it can form no precedent for a votary of ahimsa.[40]

Gandhi also applies *ahimsa* to animals by way of cow protection. This facet of *ahimsa* reveals that Gandhi does not simply consider it important not to eat, sacrifice, or experiment upon animals. These are simply nonactions. True *ahimsa* necessitates *positive* activism to ensure the welfare of all animals, for which the cow serves as a symbol.[41] Hence, Gandhi states,

He is a poor specimen of Hinduism who stops merely at cow protection when he can extend the arm of protection to other animals. The cow merely stands as a symbol, and protection of the cow is the least he is expected to undertake.[42]

Thus, for Gandhi, true *ahimsa* does not apply only to the human realm. If a person practices violence on animals, that person fails to live out nonviolence to the fullest extent. However, Gandhi realizes that in certain situations, even an advocate of *ahimsa* cannot avoid violence.[43]

Limitations of nonviolence toward nonhuman animals

Anthony Parel argues that Gandhi's *ahimsa* does not necessitate a legalistic ethics of nonkilling with regard to nonhuman animals. Instead, Gandhi aims for a balance between a utilitarian view and a position where nonhuman animals share an equal importance with humans. This middle ground permits killing in the face of extreme threats to humans.[44] However, killing is never a right of humans qua humans; rather, it is a necessary evil.

Considering Gandhi's response to episodes in which nonhuman animals such as monkeys or dogs posed an immediate threat to human welfare, Burgat claims, "Broadly speaking, the preservation of life (one's own and that of the people and animals under one's responsibility) inevitably leads to violence but it should be limited to strict necessity."[45] Even when killing is necessary, *ahimsa* mandates the highest degree of compassion possible.[46]

When an inquirer asked Gandhi how *ahimsa* applied to solving the problem of monkeys causing humans harm, he replied:

My ahimsa is my own. I am not able to accept in its entirety the doctrine of non-killing of animals. I have no feeling in me to save the lives of animals which devour or cause hurt to man. I consider it wrong to help in the increase of their progeny. Therefore, I will not feed ants, monkeys or dogs. I will never sacrifice a man's life in order to save theirs. Thinking along these lines I have come to the conclusion that to do away with monkeys where they have become a menace to the wellbeing of man is pardonable. Such killing becomes a duty. The question may arise as to why this rule should not also apply to human beings. It cannot because, however bad, they are as we are. Unlike the animal, man has been given the faculty of reason.[47]

Here, Gandhi affirms an essential distinction – reason – between humanity and all nonhuman animals. Further, this distinction grounds a unique ethic toward the human. Even so, Gandhi also posits a difference between killing in the face of an imminent danger posed by a violent creature and killing an innocent and peaceful creature for human benefit. Parel and other authors use this sole passage to frame Gandhi's view of nonviolence and animals. Even if this passage were the limit of Gandhi's writing on the subject, it contains no explicit contradiction to the extension of *ahimsa* to animals for their own sake. Notably, Gandhi here defines necessary violence toward nonhuman animals as "pardonable." That is, it requires pardon. The aim, however, is always *ahimsa* to the greatest degree possible. Where violence is required, it reveals the failure of humans to live up to the nobility of their station:

> We have not discovered a purely non-violent way of dealing with the cattle, animals, birds and the insects that come and destroy our harvests. Hence, we practise certain violence, considering it unavoidable in recognition of our own weakness. Otherwise, I know that driving away the cattle by shouting or hitting them with a stick, creating fright in the heart of a bird by throwing a pebble at it, destroying the insects by crushing them under the plough or by any other method, driving away snakes and such creatures or even permitting killing them, are all against the principle of non-violence. But since the Ashram or the inmates of the Ashram have not reached the stage of perfection, these things are being done even though they are inconsistent with the principle of non-violence. For that way alone is it possible to discover a path to moksha.[48]

Life is plagued with ethical conundrums that limit the practice of *ahimsa*. Thus, at times even an advocate of nonviolence *must* commit violence.[49] However, *ahimsa* in the fullest sense denotes brave self-sacrifice for others, including nonhuman animals.[50] Thus Gandhi maintains, "This body...has been given us only in order that we may serve all Creation with it."[51]

Gandhi's *ahimsa* in summation

Gandhi's view of *ahimsa* was shaped by his life experiences, religion, and philosophy. His initial devotion to nonviolence burgeoned out of reverence for his parents. In time, however, Gandhi developed his own passion for *ahimsa*, a passion that engendered empathy for humans and nonhumans alike. Gandhi expressed concern for nonhuman welfare by fully embracing vegetarianism, rejecting utilitarian views of animal experimentation, and repudiating animal sacrifice in the face of Vedic scholarship.

However, Gandhi also recognized the limitations set on *ahimsa* by the nature of the world. Such limitations force humanity to engage in violence against nonhuman animals. This necessity notwithstanding, Gandhi required that all such practices be carried out humanely, with the fullest level of compassion possible. Moreover, he believed that, even when necessary, such practices represented a failure to uphold *ahimsa*.

Albert Schweitzer and reverence for life

Albert Schweitzer (1875–1965) grew up in Alsace in the late nineteenth century. His father pastored a small evangelical church in a predominantly Catholic region. He began his education with a focus on Jesus in the Synoptic Gospels, through which he developed his view of Jesus as an eschatological prophet.[52] After biblical studies, he took up philosophy, all the while pursuing interests in music and medicine.

While a product of culture as much as Gandhi, Schweitzer claimed his ethics developed internally in early youth – even in spite of his context.[53] His ethics derived from intuition. As James Brabazon states,

> Out in the fields and on hillsides [Schweitzer] had already become deeply affected by the sufferings of animals, both in the course of nature and at the hands of human beings. Not that the Alsatians are particularly cruel to animals…. But country people are unsentimental about animals, sometimes indifferent. In Colmar Albert once saw an ancient pony being dragged and beaten to the knacker's yard. And there are the marks of nature's harshness in every dried-out shell of a bird caught by a cat, in every pile of rabbit's bones in the fields, every small scream in the night, every maggot that infests the dead or living flesh.[54]

From Schweitzer's youth, he displayed a genuine concern for nonhuman animals. He recalled occasions where their suffering roused deep empathy in him. Even then these feelings led to action, inasmuch as he refused to limit his prayers to human beings:

> It was quite incomprehensible to me – this was before I began going to school – why in my evening prayers I should pray for human beings only. So…I used to add silently a prayer that I had composed myself for all living creatures. It ran thus: "O, heavenly Father, protect and bless all things that have breath; guard them from all evil, and let them sleep in peace."[55]

Even so, Schweitzer did not always treat nonhuman animals with the respect his intuition engendered. He abused them and felt remorse for doing so.[56] Of all these experiences, however, his most memorable involved a friend who attempted to pressure him into shooting some birds with a homemade catapult. Just as Schweitzer took aim, church bells rang. For Schweitzer, the ringing was a "voice from heaven," calling him to remember the command of nonkilling.[57]

From such experiences, Schweitzer claimed, "There slowly grew up in me an unshakeable conviction that we have no right to inflict suffering and death on another living creature unless there is some unavoidable need for it."[58] Even as a youth Schweitzer recognized, on account of his experience, the reality of "unavoidable" violence. But these experiences formed only part of what became his foundational ethics.

In *My Life and Thought*, Schweitzer recalled his search for a foundational principle of ethics that was sufficiently world- and life-affirming. He searched many different areas of thought, including Eastern religions.[59] While he found value in them, particularly in the concept of *ahimsa*, he ultimately labeled these religions life- and world-negating.[60] He expressed disappointment with the narrow ethics of history: "The great fault of all ethics hitherto has been that they believed themselves to have to deal only with the relations of man to man."[61] Schweitzer's aim was a wider ethic. However, he felt that, in his search, he "was wandering about in a thicket in which no path was to be found."[62]

One day, while taking a journey up the Ogowe River in Africa, Schweitzer had an epiphany. While passing through a group of hippopotamuses, "there flashed upon my mind, unforeseen and unsought, the phrase, 'Reverence for Life.' The iron door had yielded: the path in the thicket had become visible."[63] This illuminated path called for the recognition of a shared experience of all creatures:

> In everything you recognize yourself again. The beetle that lies dead in your path – it was something that lived, that struggled for its existence like you, that rejoiced in the sun like you, that knew anxiety and pain like you. And now it is nothing more than decomposing material – as you, too, shall be sooner or later.[64]

Reverence for life constitutes a recognition of the community of all living things, of a commonality calling for action in favor of all life that strives to live and live well. This simple truth, realized and embraced, is reverence for life. Schweitzer held that, in this realization, "*the dissimilarity, the strangeness,* between us and other creatures is ... removed."[65]

Schweitzer's philosophical works emphasize the intuitive nature of reverence for life. Says Ara Paul Barsam, "For Schweitzer, the human body and all living beings instinctively affirm life by virtue of the fact that they *will* to stay alive."[66] Elsewhere, however, he emphasized the mystical dimension in reverence for life.[67] Schweitzer claimed, "In Jesus Christ, God is manifested as Will-to-Love."[68] Theologically, Schweitzer argued that assent to reverence for life required an inner experience of Christ as Will-to-Love.[69] This experience would be transformative, creating "a new mind and a new heart."[70] Thus Barsam notes,

> The influence of Jesus in Schweitzer's thought, and Schweitzer's belief in the activity of the Will-to-Love to transform will-to-live to a will-to-reverence, is the unacknowledged yet integral *theological* presupposition through his philosophical work.[71]

These philosophical and theological foundations of reverence for life led Schweitzer to a basic moral principle: "It is good to maintain and to encourage life; it is bad to destroy life or to obstruct it."[72]

The boundaries of reverence for life

Schweitzer left little doubt of his concern for human beings. He desired that all humans devote the same level of fervency they had for their own lives to every other human. "In the matter also of our relation to other men, the ethics of reverence for life throw upon us a responsibility so unlimited as to be terrifying."[73] This terrifying responsibility extends *to* all humans *from* all humans, regardless of social class, race, or gender. Schweitzer claimed that whatever benefited the individual belonged to the community.[74]

> It is an uncomfortable doctrine which the true ethics whisper into my ear. You are happy, they say; therefore you are called upon to give much. Whatever more than others you have received in health, natural gifts, working capacity, success, a beautiful childhood, harmonious family circumstances, you must not accept as being a matter of course. You must pay a price for them. You must show more than average devotion of life to life.[75]

For Schweitzer, reverence for life begins with human relationships. However, for the truly ethical person, it cannot end there. "A man is truly ethical when he obeys the compulsion to help all life which he is able to assist, and shrinks from injuring anything that lives."[76] Thus,

Schweitzer denounced any framework, such as the Cartesian one, that narrowed ethics to the human community.[77] He recognized his dissent from the intellectual majority: "Religious and philosophical thinkers have gone to some pains to see that no animals enter and upset their systems of ethics."[78]

Even so, Schweitzer saw in Jesus a tendency to widen the category of neighbor, which human nature seems prone to narrow. For Schweitzer, "The ethic of reverence for life is the ethic of love widened to universality."[79] This widening includes nonhuman life.[80] Thus, reverence for life mandates compassion and empathy for nonhuman animals.

Schweitzer's ethics may be described as functionally anthropocentric, in that he viewed human beings as the only creatures able to transcend the law of nature:

> Nature knows only a blind affirmation of life. The will-to-live which animates natural forces and living beings is concerned to work itself out unhindered. But in man this natural effort is in a state of tension with a mysterious effort of a different kind. Life-affirmation exerts itself to take up live-negation into itself in order to serve other living beings by self-devotion, and to protect them, even it may be, by self-sacrifice, from injury or destruction.[81]

In this sense, the ethical human lives between the irrational tensions of the will to live and the willingness to negate life that others might live.[82] In nature, the will to live dominates the propensity for self-sacrifice, resulting in a perpetual competition for survival. Human beings harbor the spiritual capacity to overcome this reality and extend the reverence they hold for their lives not only to their own kind but to all forms of the will to live.

Schweitzer's ever-present rule of expanding the boundaries of neighbor to include all life did not stop with the inclusion of animals. Life, in the most general sense, constitutes the category of ultimate ethical concern. Brabazon notes that, for Schweitzer, even grass trumped money. That is, one cannot measure the goodness of an action based on what humanity gains, even where only vegetative life is as stake. Humanity must consider all lives affected. "Life is the bottom line, not profit, not success, not conquest."[83] In Schweitzer's words,

> The essential nature of the will-to-live is determination to live itself to the full. It carries within it the impulse to realize itself to the full. It carries within it the impulse to realize itself in the highest possible

perfection. In the flowering tree, in the strange forms of the medusa, in the blade of grass, in the crystal; everywhere it strives to reach the perfection with which it is endowed. In everything that exists there is at work an imaginative force, which is determined by ideals. In us beings who can move about freely and are capable of pre-considered, purposive activity, the craving for perfection is given in such a way that we aim at raising to their highest material and spiritual value both ourselves and every existing thing which is open to our influence.[84]

Here, Schweitzer extended reverence for life even to crystals. All life, from the amoeba to the human, is a subject of intrinsic moral concern. Furthermore, anywhere necessity demands the cessation of life, reverence is violated. Thus, the truly ethical person causes no unnecessary suffering to any life, including plucking a leaf from a tree.[85]

Ultimately, for Schweitzer, the scope of reverence for life is limitless. As Marvin Meyer writes, "When Schweitzer affirmed reverence for life, he affirmed the solidarity of all living things and the moral obligation of people who live in the midst of living things."[86] For Schweitzer, a person lives out reverence for life by actively enabling the well-being of all life. Wherever the ethical person sees life in peril, he or she works to alleviate that peril.

The ethical ramifications of reverence for life for human/nonhuman relations

For Schweitzer, reverence for life constitutes a calling[87] that mandates engagement with the world for the sake of preserving life: "No one must shut his eyes and regard as non-existent the sufferings of which he spares himself the sight."[88] When the ethical person views the horrors of the world, he or she is moved to reverse them to the extent possible. This action is for the sake of those lives experiencing horror, even if "merely" a bug: "If I save an insect from a puddle, life has devoted itself to life, and the division of life against itself is ended."[89] The basic ethical ramification of reverence for life is thus to preserve all life and alleviate all suffering to the greatest extent possible.

Schweitzer enumerated some ethical practices consistent with reverence for life. First, while he did not forthrightly condemn all experiments on animals as unnecessary, he called those who engage in such practices to weigh carefully which are truly necessary. For instance, dissections that teach students what previous dissections have already taught are, for Schweitzer, inexcusable. Moreover, he claimed that because animals have benefited humans in scientific research, humanity owes a great debt to them.

> By the very fact that animals have been subjected to experiments, and have by their pain won such valuable results for suffering humanity, a new and special relation of solidarity has been established between them and us. From that springs for each one of us a compulsion to do to every animal all the good we possibly can.[90]

Included in the ethical ramifications of reverence for life, Schweitzer denounces caging and training animals:

> I never go to a menagerie because I cannot endure the sight of the misery of the captive animals. The exhibiting of trained animals I abhor. What an amount of suffering and cruel punishment the poor creatures have to endure in order to give a few moments' pleasure to men devoid of all thought and all feeling for them![91]

Schweitzer also disdained any action where humanity derived joy from the suffering of animals. Such practices, including hunting for sport, inevitably arise when one views animals as having value only in their usefulness to humanity. Considering this view, Schweitzer looked forward to a day when these violations of life would end:

> The time will come when public opinion will no longer tolerate amusements based on the mistreatment and killing of animals. The time will come, but when? When will we reach the point that hunting, the pleasure in killing animals for sport, will be regarded as a mental aberration? When will all the killing that necessity imposes upon us be undertaken with sorrow?[92]

Hence, Schweitzer held in abhorrence the harming of animals for anything other than absolute necessity. Were this principle combined with his committed belief that life, not money, formed the foundation of true ethics, many of the uses animals are put to today would fall into serious question. Exploring ever further the implications of his own thought, Schweitzer eventually became a vegetarian. Barsam quotes Erica Anderson:

> No bird or animal in the hospital village – hen or pig or sheep – is killed for food. Fish and crocodile meat brought by fisherman are

occasionally served at the table, but Schweitzer himself in recent years has given up eating either meat or fish, even the liver dumplings he used to relish and enjoy. "I can't eat anything that was alive any more" [Schweitzer said]. When a man questioned him on his philosophy and said that God made fish and fowl for people to eat, he answered, "Not at all."[93]

Schweitzer believed that society would one day realize the fault in harming animals. In the meantime, the truly ethical person should live out reverence for life as a countercultural lifestyle. "You ought to *share life* and *preserve life* – that is the greatest commandment in its most elementary form. Another, and negative, way of expressing it is this: You shall *not kill*."[94] However, like Gandhi, Schweitzer understood the limitations of his ethic.

Limitations of nonviolence toward nonhuman animals

Barsam notes that many scholars have accused Schweitzer of a deficient eschatology.[95] He also persuasively argues that this criticism fails in the face of Schweitzer's overarching theological view.[96] For Schweitzer, the eschatological kingdom of God, inaugurated with Christ, provides the vision toward which the ethical human person strives.[97] The eschatological hope lived out by Jesus forms a foundation for ethical practice. Schweitzer called this foundation "practical eschatology." Barsam states, "*Practical eschatology* is the term given to those ethical actions undertaken by humans in this world seeking to anticipate the kingdom."[98] His eschatological hope included a world where life is not divided against itself. As the human person lives toward this goal, "every act that preserves life from destruction is seen as a prelude to the new creation."[99] But the ultimate eschatological arrival of the kingdom rests on God's decisive act.[100] Hence, human beings cannot affect the full eschatological vision of the kingdom and thus must live in the tension between that which they strive for and its arrival in history. As such, the ethical person experiences discontent, for life's current state creates unavoidable tension with reverence for life. But it is also this discontent that allows the ethical person to become a great hope for the world. "The fact in itself that in the ethically developed man there has made its appearance in the world a will-to-live which is filled with reverence for life and devotion to life is full of importance for the world."[101]

Still, no person can fully live out the ethical implications of reverence for life. Schweitzer sees the world realistically.

I too am subject to division of my will-to-life against itself. In a thousand ways my existence stands in conflict with that of others. The necessity to destroy and to injure life is imposed upon me. If I walk along an unfrequented path, my foot brings destruction and pain upon the tiny creatures which populate it. In order to preserve my own existence, I must defend myself against the existence which injures it. I become a persecutor of the little mouse which inhabits my house, a murderer of the insect which wants to have its nest there, a mass-murderer of the bacteria which may endanger my life. I get my food by destroying plants and animals. My happiness is built upon injury done to my fellow-man.[102]

Schweitzer does not apply reverence for life legalistically. Rather, each concrete situation calls for balancing one's disposition with what is necessary.[103] Hence, Schweitzer fed fish to birds he rescued and killed germs for the betterment of human life. However, Schweitzer's ethic was not utilitarian. For him, reverence for life remained foundational regardless of the context. Each situation warranted thoughtful consideration of the extent to which one could uphold reverence for life. Some situations might require a necessary violation. But the person consumed by reverence for life "injures and destroys life only under a necessity which he cannot avoid, and never from thoughtlessness,"[104] because to that person "all destruction of and injury to life, under whatever circumstances they take place, [are viewed] as evil."[105]

But again, the universe is a riddle of creation and destruction:

The world is a ghastly drama of will-to-live divided against itself. One existence makes its way at the cost of another; one destroys the other. One will-to-live merely exerts its will against the other, and has no knowledge of it. But in me [the human] the will-to-live has come to know about the other wills-to-live. There is in it a yearning to arrive at unity with itself, to become universal.[106]

The state of the universe renders every effort to make all life flourish an inevitable failure. "However seriously man undertakes to abstain from killing and damaging, he cannot entirely avoid it. He is under the law of necessity, which compels him to kill and to damage both with and without his knowledge."[107] The world in which all life competes for the right to live presents endless ethical conundrums. Constantly, one must choose between one violence and another.[108] Hence, for Schweitzer, there are even times when not killing for the sake of upholding a principle would be unethical. When an animal endures prolonged suffering, active compassion may call for action to end this suffering. Even in this necessary case, however, the act of killing or causing harm remains a necessary evil.[109]

Schweitzer's reverence for life in summation

Throughout his life, Schweitzer sought to find the foundational principle in ethics that adequately captured the intuitive empathy and compassion that he felt towards all living things as a child. His embrace and study of Christianity, particularly Jesus in the gospels, his exploration of Eastern religions, and his love of philosophy and ethics all contributed to his discovery of this principle, which he labeled "reverence for life." Its boundaries are endless, including human beings, nonhuman animals, plants, and even microorganisms and minerals. Applying the principle requires thoughtfulness, for it highlights the tension between reality and hope. However, even when one cannot avoid the necessity of violence, partaking in it remains a violation of reverence for life, albeit an unavoidable one. The goal of creation includes the redemption of all suffering creatures in the context of a new creation. The eschaton calls for action that works to promote life and assuage suffering to whatever degree possible.

Mohandas Gandhi and Albert Schweitzer: a comparison

I have delineated the foundations for extending moral concern to nonhuman animals in the thought of both Gandhi and Schweitzer according to the common categories of historical development and the boundaries, ethical ramifications, and limitations of their ethics. Here I offer something by way of comparing the two approaches. The comparison highlights the major point of convergence between Gandhi and Schweitzer: the dismantling of an anthropocentrism that releases humans from direct moral obligations to animals by denying them intrinsic value. Such a convergence suggests that the alternative traditions in Christianity – especially those that recognize humanity's unique capacity to extend direct moral concern to nonhuman animals – open new spaces within which to dialogue with other religious traditions.

Both Gandhi and Schweitzer drew upon both their own religious traditions and others to establish their positions. Gandhi saw in Jesus an affirmation of nonviolence[110] and in the protology and eschatology of Christianity a clear affirmation of vegetarianism as an ideal.[111] Schweitzer, while rejecting the general *ahimsa* of "Eastern thought" as insufficiently life- and world-affirming, praised Gandhi's active appropriation of the concept: "The fact that Gandhi has united the idea of Ahimsa to the idea of activity directed on the world has the importance not merely of an event in the thought of India but in that of humanity."[112]

Both thinkers believed that their ideals of nonviolence transcended the revealed truth of their religious traditions. Both saw in their traditions an affirmation that the human being, capable of compassion and solidarity, constitutes a great hope for a tumultuous and competitive world. The human can transcend what appears to be the natural state of the cosmos and live out a divinely revealed ethic. Gandhi held that humanity's rationality, while constituting a greatness that surpasses the lower creatures, also constitutes a deep responsibility to care for those creatures. For Gandhi, "Man's destiny is to replace the law of the jungle with the law of conscious love."[113] Schweitzer maintained that humanity, while fundamentally united to all life in its will to live, nonetheless could move beyond the "blind affirmation of life" in nature and, by the Spirit, be renewed to a will-to-love in which reverence for life became possible.[114] In this sense both Gandhi and Schweitzer adopted a functional anthropocentrism not all that dissimilar in its roots from the functional readings of the *imago Dei* discussed in Chapters 3 and 5 and the priestly role of humanity discussed in Chapter 7. Humans are not the center of the world in the sense of being the measure of all things; rather, they bear a central responsibility to detect and honor that all existence bears a measure of value in and of itself.

In line with this claim, both Gandhi and Schweitzer extended their ethical principles to include nonhuman animals. They also delineated similar ethical ramifications of their principles. Both provided critiques of religious animal sacrifice. Both affirmed nonviolence as an ideal and decried cruel treatment of nonhuman animals for human amusement and benefit. Both called for humans to take positive action and rise above the apparent laws of nature – to witness to a law of love in the midst of nature.

However, Gandhi and Schweitzer also both affirmed that the world necessitates some violence toward nonhuman animals. Each recognized that, for whatever reason, the competition of biological existence is unavoidable. There will be cases in which humans must choose between their own lives and the lives of nonhumans. Nonetheless, both Gandhi and Schweitzer ardently affirmed that even violence arising out of vital necessity constitutes an evil – either a failure of living out *ahimsa* or a violation of the reverence due to all life. That is, even vitally necessary acts of violence require pardoning and, when possible, compensation.

While these similarities are substantial, there are also important differences between Gandhi and Schweitzer regarding nonviolence. Two such differences are worth mentioning here. They are (1) the foundational constitution of the human person and this foundation's relevance to anthropocentrism and (2) the criterion for the application of nonviolence and this criterion's effect on the inclusiveness of each thinker's principle.

First, Gandhi emphasizes that humans, as rational beings, are greater than the lower creatures that lack reason. While he accepts that killing monkeys is a "pardonable" duty where they have become "a menace to the wellbeing of man," he refuses to accept that killing another human can ever fall into such a category: "It cannot because, however bad, they are as we are. Unlike the animal, man has been given the faculty of reason."[115] This view of the constitution of the human person suggests that for Gandhi, the human's greatness over the nonhuman world is an objective reality grounded in the faculty of reason, a vision of the human person quite consistent with much of the history of philosophy, including the view of Aquinas explored in Chapter 1. However, one ought not to overstate Gandhi's position here. The essential difference does not deny animals the right to life, as much of that philosophical tradition does. Earlier in his life Gandhi claimed that the notion of cow protection "puts the animal creation on the same level with man so far as the right to live is concerned."[116] Still, Gandhi accepted a hierarchy based on objective and substantial differences in creatures.

Schweitzer, on the other hand, while accepting humanity's unique capacity to become will-to-love, nonetheless emphasized how an ontology of the will breaks down the dissimilarity between humans and nonhumans. All things will to live; thus, "in everything you recognize yourself." All things experience struggle, joy, and anxiety. In these shared experiences of will to live, "*the dissimilarity, the strangeness*, between us and other creatures is...removed."[117] Thus Schweitzer, in applying such experiences to all creatures that will to live, rejected the Cartesian emphasis on the reasoning individual. In place of what Schweitzer called the "paltry, arbitrarily chosen beginning" of Descartes's *cogito ergo sum*, he advocated the knowledge that "I am life which wills to live." However, because one must not separate inner knowledge from experience with the world, the dictum expands to "I am life which wills to live, in the midst of life which wills to live."[118] This relational realization is the foundation of Schweitzer's ethics. In this sense, Schweitzer's view is amenable to a relational ontology, as humanity's will to live is always and already in the midst of a world filled with others that will to live.

Lastly on this difference, while Schweitzer's application of the ethic of reverence for life favors humans over bacteria in practice, he did not attempt to ground this gradation of concern in an objective constitution of the human person, such as the faculty of reason.[119] Says Schweitzer, "I'll be damned if I recognize any *objectively valid* distinctions in life. Every life is sacred."[120]

This first disparity between Gandhi and Schweitzer highlights a difference in the anthropocentric tendencies of each thinker. For Gandhi, the heightened status of the human person is an objective reality based on humanity's capacity for reason. For Schweitzer, choosing a human over a tree is a subjective (albeit necessary) departure from the fundamental commonality of all life. At any rate, both thinkers maintained that anthropocentrism neither justifies violence in any situation nor removes direct moral concern for other creatures. The anthropocentrism of both Gandhi and Schweitzer, because it is fundamentally functional, is wholly compatible with the recognition that all life bears intrinsic value. Humans are first and foremost those creatures responsible for all others, not those entitled above all others.

Secondly (and connected to the above disparity), Gandhi and Schweitzer differed in the scope of their application of nonviolence. They agreed that humans ought to seek the welfare of nonhuman animals through action and nonviolence. Much as Jeremy Bentham did, Gandhi accepted suffering as the insuperable line upon which one ought to ground direct moral concern. Concerning nonviolence, then, Gandhi's emphasis was on sentient creatures.

Contrarily, Schweitzer replaced both the lines of rationality and sentience with the line of will to live. For Schweitzer, then, the ethics of nonviolence applied to all things that strive to live, from grass to beetles to fish to pelicans to humans. Schweitzer was quite accurate, then, when he claimed, "The ethic of reverence for life is the ethic of love widened to universality."[121]

Conclusion

I could at this point evaluate the differences between Gandhi and Schweitzer and offer an assessment of the strengths and weaknesses of each.[122] However, since I am here fundamentally interested in how alternatives to the dominant tradition of Christianity regarding nonhuman animals open spaces for dialogue, I focus my conclusion, rather, on Schweitzer's break with that tradition. It is worth noting that *every* similarity I listed between Gandhi and Schweitzer is an area in which Schweitzer rejected the positions promulgated by Aquinas. Reason witnesses to the claim nonhumans lay upon humans. Humans bear a responsibility, based on their unique capacities, to protect each nonhuman life for its own sake. The end of all life is the hope for a world in which divisions end. Without the claims that Schweitzer made from his Christian framework, the areas of common affirmation with Gandhi would not exist. Of course, I do not intend such a claim to intimate that breaking with the dominant tradition is appropriate merely because it creates common ground with other religious viewpoints. Rather, my point is simply that in exploring the alternative traditions of their religious history, Christians can find surprising areas of convergence with other religious traditions. The dialogue such a discovery facilitates can only help improve and strengthen these alternative Christian views. They will also encourage interreligious practice in areas of animal welfare and political reform.

Conclusion

By way of conclusion, I want first to reiterate a point I make in the Introduction. This book's intent is not to argue that the dominant tradition is wrong. My aim has simply been to delineate the dominant tradition and cast light upon its discontents in Christian history, thereby highlighting alternative strands of tradition. It is, however, my opinion that, at the very least, the dismantling of the dominant tradition's anthropocentrism is a better form of Christianity and is more applicable to the context in which we find ourselves. Even so, I offer no accusations that the dominant tradition is *objectively* deficient.

Moving beyond this claim, I can summarize the contents of the dominant tradition and its alternatives in a single question. What kind of world did God create? The subquestions are as follows: Did God create a world divided into persons and things? A world in which some creatures have the right to cause others to suffer and die even when there is no vital necessity to do so? A world of holistic harmony in the midst of competitive violence?

For the dominant tradition the answer to these subquestions is yes. Humans alone bear intrinsic value. God, in fact, has ordained this unique status for humans. On account of their special place, humans have the right to harm and kill other creatures for the sake of their own well-being, provided such actions are not detrimental to the common good of humanity.

The alternative strands, when combined and critically retrieved, open the door to a different vision of the world: a world in which the category of "person" does not justify violence against creatures that fall outside that category but rather grounds loving concern for those creatures; a world in which entitlements predicated upon superiority ground, not a food chain, but a chain of responsibility to express love and compassion, where even vital necessity leaves one penitent in the face of violence, and where humans long for the transfiguration of the universe – the new creation of cosmic peace. It is a world in which humans not only seek the presence of God *in the world* but also seek to witness to the love of God *for the world*.

These two visions of God's creation are radically different. However, Christianity has foundations that can support both visions. So which ought we to choose? I think we ought to choose the latter. We should live life *as if* God's love of the world is in no way limited to human beings but is wide enough to include the entire cosmos. Bearing *this* God's image, we should seek to emulate that love, choosing the path of self-sacrifice for the sake of the nonhuman other. Such an emulation witnesses to the God who does not lord greatness over and against the world but becomes vulnerable for its sake. It witnesses to the peaceful and other-affirming Creator of Genesis 1. It witnesses to the protological vision of peace and the eschatological hope for the dissolution of cosmic inequity. In such an emulation, humans becomes sacraments of the divine presence – they reflect the divine image – to the nonhuman world. Humans become "humans for the world" just as God is "God for us."

Implicit in the title of this book is a question: What is the status of animals in Christianity? The answer is that it depends on which tradition of Christianity one engages. But I think humans would do well, in the face of Elohim's peace versus Marduk's warfare, to ask another question: What if God treated humans the way humans treat nonhuman animals? If the answer to that question is a horrible thought, humans ought to reflect on which God they are actually imaging to the nonhuman creation.

Notes

1 Thomas Aquinas and the Dominant Tradition

This chapter is a modified version of an earlier published work. See R. P. McLaughlin (2012). "Thomas Aquinas's Eco-Theological Ethics of Anthropocentric Conservation," *Horizons* 39, 1: 69–97.

1. L. White (2000), "The Historical Roots of Our Ecological Crisis." Reprinted in J. Berry (ed.), *The Care of Creation: Focusing Concern and Action*. Downers Grove, IL: Inter-Varsity Press, 2000, p. 38.
2. P. Singer (1975), *Animal Liberation: A New Ethics for Our Treatment of Animals* (New York: Avon Books), p. 203.
3. R. D. Ryder (1989), *Animal Revolution: Changing Attitudes towards Speciesism* (Cambridge, MA: Basil Blackwell), p. 43.
4. G. Steiner (2005), *Anthropocentrism and Its Discontents: The Moral Status of Animals in the History of Western Philosophy* (Pittsburgh: University of Pittsburgh Press), p. 126.
5. R. N. Wennberg (2003), *God, Humans, and Animals: An Invitation to Enlarge Our Moral Universe* (Grand Rapids, MI: Eerdmans), p. 121.
6. A. Linzey (1995), *Animal Theology* (Chicago: University of Illinois Press), p. 19.
7. P. Santmire (1985), *The Travail of Nature: The Ambiguous Ecological Promise of Christian Theology* (Minneapolis: Fortress Press), pp. 91–92.
8. J. Berkman (2009), "Towards a Thomistic Theology of Animality," in C. Deane-Drummond and D. Clough (eds), *Creaturely Theology: On God, Humans and Other Animals* (London: SCM Press), p. 24.
9. Berkman, "Towards a Thomistic Theology of Animality," p. 24.
10. A. Clifford (1996), "Foundations for a Catholic Ecological Theology of God," in D. Christiansen and W. Grazer (eds), *"And God Saw That It Was Good": Catholic Theology and the Environment* (Washington, DC: US Catholic Conference), p. 40.
11. See C. Deane-Drummond (2008), *Eco-Theology* (Winona, MN: Anselm Academic), pp. 103–104; 213–214, n. 23.
12. J. Schaefer (2009), *Theological Foundations for Environmental Ethics: Reconstructing Patristic & Medieval Concepts* (Washington, DC: Georgetown University Press), pp. 8–9.
13. W. French (1993), "Beast Machines and the Technocratic Reduction of Life," in C. Pinches and J. B. McDaniel (eds), *Good News for Animals? Christian Approaches to Animal Well-Being* (New York: Orbis), p. 39.
14. M. Wynn (2010), "Thomas Aquinas: Reading the Idea of Dominion in the Light of the Doctrine of Creation," in D. G. Horrell, C. Hunt, C. Southgate, and F. Stavrakopoulou (eds), *Ecological Hermeneutics: Biblical, Historical and Theological Perspectives* (New York: T & T Clark), pp. 154–167.
15. W. Jenkins (2008), *Ecologies of Grace: Environmental Ethics and Christian Theology* (New York: Oxford University Press), p. 150.

16. T. Aquinas (1265/1946), *Summa Theologica* (hereafter *ST*), translated by Fathers of the English Dominican Province (New York: Benzinger), 1.5.3.
17. *ST*, 1.47.2
18. See *ST*, 1.78.1. See also J. Barad (1995), *Aquinas on the Nature and Treatment of Animals* (San Francisco: International Scholars Publications), pp. 29–30.
19. See *ST*, 1.79.2.
20. See *ST*, 1.78.1; T. Aquinas (1955–1957), *Summa contra Gentiles* (hereafter *SCG*), Joseph Kenny (ed.) (New York: Hanover House), II.66. Even within the realm of sensation, in which Aquinas considers five exterior and four interior powers, he posits a distinction between humans and nonhumans. See *ST*, 1.78.4; 1.79.6; 1.81.3.
21. *ST*, I.76.5.
22. Aquinas posits that the human, containing all qualities of souls, is a microcosmic being that "is in a manner composed of all things" (*ST*, 1.91.1). See also *ST*, 1.96.2; 1.75.4; 1.77.2. Aquinas accepts that the different dimensions of the soul are unified (*ST*, 1.76.3; *SCG*, II.58). Furthermore, the unified human soul (vegetative, sensitive, and rational) is substantially unified to the human body as its form (*ST*, 1.76.6). Even so, "some operations of the soul are performed without a corporeal organ, as understanding and will" (*ST*, 1.77.5). Thus, Aquinas posits that the intellectual powers of the soul do not have the soul-body composite as their subject. Hence, when the human body dies, the powers of the soul that depend on corporeal organs become dormant in the soul. See *ST*, 1.77.8.
23. *ST*, 1.93.6.
24. *ST*, 1.93.6.
25. *ST*, 1.45.7; 1|2.62.1.
26. *ST*, 1|2.1.8; also *ST*, 1.1.8.
27. *ST*, 1|2.2.8.
28. While the vision of God is the shared end of all humanity, Aquinas argues that "fellowship of friends is not essential to [perfect] happiness." However, "fellowship of friends conduces to the well-being of happiness." *ST*, 1|2.4.8. Bonnie Kent asserts that Aquinas understands the ultimate telos of humanity to be a communal affair. B. Kent (2002), "Habits and Virtues (Ia IIae, pp. 49–70)," in S. J. Pope (ed.), *The Ethics of Aquinas* (Washington, DC: Georgetown University Press), p. 126.
29. *ST*, 1|2.3.8.
30. *SCG*, III.37.
31. *ST*, 1|2.62.1. Also, J. Porter (1990), *The Recovery of Virtue: The Relevance of Aquinas for Christian Ethics* (Louisville, KY: Westminster / John Knox Press), p. 53.
32. *ST*, 1|2.4.5.
33. *ST*, 1|2.4.7. Happiness in the temporal realm is always imperfect for Aquinas. See *SCG*, III.48.
34. *ST*, 1.79.2. According to Aquinas's redactor, this dependence will cease at the resurrection (*ST*, S3.81.4).
35. See *ST*, 1|2.1.6.
36. S. J. Pope (2002), "Overview of the Ethics of Thomas Aquinas," in S. J. Pope (ed.), *The Ethics of Aquinas* (Washington, DC: Georgetown University Press), p. 32. See also A. MacIntyre (2007), *After Virtue: A Study in Moral Theory*, 3rd ed. (South Bend, IN: University of Notre Dame Press), pp. 53, 185.

37. *SCG*, III.34–35; *ST*, 1|2.65.2. See also Kent, "Habits and Virtues," pp. 121–122.
38. *ST*, 1|2.65.2.
39. S. Pinckaers (2002), "The Source of Ethics of St. Thomas Aquinas," in S. J. Pope (ed.), *The Ethics of Aquinas* (Washington, DC: Georgetown University Press), p. 23.
40. Pope, "Overview of the Ethics of Thomas Aquinas," p. 34.
41. Kent, "Habits and Virtues," p. 125. Consider also how Aquinas links martyrdom, charity, and fortitude. Aquinas, *ST*, 1|2.6.3, 2|2.124.3.
42. See Kent, "Habits and Virtues," p. 118.
43. D. Hollenbach (2002), *The Common Good and Christian Ethics* (New York: Cambridge University Press), p. 123.
44. *ST*, 1|2.65.2. See also J. A. Herdt (2008), *Putting on Virtue: The Legacy of Splendid Vices* (Chicago: University of Chicago Press), pp. 84–87. Herdt rightly notes that infused virtues do not replace the acquired virtues. Indeed, "cases of outright conflict between the two are the exception rather than the rule." Herdt, *Putting on Virtue*, p. 87.
45. Hollenbach, *The Common Good*, p. 123.
46. *ST*, 1.1.2; *SCG*, III.2. See also Pope, "Overview of the Ethics of Thomas Aquinas," p. 32.
47. *ST*, 1.5.1, 4. For a helpful explanation on the distinction between beings as good and the telos of beings as their good, see Porter, *The Recovery of Virtue*, pp. 35–47.
48. *SCG*, III.17.
49. This theocentric cosmology constitutes a central focus in applying Aquinas's thought to modern ecological concerns. See Berkman, "Towards a Thomistic Theology of Animals," p. 24.
50. *ST*, 1.65.2.
51. *ST*, 1.47.1.
52. *ST*, 1.47.2.
53. See *ST*, 1|2.1.8; *SCG*, III.18.
54. See *ST*, 1.91.3; *SCG*, III.22. See also Schaefer, *Theological Foundations*, pp. 22–24.
55. *SCG*, III.20.3.
56. *ST*, 1.96.1.
57. *SCG*, III.112. "Slave" here denotes that animals are, by nature, at the disposal of humanity's pursuit of the good.
58. See *ST*, 1.96.1.
59. *ST*, 1.91.4.
60. Berkman, "Towards a Thomistic Theology of Animality," p. 24.
61. *SCG*, III.112.3.
62. D. Kinsley (1995), *Ecology and Religion: Ecological Spirituality in Cross-Cultural Perspective* (Upper Saddle River, NJ: Prentice Hall), p. 109.
63. Santmire, *Travail of Nature*, p. 91.
64. A. Linzey (2009), *Why Animal Suffering Matters: Philosophy, Theology, and Practical Ethics* (New York: Oxford University Press), p. 14.
65. For example, Wynn, "Thomas Aquinas," pp. 158–162.
66. *ST*, S3.91.1.
67. *ST*, 1.65.2.

68. *ST*, S3.91.1.
69. On the inclusion of simple nonhuman matter, compare *ST*, S3.91.1, with *ST*, 1.65.1.
70. *ST*, S3.91.5. See also *SCG*, IV.97.5. On humanity's animal life ceasing, see *SCG*, IV.83–86.
71. *ST*, 1|2.1.8.
72. Aquinas is explicit on this point. *ST*, 1|2.1.8.
73. C. Leget (2005), "Eschatology," in R. V. Nieuwenhove and J. Wawrykow (eds), *The Theology of Thomas Aquinas* (South Bend, IN: Notre Dame University Press), p. 370.
74. *ST*, 1.75.6; *SCG*, II.79.
75. For Aquinas, the difference between the nonhuman and the human soul is that the latter is self-subsistent. See Aquinas, *ST*, 1.75.2–3.
76. *ST*, 1.75.6.
77. *SCG*, IV.97.5.
78. *ST*, 1|2.25.3. For further foundations for excluding animals from charity, see *ST*, 2|2.25.3.
79. Jenkins, *Ecologies of Grace*, pp. 140–141. On this point, see also E. Schockenhoff (2002), "The Theological Virtue of Charity," in S. J. Pope (ed.), *The Ethics of Aquinas* (Washington, DC: Georgetown University Press), pp. 251–254.
80. See *ST*, 1.65.1. See also Aquinas's view on animals arising out of the death of other animals. *ST*, 1.72.
81. *ST*, 1.96.1.
82. *ST*, 1.72.
83. Given Aquinas's rejection of an edenic state in conjunction with his claim that it is *natural* for humans to use animals for food and clothing, it is odd that Jenkins claims that Aquinas holds that humanity, in innocence, would not have used animals for food. Jenkins provides no reference to Aquinas at this point. See Jenkins, *Ecologies of Grace*, p. 135. Nonetheless, Jenkins provides a wonderful overview of Aquinas's engagement with natural evil and the notion of the Fall. See Jenkins, *Ecologies of Grace*, pp. 144–148.
84. *SCG*, III.117.2; also 117.3.
85. *SCG*, III.111.
86. *SCG*, III.117.2.
87. *ST* 1|2.1.6.
88. The term "resources" is used in modern magisterial documents of the Catholic Church, which I address in Chapter 2.
89. *ST* 2|2.64.1.
90. *SCG*, III.112.13.
91. Clifford, "Foundations," p. 39; on this point, see also Jenkins, *Ecologies of Grace*, pp. 125–127.
92. Jenkins, *Ecologies of Grace*, p. 131.
93. J. E. Salisbury (1998), "Attitudes toward Animals: Changing Attitudes throughout History," in M. Bekoff and C. A. Meaney (eds), *Encyclopedia of Animal Rights and Animal Welfare* (Westport, CT: Greenwood Press), p. 78.
94. See Steiner, *Anthropocentrism and Its Discontents*, p. 131; Wennberg, *God, Humans, and Animals*, p. 121.
95. Aquinas, *ST*, 2|2.141.3; *SCG*, III.129. Also, J. Shaefer (2005), "Valuing Earth Intrinsically and Instrumentally: A Theological Framework for Environmental

Ethics," *Theological Studies* 66, p. 792. Aquinas holds that God charges the human creature (as rational) with maintenance of the created order. *SCG*, III.78; *ST*, 1.64.4; Porter, *The Recovery of Virtue*, pp. 61, 178.
96. Aquinas, *SCG*, III.112.
97. *SCG*, III.112.
98. *ST*, 2|2.64.1.

2 The Dominant Tradition and the Magisterium

1. See W. French (1993), "Beast Machines and the Technocratic Reduction of Life," in C. Pinches and J. B. McDaniel (eds), *Good News for Animals? Christian Approaches to Animal Well-Being* (New York: Orbis Books), pp. 24–43.
2. See, for example, T. Berry (1990), *The Dream of the Earth* (San Francisco: Sierra Club Books).
3. See J. Schaefer (2009), *Theological Foundations for Environmental Ethics: Reconstructing Patristic & Medieval Concepts* (Washington, DC: Georgetown University Press).
4. Deborah Jones heads up an online effort, including the publication entitled *The Ark*, to put animal welfare on the Catholic agenda. See www.all-creatures. org/ca/index.html.
5. *Nostra Aetate*, 5. All citations from the Second Vatican Council are available at www.vatican.va/archive/hist_councils/ii_vatican_council/index.htm.
6. *Apostolicam Actuositatem*, 8.
7. *Apostolicam Actuositatem*, 8.
8. *Gaudium et Spes*, 5.
9. Elsewhere there is some ambiguity as to whether "image" and "likeness" are synonymous or nuanced in magisterial thought. For example, compare sections 225, 705, and 1700 of *The Catechism of the Catholic Church: With Modifications from the Editio Typica* (1995; New York: Doubleday).
10. See *Gaudium et Spes*, 22; *Lumen Gentium*, 2, 7.
11. *Gaudium et Spes*, 22.
12. *Gaudium et Spes*, 17.
13. *Gaudium et Spes*, 17.
14. *Gaudium et Spes*, 19.
15. *Gaudium et Spes*, 24.
16. *The Catechism of the Catholic Church*, 1700.
17. Paul VI (1967), *Populorum Progressio*, 15–16, www.vatican.va/holy_father/ paul_vi/encyclicals/index.htm.
18. *Populorum Progressio*, 42.
19. John XXIII (1963), *Pacem in Terris*, 121, www.vatican.va/holy_father/john_ xxiii/encyclicals/index.htm. John XXIII is clear that rights are predicated upon personhood, a category unique to the human creature; *Pacem in Terris*, 9.
20. See John Paul II (1979), *Redemptoris Hominis*, 14, 17–18, www.vatican.va/ holy_father/john_paul_ii/encyclicals/documents/.html.
21. D. Hollenbach (2007), *The Common Good and Christian Ethics* (New York: Cambridge University Press), p. 7.
22. *Gaudium et Spes*, 69; italics added.
23. See *Apostolicam Actuositatem*, 8.

24. *Gaudium et Spes*, 24; italics added.
25. *Gaudium et Spes*, 25.
26. Citations from *Peace with God the Creator, Peace with All of Creation* are from www.vatican.va/holy_father/john_paul_ii/messages/peace/index.htm.
27. Pope John Paul II and Patriarch Bartholomew I (2002), *Common Declaration on Environmental Ethics*, www.vatican.va/holy_father/john_paul_ii/speeches/2002/june/index.htm.
28. *Peace with God the Creator*, 1.
29. *Peace with God the Creator*, 3.
30. *Peace with God the Creator*, 5,
31. *Peace with God the Creator*, 8.
32. *Peace with God the Creator*, 7.
33. *Peace with God the Creator*, 8–9.
34. The pope's view of nature is here overly optimistic. For a critique of such optimism, see L. H. Sideris (2003), *Environmental Ethics, Ecological Theology, and Natural Selection* (New York: Columbia University Press).
35. *Peace with God the Creator*, 13.
36. *Peace with God the Creator*, 15.
37. John Paul II and Bartholomew I, *Common Declaration*.
38. John Paul II and Bartholomew I, *Common Declaration*.
39. Pope Benedict XVI (2011), "If You Want to Cultivate Peace, Protect Creation: Message for the 2010 World Day of Peace," in T. Winright (ed.), *Green Discipleship: Catholic Theological Ethics and the Environment* (Winona, MN: Anselm Academic), pp. 61–71.
40. *If You Want to Cultivate Peace*, 1 (p. 61).
41. *If You Want to Cultivate Peace*, 2 (p. 61).
42. *If You Want to Cultivate Peace*, 4 (p. 63).
43. *If You Want to Cultivate Peace*, 12 (p. 70).
44. *If You Want to Cultivate Peace*, 8 (p. 66).
45. *If You Want to Cultivate Peace*, 6 (p. 64).
46. *If You Want to Cultivate Peace*, 6 (p. 64).
47. *If You Want to Cultivate Peace*, 6 (p. 65).
48. Nor does Benedict make mention of the eschatological inclusion of creation. He does not follow John Paul II in including Romans 8 as an indicator of such a future. This point is not altogether surprising, given that the pope's masterful text on eschatology (written as Cardinal Joseph Ratzinger) makes virtually no mention of the role of the cosmos in the doctrine. See J. Ratzinger (1988), *Eschatology: Death and Eternal Life*, 2nd ed., translated by M. Waldstein (Washington, DC: Catholic University of America Press). In addition, Benedict received a critique from Jürgen Moltmann regarding his exclusion of the new creation in the encyclical *Spe Salvi*. See J. Moltmann (2009), "Horizons of Hope," *Christian Century* (May 20): 31–33.
49. *If You Want to Cultivate Peace*, 7 (p. 65).
50. *If You Want to Cultivate Peace*, 11 (p. 69).
51. Benedict XVI (2009), *Caritas in Veritate*, 7 (see also 21), www.vatican.va/holy_father/benedict_xvi/encyclicals/index_En.htm.
52. All citations are from www.usccb.org/sdwp/ejp/bishopsstatement.shtml (accessed September 2009).
53. *Renewing the Earth*, I.A.

54. *Renewing the Earth*, II.A.
55. *Renewing the Earth*, II.B.
56. *Renewing the Earth*, III.A.
57. *Renewing the Earth*, III.B; italics added.
58. *Renewing the Earth*, III.B.
59. *Renewing the Earth*, III.C.
60. *Renewing the Earth*, II.A.
61. *Renewing the Earth*, II.A.
62. *Renewing the Earth*, III.D.
63. *Renewing the Earth*, III.F.
64. *Renewing the Earth*, III.G; also V.A.
65. *Renewing the Earth*, III.E.
66. *Renewing the Earth*, III.E.
67. *Renewing the Earth*, IV.A.
68. *Renewing the Earth*, IV.B.
69. *Renewing the Earth*, IV.C.
70. *Renewing the Earth*, V.B.
71. A 2003 pastoral letter, "You Love All That Exists... All Things Are Yours, God, Lover of Life..." www.cccb.ca/site/Files/pastoralenvironment.html (accessed September 2009).
72. *You Love All That Exists*, 3.
73. *You Love All That Exists*, 2.
74. *You Love All That Exists*, 6; italics added.
75. *You Love All That Exists*, 7; italics added.
76. The document is reprinted in A. Linzey and T. Regan (eds), *Animals and Christianity: A Book of Readings* (New York: Crossroad, 1989), pp. 167–170.
77. A. Linzey (1998), *Animal Gospel* (Louisville, KY: Westminster / John Knox Press), p. 57. For Linzey's critique of the catechism's engagement with animals, see Linzey, *Animal Gospel*, pp. 56–63.
78. Linzey, *Animal Gospel*, p. 61.
79. Linzey, *Animal Gospel*, p. 62.
80. Linzey, *Animal Gospel*, p. 57. These paragraphs are 2415–2418 (p. 640).
81. *Catechism*, 356 (p. 101); *Gaudium et Spes*, 24.
82. *Catechism*, 356 (p. 102).
83. *Catechism*, 357 (p. 102).
84. *Catechism*, 358 (p. 102).
85. *Catechism*, 374 (p. 106).
86. *Catechism*, 376 (p. 107).
87. *Catechism*, 379 (p. 107).
88. *Catechism*, 400 (p. 112); italics added.
89. See *Catechism*, 400 (p. 112).
90. The catechism follows Augustine's ordering of the Ten Commandments, thus placing what most Protestant churches tend to label the eighth commandment as the seventh. On this point, see *Catechism*, 2064–2068 (pp. 557–558).
91. See *Catechism*, 2168–2195 (pp. 580–586).
92. The passage extends rest to Israel's livestock.
93. *Catechism*, 2401 (p. 636); italics added.
94. *Catechism*, 2415 (p. 640); italics added.
95. *Catechism*, 2415 (p. 640); italics added.

96. J. Rickaby (1919), *Moral Philosophy: Ethics, Deontology and Natural Law*, 4th ed. (New York: Longmans, Green), pp. 248–249.
97. *Catechism*, 2415 (p. 640).
98. *Catechism*, 2415 (p. 640).
99. *Catechism*, 2415 (p. 640).
100. *Catechism*, 2416 (p. 640).
101. *Catechism*, 2416 (p. 640).
102. Linzey maintains that such is the case; *Animal Gospel*, 58–59.
103. *Catechism*, 2417 (p. 640).
104. *Catechism*, 2417 (p. 640).
105. *Catechism*, 2418 (p. 640).
106. *Catechism*, 2418 (p. 640).
107. Linzey, *Animal Gospel*, 60.
108. Linzey, *Animal Gospel*, 60.
109. Ironically, the passage that is most often used in magisterial pronouncements to support this claim (from Romans 8) was read by Augustine as applying only to humans. See Augustine (1982), *Augustine on Romans*, edited by P. F. Landers (Chico, CA: Scholars Press), p. 23.

3   Theology and the Reconfiguration of Difference

This chapter is a modified version of an earlier published work. See R. P. McLaughlin (2011), "*Noblesse Oblige*: Theological Differences between Humans and Animals and What They Imply Morally." *Oxford Journal of Animal Ethics* 1, 2 (Fall): 132–149.

1. R. Wallace (1995), *Braveheart* (early draft), www.imsdb.com/scripts/Braveheart.html (accessed May 15, 2009).
2. I. Kant (1785/1998), *The Groundwork of the Metaphysics of the Moral*, translated by M. Gregor (New York: Cambridge University Press).
3. R. Descartes (1637/1985), "Discourse on the Method," translated by J. Cottingham, R. Stoothoff, and D. Murdoch, in *The Philosophical Works of Descartes* (New York: Cambridge University Press), V.
4. T. Aquinas (1265/1946), *Summa Theologica*, translated by the Fathers of the English Dominican Province (New York: Benzinger), 1.93.6.
5. Augustine (1948), *City of God*, in W. J. Oates (ed.), *Basic Writings of Saint Augustine* (New York: Random House), XII.23.
6. Nonetheless, I do not believe that Jesus denied nonhuman animals what today one might consider direct moral concern. For considerations, see Richard Bauckham's two entries (1998): "Jesus and Animals I: What Did He Teach?" and "Jesus and Animals II: What Did He Practice?" in A. Linzey and D. Yamamoto (eds), *Animals on the Agenda: Questions about Animal Ethics for Theology and Ethics* (Chicago: University of Illinois Press), pp. 33–48, 49–60.
7. Genesis 1:26–28.
8. Irenaeus (1868), *Against Heresies*, in A. Roberts and J. Donaldson (eds), *The Ante-Nicene Christian Library* (Edinburgh: T. & T. Clark), IV.4.3.
9. Ephrem (1994), *Commentary on Genesis*, in K. McVey (ed.), *St. Ephrem the Syrian: Selected Prose Works*, translated by E. G. Mathews and J. P. Amar (Washington, DC: Catholic University of America Press), 2.4.

10. Gregory of Nyssa (1988), *On the Making of Man*, in P. Schaff and H. Wace (eds), *Nicene and Post-Nicene Fathers of the Christian Church* (Grand Rapids, MI: Eerdmans), 16.9.

11. S. J. Grenz (2001), *The Social God and the Relational Self: A Trinitarian Theology of the Imago Dei* (Louisville, KY: Westminster / John Knox Press), p. 143.

12. N. Habel (2011), *The Birth, the Curse and the Greening of Earth: An Ecological Reading of Genesis 1–11* (Sheffield, UK: Sheffield Phoenix Press), 35.

13. Grenz, *The Social God*.

14. D. Clough (2009), "All God's Creatures: Reading Genesis on Human and Nonhuman Animals," in S. C. Barton and D. Wilkinson (eds), *Reading Genesis after Darwin* (New York: Oxford University Press), pp. 145–148.

15. J. R. Middleton (2005), *The Liberating Image: The Imago Dei in Genesis 1* (Grand Rapids, MI: Brazos Press), pp. 18–19.

16. D. J. Hall (1986), *Imaging God: Dominion as Stewardship* (Grand Rapids, MI: Eerdmans), p. 90.

17. Hall, *Imaging God*, p. 90.

18. See M. Erickson (1998), *Christian Theology*, 2nd ed. (Grand Rapids, MI: Baker Books), pp. 519–534 (esp. 529–532).

19. N. M. Sarna (1989), *The JPS Torah Commentary: Genesis* (Philadelphia: Jewish Publication Society), 12. Sarna, however, maintains that the *imago* has a functional dimension.

20. B. M. Ashley, J. K. deBlois, and K. D. O'Rourke (2006), *Health Care Ethics: A Catholic Theological Analysis* (Washington, DC: Georgetown University Press), p. 40.

21. Middleton, *The Liberating Image*, pp. 50–55; W. S. Towner (2005), "Clones of God: Genesis 1:26–28 and the Image of God in the Hebrew Bible," *Interpretation* 59: 341–356.

22. W. Sibley Towner (2001), *Genesis* (Louisville, KY: Westminster / John Knox Press), 28.

23. Habel describes Towner's functional reading of the *imago* as "boldly anthropocentric" (Habel, *The Birth, the Curse and the Greening of Earth*, 36). However, it should be noted that there is a difference between an *ontological* anthropocentrism, in which human beings bear a substantialistic status that elevates them above (and often against) the rest of the created order, and a *functional* anthropocentrism, in which humans are entrusted with a grave responsibility in the midst of (and often for) the rest of the created order.

24. Middleton, *The Liberating Image*, p. 53; emphasis in original.

25. Middleton, *The Liberating Image*, p. 55.

26. Middleton, *The Liberating Image*.

27. Middleton, *The Liberating Image*; Towner, "Clones of God."

28. E. Wolde (1995), *Stories of the Beginning: Genesis 1–11 and Other Creation Stories* (Ridgefield, CT: Morehouse), p. 28.

29. T. Fretheim (2006), *God and World in the Old Testament: A Relational Theology of Creation* (Nashville: Abingdon Press), p. 52; emphasis in original. See also Towner, "Clones of God," p. 352.

30. Fretheim, *God and World*, p. 48.

31. Towner, "Clones of God," p. 348.

32. C. M. LaCugna (1993), *God for Us: The Trinity and Christian Life* (San Francisco: Harper).

33. Though, admittedly, less evident are the ethical implications one might draw.
34. Irenaeus, *Against Heresies*, 11.
35. Gregory of Nyssa, *On the Making of Man*.
36. N. V. Harrison (2008), "The Human Person as the Image and Likeness of God," in M. B. Cunningham and E. Theokritoff (eds), *The Cambridge Companion to Orthodox Christian Theology* (New York: Cambridge University Press), p. 86.
37. Harrison, "The Human Person," p. 86.
38. K. Ware (1999), "The Soul in Greek Christianity," in M. James and C. Crabbe (eds), *From Soul to Self* (New York: Routledge), p. 64.
39. Ware, "The Soul in Greek Christianity," p. 64.
40. Linzey, *Why Animal Suffering Matters*.
41. Linzey, *Why Animal Suffering Matters*, p. 12.
42. Linzey, *Why Animal Suffering Matters*, pp. 11–29.
43. Linzey, *Why Animal Suffering Matters*, p. 15.
44. Linzey, *Animal Theology*, p. 82.
45. I address this point in greater detail in Chapter 5.
46. Linzey, *Why Animal Suffering Matters*, p. 17.
47. Linzey, *Why Animal Suffering Matters*, p. 23.
48. Linzey, *Why Animal Suffering Matters*, p. 24.
49. Linzey, *Why Animal Suffering Matters*, p. 27.
50. Linzey, *Animal Theology*, p. 32.
51. Linzey, *Animal Theology*, p. 47.
52. Linzey, *Animal Theology*, p. 71.
53. Linzey, *Animal Theology*, p. 57.
54. See Linzey, *Animal Theology*.
55. LaCugna, *God for Us*, p. 396
56. LaCugna, *God for Us*, p. 290.
57. D. Yarri (2005), *The Ethics of Animal Experimentation: A Critical Analysis and Constructive Proposal* (New York: Oxford University Press), p. 115.
58. Yarri, *The Ethics of Animal Experimentation*, p. 116.
59. Yarri, *The Ethics of Animal Experimentation*, p. 116.
60. N. Phelps (2002), *The Dominion of Love: Animal Rights according to the Bible* (New York: Lantern Books), p. 45
61. Phelps, *Dominion of Love*, p. 15.
62. For a more detailed account of Moltmann's potential contribution in relation to animal welfare, see R. P. McLaughlin, "Anticipating a Maximally Inclusive Eschaton: Jürgen Moltmann's Potential Contribution to Animal Theology," *Oxford Journal of Animal Ethics*, forthcoming.
63. J. Moltmann (1993), *The Crucified God: The Cross of Christ as the Foundation and Criticism of Christian Theology*, translated by R. A. Wilson and J. Bowden (Minneapolis: Fortress Press).
64. J. Moltmann (1996), *The Coming of God: Christian Eschatology*, translated by M. Kohl (Minneapolis: Fortress Press).
65. Moltmann borrows this phrase from Albert Schweitzer, whom I engage in passing below and in much greater detail in Chapter 8.
66. J. Moltmann (1992), *The Spirit of Life: A Universal Affirmation*, translated by M. Kohl (Minneapolis: Fortress Press), p. 172.

67. A. Schweitzer (2002), "First Sermon on Reverence for Life," in M. and K. Bergel (eds), *Reverence for Life: The Ethics of Albert Schweitzer for the Twenty-first Century* (Syracuse, NY: Syracuse University Press).
68. A. Schweitzer (1946), *Civilization and Ethics* (London: Adam and Charles Clark). See also P. Barsam (2008), *Reverence for Life: Albert Schweitzer's Great Contribution to Ethical Thought* (New York: Oxford University Press).
69. S. Hauerwas and J. Berkman (1993), "A Trinitarian Theology of the 'Chief End' of 'All Flesh'," in C. Pinches and J. B. McDaniel (eds), *Good News for Animals? Christian Approaches to Animal Well-Being* (New York: Orbis Books), p. 71.
70. For a consideration of angels, see below.
71. Fretheim, *God and World*, 2005; Middleton, *The Liberating Image*, 2005.
72. Wolde, *Stories of the Beginning*, p. 193.
73. I explore the disparity between Elohim and Marduk in greater detail in Chapter 5.
74. W. Brueggemann (1982), *Genesis* (Atlanta: John Knox Press).
75. T. Fretheim (1991), *Exodus* (Atlanta: John Knox Press).
76. Hosea 11:1–4, 8–9.
77. D. Bonhoeffer (1971), *Letters and Papers from Prison* (London: SCM Press), p. 361.
78. Luke 19:41–44.
79. John 11:32–36.
80. John 12:20–36.
81. Moltmann, *The Crucified God*, p. 205.
82. Philippians 2:6–7; NIV. The reason I use the NIV for this quote is that I believe it more accurately reflects the Greek text. The NRSV, for instance, adds the word "though" to this verse, suggesting that *although* Jesus "was in the form of God, he did not regard equality with God as something to be exploited." But there is no word for "though" in the Greek. The addition of the word might seem implicit, as the verse appears to be contrasting who/what Jesus was (the form of God) and how Jesus viewed what/who he was (not exploitatively). But the addition of "though" suggests that Jesus performs his kenotic action despite the reality that he is "in the form of God." However, the syntax in Greek (*hos en morphē*) permits a strong possibility for reading the text thus: "*Because* Jesus was in the form God, he did not regard equality with God as something to be exploited." This translation suggests that kenosis is constitutive of divinity. That is, because Jesus was God, he engaged in kenotic love. The translation depends on how one translates the participle at the beginning of verse 6.
83. G. D. Fee (1995), *Paul's Letter to the Philippians* (Grand Rapids, MI: Eerdmans), p. 208.
84. M. Bockmuehl (1998), *Black's New Testament Commentary: The Epistle to the Philippians* (Peabody, MA: Hendrickson), p. 133.
85. Linzey, *Why Animal Suffering Matters*, p. 15.
86. Matthew 23:11.
87. Genesis 12:2–3.
88. Fretheim, *God and World*, p.103.
89. Jonah, 4:11.

90. The interpretation I offer of the book of Jonah is well represented in biblical scholarship. However, it is also contested as to whether or not the issue of inclusion of the nonelect is the central didactic emphasis of the narrative. While I can accept that it is not, I hold the issue is nonetheless in the purview of the author. For considerations, see R. P. McLaughlin (2013), "Jonah and the Religious Other: An Exploration in Biblical Inclusivism," *Journal of Ecumenical Studies* 48, 1 (Winter): 72–75.
91. John 8:39b.
92. I offer this brief consideration in the case of angels. Psalm 8 states that God created humanity "a little lower than *elohim*" (Psalm 8:5). The NRSV translates *elohim* as "God," which is consistent with the use of the word in Genesis 1: "In the beginning...*elohim* created the heavens and the earth" (Genesis 1:1). The Septuagint, however, does not render *elohim* as *theos* but rather *angelous*. If *angelous* is accepted as a viable reading of the psalm, then angels are above humans (at least temporarily) in the hierarchy of creation. Yet angels frequently serve as aids to humanity, not exploitative agents. In fact, when spiritual beings exploit humans for their own benefit, people tend to refer to such activity as *demonic*. Interestingly, Linzey finds just such a reading in a sermon from John Henry Newman, who refers to harming innocent animals as "satanic" (see *Why Animal Suffering Matters*, p. 39). Likewise, Towner asks whether, when nonhuman creatures experience the dominion of humanity, they experience it as that of God or something satanic ("Clones of God," p. 348). Finally, Phelps states, "Suppose for a moment that the angels adopted the aristocracy theory and treated us the way we treat animals. Would we believe that they were reflecting the image of a loving, compassionate God? Would we believe that they were angels or demons? Would they, in fact, be angels in demons?" Phelps, *Dominion of Love*, p. 49.
93. I am aware that the biblical witness is not without ambiguity in the categorical relationships I have explored. According to the Scriptures, God floods the created order, commands the elect to slaughter the nonelect in holy war, and prescribes the slaughter of animals in sacrifice. What I attempt to retrieve in this section is redemptive direction of the drama of salvation.
94. Linzey, *Why Animal Suffering Matters*, p. 29.
95. For many scholars, the question of sentience provides the proper border for moral concern. This border leaves ambiguous the ethical engagement of other creatures, such as insects, and other forms of life, such as plants. On this point, see Linzey, *Animal Theology*, p. 74; Linzey, *Why Animal Suffering Matters*, p. 137; Phelps, *Dominion of Love*, p. 42. My focus in the present work is animals. However, I find the line of sentience inadequate for establishing direct moral concern. I address this point more thoroughly in my forthcoming work, *Preservation and Protest*.

4 *In Via* toward an Animal-Inclusive Eschaton

This chapter is a modified version of an earlier work. See R. P. McLaughlin (2011), "Evidencing the Eschaton: Progressive-Transformative Animal Welfare in the Church Fathers." *Modern Theology* 27, 1 (January 2011): 121–146.

1. Irenaeus of Lyons (1996), *Irenaeus: Against Heresies*, in A. Roberts and J. Donaldson (eds), *Ante-Nicene Fathers*, vol. 1 (Grand Rapids, MI: Eerdmans), 5.33.4.
2. See R. M. Grant (1999), *Early Christians and Animals* (New York: Routledge), pp. 75–76.
3. Theophilus of Antioch (1880), *Letter to Autolycus*, in A. Roberts and J. Donaldson (eds), *Ante-Nicene Christian Library: Translations of the Writings of the Fathers*, vol. 3 (Edinburgh: T. & T. Clark), II.16 (pp. 83–84).
4. Irenaeus, *Against Heresies*, 5.33.4.
5. M. C. Steenberg (2008), *Irenaeus on Creation: The Cosmic Christ and the Saga of Redemption* (Boston: Brill), p. 94.
6. See Irenaeus (2002), *Irenaeus' Demonstration of the Apostolic Preaching: A Theological Commentary and Translation*, I. M. Mackenzie, with the translation of the text of the *Demonstration* by J. A. Robinson (Burlington, VT: Ashgate), p. 193.
7. Irenaeus, *Demonstration*, p. 61.
8. Ephrem the Syrian (1994), *Commentary on Genesis*, in K. McVey (ed.), *St. Ephrem the Syrian: Selected Prose Works*, translated by E. G. Mathews and J. P. Amar (Washington, DC: Catholic University of America Press), 2.9.3.
9. I deal with Ephrem's view of the Fall below.
10. Ephrem the Syrian (1989), *Hymns on Paradise*, introduction and translation by S. Brock (Crestwood, NY: St. Vladimir's Press), IX.1.
11. Steenberg, *Irenaeus*, pp. 49–60.
12. Irenaeus, *Demonstration*, p. 12.
13. Irenaeus, *Demonstration*, p. 14.
14. See P. Bouteneff (2008), *Beginnings: Ancient Christian Readings of the Biblical Creation Narratives* (Grand Rapids, MI: Baker Academic), p. 80.
15. D. Minns (1994), *Irenaeus* (Washington, DC: Georgetown University Press), p. 57. Also, Bouteneff, *Beginnings*, p. 77.
16. Irenaeus, *Against Heresies*, 5.29.1.
17. Irenaeus, *Demonstration*, p. 11; brackets mine.
18. Steenberg, *Irenaeus*, p. 149; italics added.
19. Irenaeus, *Against Heresies*, 5.32.1.
20. Irenaeus, *Against Heresies*, 5.32.1.
21. See Steenberg, *Irenaeus*, p. 168.
22. Steenberg, *Irenaeus*, p. 154.
23. Steenberg, *Irenaeus*, p. 168.
24. Again, here Irenaeus follows Theophilus, who writes, "When man transgressed, they [the animals] transgressed with him." Likewise, "When...man again shall have made his way back to his natural condition, and no longer does evil, those [the animals] also shall be restored to their original gentleness." Theophilus, *Letter to Autolycus*, II.17.
25. Irenaeus, *Demonstration*, p. 33–34.
26. Irenaeus, *Demonstration*, p. 37.
27. Steenberg, *Irenaeus*, p. 8.
28. Steenberg, *Irenaeus*, p. 9.
29. Brock, Introduction to *Hymns on Paradise*, p. 72.
30. Ephrem, *Commentary on Genesis*, 2.9.3.
31. Ephrem, *Commentary on Genesis*, 6.9.3.
32. Ephrem, *Commentary on Genesis*, 2.9.3.

33. For Ephrem, the Fall is both instantaneous and progressive. See Ephrem, *Hymns on Paradise*, I.10.
34. These are my brackets, not the editor's.
35. Ephrem, *Commentary on Genesis*, 6.9.3.
36. The editors of The Church Fathers series note this resemblance to Eden: "In Ephrem's hymns, this peace on the ark is sign of a new beginning, of a pre-Fall state, and is thus also a type of the Church." Ephrem, *Selected Prose Works*, p. 139, n. 284. This point is not lost on modern writers. See, for example, M. Northcott (2009), "'They Shall Not Hurt or Destroy in All My Holy Mountain' (Isaiah 65.25): Killing for Philosophy and A Creaturely Theology of Non-Violence," in C. Deane-Drummond and D. Clough (eds), *Creaturely Theology: On God, Humans and Other Animals* (London: SCM Press), p. 235.
37. T. Kronholm (1978), *Motifs from Genesis 1–11 in the Genuine Hymns of Ephrem the Syrian* (Lund, Sweden: Gleerup), p. 186.
38. Kronholm, *Motifs from Genesis 1–11*, p. 186.
39. See Ephrem, *Hymns on Paradise*, 2.12–13.
40. Ephrem, *Commentary on Genesis*, 6.10.1.
41. See Ephrem, *Hymns on Paradise*, 5.17.
42. Ephrem, *Commentary on Genesis*, 1.31.2; brackets added by the editors.
43. Ephrem, *Commentary on Genesis*, 2.15.
44. Ephrem, *Commentary on Genesis*, 2.14.2.
45. Ephrem, *Commentary on Genesis*, 2.14.2.
46. Ephrem (1847), 36th Rhythm; *Selected Works of S. Ephrem the Syrian*, translated by J. B. Morris (Oxford: Oxford University Press), p. 218. The glory was underneath – hidden by Christ's garments of clothes and flesh – because Christ set it aside to take up the clothing of humanity. See Brock, Introduction to *Hymns on Paradise*, p. 66.
47. Ephrem (1989), *Hymns on Nativity*, in *Ephrem the Syrian: Hymns*, translated by K. E. McVey (Mahwah, NJ: Paulist Press), 16.11.
48. Ephrem, *Hymns on Nativity*, 23.13.
49. Ephrem (1989), *Hymns on Virginity*, in *Ephrem the Syrian: Hymns*, translated by K. E. McVey (Mahwah, NJ: Paulist Press), 16.9.
50. See Brock, Introduction to *Hymns on Paradise*, pp. 66–72. I am indebted to Brock's work in this section, drawing also upon his summary of divinization. Brock, Introduction to *Hymns on Paradise*, pp. 72–74.
51. Brock, Introduction to *Hymns on Paradise*, pp. 67–68.
52. I here focus only on historical voices that offer an alternative tradition to the dominant view.
53. Isaac of Nineveh (1984), *The Ascetical Homilies of St. Isaac the Syrian*, Dana Miller (ed.) (Boston, MA: Holy Transfiguration Monastery), p. 383.
54. Isaac of Nineveh (1969), *Mystic Treatises*, translated from Bedjan's Syriac text with an introduction and registers by A. J. Wensinck (Wiesbaden), LXXIV.
55. See V. Lossky (1976), *The Mystical Theology of the Eastern Church* (Crestwood, NY: St. Vladimir's Seminary Press), ch. 5.
56. Lossky, *The Mystical Theology of the Eastern Church*, 111; italics added.
57. See D. Jackson (2007), *Marvelous to Behold: Miracles in Medieval Manuscripts* (London: British Library), p. 28.
58. Pseudo-Matthew, 18, www.gnosis.org/library/psudomat.htm (accessed June 25, 2009).

59. Pseudo-Matthew, 19.
60. Bauckham, "Jesus and Animals II: What Did He Practice?" in *AA*, p. 56.
61. Bauckham, "Jesus and Animals II: What Did He Practice?" p. 58. The meaning of Mark 1:13 is quite divisive in modern scholarship. For examples of agreement with Bauckham's interpretation, see M. Healy (2008), *The Gospel of Mark* (Grand Rapids, MI: Baker Academic), p. 38; M. E. Boring (2006), *Mark: A Commentary* (Louisville, KY: Westminster / John Knox Press), p. 48; J. B. Gibson (1994), "Jesus' Wilderness Temptation according to Mark," *Journal for the Study of the New Testament* 53 (March): 19. For examples of those who conclude that the wild animals intensify Jesus's suffering in the wilderness, see R. J. Kernaghan (2007), *Mark* (Downers Grove, IL: Inter-Varsity Press), p. 40; A. Y. Collins (2007), *Mark: A Commentary*, Harold W. Attridge, ed. (Minneapolis: Fortress Press), p. 153.
62. Bauckham, "Jesus and Animals II: What Did He Practice?" p. 59.
63. For different examples, see Northcott, "A Creaturely Theology of Non-Violence," pp. 246–247.
64. I again select examples that highlight alternatives to the dominant tradition. There are both positive and negative interactions between saints and animals. See I. S. Gilhus (2006), *Animals, Gods and Humans: Changing Attitudes to Animals, in Greek, Roman, and Early Christian Ideas* (New York: Routledge), chs. 9–10.
65. On Silouan, see K. Ware (1999), "The Soul in Greek Christianity," in M. James and C. Crabbe (eds.), *From Soul to Self* (New York: Routledge), p. 65. On Anselm, see D. Alexander (2008), *Saints and Animals in the Middle Ages* (Rochester, NY: Boydell Press), p. 1. For a response to Alexander's demythologizing of the hagiographies, see McLaughlin, "Evidencing the Eschaton," pp. 143–144, n. 76.
66. In Denis's case, the animal found refuge in the vicinity of his shrine after the saint's martyrdom. See Jackson, *Marvelous to Behold*, p. 35. On Giles, see Jackson, *Marvelous to Behold*, pp. 38–40.
67. Jackson, *Marvelous to Behold*, p. 40.
68. This narrative is not in the *Virtues* but is attributed in other sources. See T. Vivian (2003), "The Peaceable Kingdom: Animals as Parables in the *Virtues of Saint Macarius*," *Anglican Theological Review* 85, 3 (Summer): 487–488.
69. Vivian, "The Peaceable Kingdom," p. 489.
70. Vivian, "The Peaceable Kingdom," p. 479.
71. I have in mind here not only the dominant tradition I examine in Chapter 1 but also the work of deep ecologists and creation spiritualists. See, for examples, M. Fox (1991), *Creation Spirituality: Liberating Gifts for the Peoples of the Earth* (San Francisco: HarperCollins); R. R. Ruether (1992), *Gaia and God: An Ecofeminist Theology of Earth Healing* (New York: HarperCollins Publishers); C. DeWitt (2011), *Earthwise: A Guide to Hopeful Creation Care*, 3rd ed. (Grand Rapids, MI: Faith Alive Christian Resources).
72. Certainly, theologians and ethicists who do not accept the framework I have delineated would not, unless moved by some other reason, accept the ethical implications of that framework. However, the acceptance of such a framework does not necessarily secure the ethical implications either. At stake is the question of the extent to which eschatology should affect ethical practice in the present. Karl Barth, for example, is careful not to overstate the ethical

implications of the eschaton. In his view, what is required is a proper outlook about how and for what purpose killing occurs. See A. McIntosh (2009), "Human and Animal Relations in the Theology of Karl Barth," *Pacifica* 22, 1 (February): 23–24.

73. Isaac of Nineveh, *Mystical Treatises*, LXXIV.

5 Breaking with Anthropocentrism: Genesis 1

1. See T. Fretheim (2005), *God and World in the Old Testament: A Relational Theology of Creation*. (Nashville: Abingdon Press), p. 48.
2. J. Johnson (2005), "Genesis 1:26–28," *Interpretation* 59 (April): 176–178.
3. By "Priestly author" I am here subscribing to a source theory in which strands of Genesis (including Genesis 1 and 9:1–3) are the work of a member of Israel's priesthood, probably during the Babylonian exile. R. W. L. Moberly (2009), *The Theology of the Book of Genesis* (New York: Cambridge University Press), p. 49. It is my focus on this strand of the narrative that draws my attention to the first creation narrative as opposed to the second (in Genesis 2).
4. B. T. Arnold (2009), *Genesis* (New York: Cambridge University Press), p. 30. Arnold cautions that the "polemical nature of Gen 1 has been overstated and is not the primary *raison d'etre* for the chapter" (Arnold, *Genesis*, p. 30).
5. J. McKeown (2008), *Genesis* (Grand Rapids, MI: Eerdmans), p. 12.
6. See Moberly, *The Theology of the Book of Genesis*, pp. 50–54.
7. This translation of the *Enuma Elish* is found in E. V. Wolde (1995), *Stories of the Beginning: Genesis 1–11 and Other Creation Stories* (Ridgefield, CT: Morehouse), pp. 189–194. This particular passage is found on p. 193.
8. D. W. Cotter (2003), *Genesis* (Collegeville, MN: Liturgical Press), p. 10.
9. This difference regarding humanity's position vis-à-vis the gods is also evident in the *Epic of Atrahasis*. On this point, see also J. R. Middleton (2005), *The Liberating Image: The Imago Dei in Genesis 1* (Grand Rapids, MI: Brazos Press), p. 133; W. Brueggemann (1982), *Genesis* (Atlanta: John Knox Press), p. 79; T. Fretheim (1994), *Genesis* (Nashville: Abingdon Press), p. 65, 77.
10. J. R. Middleton (2004), "Created in the Image of Violent God? The Ethical Problem of the Conquest of Chaos in Biblical Creation Narratives," in *Interpretation* 58/4 (October): 341–355.
11. Middleton, "Violent God," 342–343.
12. See Middleton, "Violent God," 343–344.
13. Middleton, "Violent God," 344. For exceptions and considerations thereof, see 344–348.
14. Middleton, "Violent God," 352.
15. Arnold, *Genesis*, p. 30.
16. Arnold, *Genesis*, p. 32.
17. On this point, see also R. Bauckham (2012), "Humans, Animals, and the Environment in Genesis 1–3," in N. MacDonald, M. W. Elliot, and G. Macaskill (eds), *Genesis and Christian Theology* (Grand Rapids, MI: Eerdmans), pp. 183–184.
18. Middleton, "Violent God," 352–353. Middleton's claim is based on Genesis 1:21, in which God creates the *tanninim* ("monsters").

19. This claim is quite literal given the order of creation. First, God creates the biome of the creature and then places that creature in the biome.
20. Middleton, "Violent God," 354.
21. Arnold, *Genesis*, p. 43.
22. Arnold, *Genesis*, p. 44.
23. See, respectively, Genesis 1, vv. 20, 24, and 26.
24. On this point, see Chapter 3.
25. Arnold, *Genesis*, p. 45.
26. Arnold, *Genesis*, p. 45. See also G. J. Wenham (1982), *Genesis 1–15* (Waco, TX: Word Books), p. 33.
27. G. V. Rad (1961), *Genesis: A Commentary*, translated by John H. Marks (Philadelphia: Westminster Press), p. 57.
28. K. A. Matthews (1995), *Genesis 1–11:26* (Nashville: B&H), p. 164.
29. Arnold, *Genesis*, p. 45. Other biblical scholars offer a more relational and anthropocentric (in terms of status) reading of the *imago*. See McKeown, *Genesis*, p. 27; N. M. Sarna (1989), *Genesis* (Philadelphia: Jewish Publication Society), p. 12; B. K. Waltke with C. J. Fredericks (2001), *Genesis: A Commentary* (Grand Rapids, MI: Zondervan), p. 65. For a substantialistic interpretation in biblical scholarship, see R. R. Reno (2010), *Genesis* (Grand Rapids, MI: Brazos Press), pp. 52–53.
30. Genesis 1:29–30.
31. C. Westermann (1984), *Genesis 1–11: A Commentary*, translated by J. J. Scullion (Minneapolis: Augsburg), p. 159.
32. Westermann, *Genesis 1–11*, p. 162.
33. von Rad, *Genesis*, p. 59.
34. See this accusation in L. White (2000), "The Historical Roots of Our Ecological Crisis," reprinted in *The Care of Creation: Focusing Concern and Action*, R. J. Berry, ed. (Downers Grove, IL: Inter-Varsity Press), pp. 31–42.
35. Westermann, *Genesis 1–11*, p. 165.
36. See D. J. Hall (1986), *Imaging God: Dominion as Stewardship* (Grand Rapids, MI: Eerdmans), p. 246 (scriptural index).
37. Middleton, *The Liberating Image*, p. 52.
38. W. Brueggemann (2003), *Introduction to the Old Testament: The Canon and Christian Imagination* (Louisville, KY: Westminster / John Knox Press), p. 418.
39. Westermann, *Genesis 1–11*, p. 164.
40. Reno, *Genesis*. He does offer an implicit significance in reference to Genesis 9:1–3. See Reno, *Genesis*, p. 124.
41. Arnold, *Genesis*.
42. See Cotter, *Genesis*, p. 11.
43. W. S. Towner (2001), *Genesis* (Louisville, KY: Westminster / John Knox Press).
44. In his commentary on Genesis 9:3, McKeown notes that the original diet of humanity was vegetarian. McKeown, *Genesis*, p. 64.
45. McKeown, *Genesis*, p. 218.
46. McKeown, *Genesis*, p. 228.
47. B. Bandstra (2008), *Genesis 1–11: A Handbook on the Hebrew Text* (Waco, TX: Baylor University Press), p. 102; italics added.
48. Bandstra, *Genesis 1–11*, p. 102.

49. Bandstra emphasizes the import of humanity's use of the created material from the third day. However, I argue that the implicit dietary limitation (that is, what is *not* given for food) is theologically significant in the development of creation (Bandstra, *Genesis 1–11*, p. 102).
50. Arnold, *Genesis*, p. 129.
51. Fretheim, *God and World*, p. 51.
52. Brueggemann, *Genesis*, pp. 34–35.
53. B. C Birch, W. Brueggemann, T. E. Fretheim, and D. L. Peterson (2005), *A Theological Introduction to the Old Testament*, 2nd ed. (Nashville: Abingdon Press), p. 219.
54. Sarna, *Genesis*, pp. 13–14.
55. Sarna, *Genesis*, p. 60; italics added.
56. For a similar reading, see Waltke, *Genesis*, p. 144.
57. Matthews, *Genesis 1–11:26*, p. 175.
58. Westermann, *Genesis 1–11*, pp. 164–165.
59. Westermann argues that such reluctance is evident in other cosmogonies of the ancient Near East. See Westermann, *Genesis 1–11*, pp. 162–164.
60. Bauckham, "Humans, Animals, and the Environment in Genesis 1–3," pp. 183–184.
61. Bauckham, "Humans, Animals, and the Environment in Genesis 1–3," p. 184.
62. Westermann, *Genesis 1–11*, p. 162.
63. See Genesis 3:21. On these arguments, see Wenham, *Genesis 1–15*, pp. 25–26.
64. Arnold, *Genesis*, p. 108.
65. Genesis 9:1–3.
66. Arnold, *Genesis*, p. 109.
67. On this particular comparison between Genesis 1 and 9, see Reno, *Genesis*, p. 124.
68. Matthews, *Genesis 1–11:26*, p. 401.
69. Arnold, *Genesis*, p. 109.
70. McKeown, *Genesis*, p. 64.
71. See Genesis 9:6.
72. Genesis 9:2.
73. The term is used to describe the proper disposition before God (Psalms 9:20 and 76:11). Yet even in such instances, the term appears negatively. For example, in Isaiah 8, Israel is warned that God is their punisher for their deeds. Thus they ought to fear God, not other nations.
74. See Deuteronomy 4:34 and 11:25, respectively. On Egypt, see also Jeremiah 32:31.
75. See 1 Samuel 2:4 and Jeremiah 46:5, respectively.
76. Job 41:33.
77. See Leviticus 25:53; 26:17; Numbers 24:19; Psalms 110:2; Isaiah 41:2.
78. 1 Kings 9:23; Isaiah 14:2.
79. Since the term *kabash* refers to the earth and not the animals, I do not address it here.
80. See Towner, *Genesis*, p. 28.
81. W. S. Towner (2005), "Clones of God: Genesis 1:26–28 and the Image of God in the Hebrew Bible," *Interpretation* 59 (October): 347–348.

82. Fretheim, *Genesis*, p. 346.
83. Leviticus 25:43.
84. See Middleton, *The Liberating Image*, pp. 50–54.
85. For a consideration of the etymology of *radah*, see Towner, *Genesis*, pp. 28–29.
86. On a positive reading of *kabash* and *radah*, see McKeown, *Genesis*, p. 27.
87. Towner, *Genesis*, p. 28.
88. Cotter, *Genesis*, p. 18.
89. von Rad, *Genesis*, p. 127.
90. Cotter, *Genesis*, pp. 59–60.
91. I recognize that Genesis 1 does not exhaust the creation narratives of Israel. Moberly's words should be heeded: "Genesis 1 is by no means the only picture of the world in the Bible," Moberly, *The Theology of the Book of Genesis*, p. 66.
92. Reno, *Genesis*, p. 124.
93. Matthews, *Genesis 1–11:26*, p. 400.
94. Matthews, *Genesis 1–11:26*, p. 400.
95. Sarna, *Genesis*, p. 60.
96. Waltke, *Genesis*, p. 144.
97. Genesis 6:11–12.
98. Equally unwarranted is von Rad's claim: "Obviously ch. 9.2 assumes that until then the paradisiacal peace had ruled among the creatures" (von Rad, *Genesis*, p. 127). The notion that "all flesh" was corrupted (Genesis 6) mitigates the validity of von Rad's claim.
99. Towner, *Genesis*, p. 85.
100. As I noted in Chapter 4, this vision of humanity reestablishing the peace with creation is well attested in the lives of the saints.
101. See Genesis 9:6.
102. It is possible that God's allowance of violence is predicated upon his own action of violence against his creation in the flood narrative. Could it be that the *imago Dei* changed in the face of Elohim's own act of violence?
103. Westermann cautions against interpreting the dominion of Genesis 1 and the "fear and dread" of Genesis 9 as antithetical. Westermann, *Genesis 1–11*, p. 462. This new language expresses a cosmic tension that will be overcome in the eschaton. Westermann, *Genesis 1–11*, pp. 462–463.
104. N. Habel (2011), *The Birth, the Curse and the Greening of Earth: An Ecological Reading of Genesis 1–11* (Sheffield, UK: Sheffield Phoenix Press), 107.
105. Or perhaps it reflects the violent re-creation of Elohim as opposed to the nonviolent creation that preceded it.
106. David Clough (2009), "All God's Creatures: Reading Genesis on Human and Nonhuman Animals," in Stephen C. Barton and David Wilkinson (eds), *Reading Genesis after Darwin* (New York: Oxford University Press), pp. 156–157.
107. Bauckham, "Humans, Animals, and the Environment in Genesis 1–3," pp. 184–185.
108. For a much deeper analysis of this point, see R. P. McLaughlin, *Preservation and Protest: Theological Foundations for an Eco-Eschatological Ethics* (Minneapolis: Fortress Press), forthcoming.

6 Breaking with Conservationism: Isaiah 11:1–9

1. G. M. Tucker (1994), *Isaiah-Ezekiel* (Nashville: Abingdon Press), p. 31.
2. See, for example, O. Kaiser (1983), *Isaiah 1–12: A Commentary*, translated by John Bowden (Philadelphia: Westminster Press), p. 260. For a summary of the options in this debate, see B. S. Childs (2001), *Isaiah* (Louisville, KY: Westminster / John Knox Press), pp. 99–100.
3. A. Motyer (1999), *Isaiah* (Downers Grove, IL: Inter-Varsity Press), p. 15; W. S. Lasor, D. A. Hubbard, and F. W. Bush (1996), *Old Testament Survey: The Message, Form, and Background of the Old Testament*, 2nd ed. (Grand Rapids, MI: Eerdmans), p. 280; S. A. Irvine (1990), *Isaiah, Ahaz, and the Syro-Ephraimitic Crisis* (Ann Arbor: University of Michigan Press), p. 273; J. Jensen (1984), *Isaiah 1–39* (Wilmington, DE: Michael Glazier), p. 130.
4. U. F. Berges (2012), *The Book of Isaiah: Its Composition and Final Form*, translated by Millard C. Lind (Sheffield, UK: Sheffield Phoenix Press), p. 34.
5. Berges, *The Book of Isaiah*, pp. 112–113.
6. A. J. Heschel (1962), *The Prophets* (New York: Harper Perennial), p. 76; Tucker, *Isaiah*, p. 36.
7. J. D. W. Watts (1982), *Isaiah 1–33* (Waco, TX: Word Books), p. xxv.
8. 2 Kings 15:3; 2 Chronicles 26:4.
9. 2 Kings 14:25–27.
10. In fact, in 742 BCE Judah subjugated itself as an Assyrian vassal, paying tributary fees to the nation. See Watts, *Isaiah 1–33*, pp. 80–81; Tucker, *Isaiah*, p. 36.
11. Heschel, *The Prophets*, p. 78.
12. Isaiah 7:1–17.
13. Childs, *Isaiah*, 100.
14. Childs, *Isaiah*, 102.
15. Isaiah 1:23c.
16. Isaiah 1:25a.
17. Isaiah 1:26b.
18. Isaiah 1:22–23.
19. Isaiah 3:15.
20. Isaiah 5:7.
21. Isaiah 10:1–2.
22. Isaiah 5:15.
23. See Isaiah 7:1–9.
24. Isaiah 8:6.
25. Isaiah 8:7–8.
26. Isaiah 10:5.
27. Isaiah 10:6; italics added.
28. Isaiah 10:12.
29. Isaiah 10:12.
30. See Isaiah 8:5–8.
31. Isaiah 9:7.
32. Isaiah 9:6–7; 11:1–5.
33. Isaiah 9:7b; 11:3–4.
34. Isaiah 9:7a; 11:6–9.
35. Berges, *The Book of Isaiah*, p. 113.

36. Childs, *Isaiah*, p. 99.
37. Berges, *The Book of Isaiah*, p. 34.
38. Tucker, *Isaiah*, p. 139. On the other hand, see J. Blenkinsopp (2000), *Isaiah 1–39* (New York: Doubleday), p. 263; H. Wildberger (1990), *Isaiah 1–12*, translated by T. H. Trapp (Minneapolis: Fortress Press), p. 465.
39. See Job 14:7–8.
40. W. Brueggemann (1998), *Isaiah 1–39* (Louisville, KY: Westminster / John Knox Press), p. 99.
41. This point stands in contrast to those who argue for a later date for ch. 11 (after Isaiah of Jerusalem) based on the "stump" representing the abolishment of the Davidic dynasty. For example, S. H. Blank (1958), *Prophetic Faith in Isaiah* (New York: Harper), pp. 161–164.
42. Wildberger suggests that the verb tense of this section, which varies from 9:1–6, clearly places this passage as a promise. See Wildberger, *Isaiah 1–12*, p. 463.
43. Watts, *Isaiah 1–33*, p. 208.
44. Isaiah 11:2.
45. Isaiah 11:2.
46. Isaiah 11:9.
47. See Job 28:28; Proverbs 1:7; Sirach 1:12. On this point, see Jensen, *Isaiah 1–39*, p. 132.
48. Wildberger argues for a more radical reading here, writing that the Messiah "is more than first among equals; he stands in a relationship with the people as God's proxy, has responsibilities connected with an incomparable task, and acts in unquestioned authority." Wildberger, *Isaiah 1–12*, pp. 473–474. See also, J. Goldingay (2001), *Isaiah* (Peabody, MA: Hendrickson), p. 84.
49. Isaiah 11:3.
50. C. Seitz (1993), *Isaiah 1–39* (Louisville, KY: John Knox Press), p. 105; Jensen, *Isaiah 1–39*, pp. 105, 133.
51. Isaiah 11:4.
52. Tucker, *Isaiah 1–39*, p. 141.
53. Wildberger, *Isaiah 1–12*, pp. 477–478.
54. See Brueggemann, *Isaiah 1–39*, p. 102; Blenkinsopp, *Isaiah 1–39*, p. 265.
55. See Psalms 33:4; 40:10; 92:2.
56. On the Davidic covenant, see 2 Samuel 7. Of particular significance for this covenant is 2 Samuel 7:16, YHWH's promise for an everlasting Davidic throne.
57. See Psalms 7:17; 9:8, 50:6; 97:2.
58. See Isaiah 1:26; 16:4b-5; 32:14–20.
59. Psalm 36:6.
60. Isaiah 11:9.
61. J. A. Alexander (1992/1867), *Commentary on Isaiah* (Grand Rapids, MI: Kregel Classics), p. 253. Alexander casts his lot with these interpretations. Alexander, *Commentary on Isaiah*, p. 248. He maintains that the main point is that the "pacific effects of true religion" are ultimately aimed at the well-being of the human creature. Alexander, *Isaiah*, pp. 253–254.
62. E. J. Kissane (1941), *The Book of Isaiah* (Dublin: Browne and Nolan), p. 132.
63. Kissane, *Isaiah*, p. 143.
64. Goldingay, *Isaiah*, p. 85.
65. See Chapter 4 of the present work.

66. W. E. Vine (1971), *Isaiah: Prophecies, Promises, Warning* (Grand Rapids, MI: Zondervan), p. 49.
67. Vine, *Isaiah*, 50.
68. Wildberger, *Isaiah 1–12*, p. 467.
69. Wildberger, *Isaiah 1–12*, p. 467.
70. Wildberger, *Isaiah 1–12*, p. 481. However, for Wildberger the lack of allegory does not suggest hope for a literal future. Wildberger, *Isaiah 1–12*, p. 481.
71. G. V. Smith (2007), *Isaiah 1–39* (Nashville: B&H), p. 269.
72. Smith, *Isaiah 1–39*, p. 269.
73. See Tucker, *Isaiah 1–39*, p. 142.
74. Isaiah 1:3.
75. Isaiah 1:30.
76. Isaiah 5:7.
77. Isaiah 5:29a.
78. Isaiah 8:7.
79. Isaiah 10:14.
80. See Isaiah 10:33–34.
81. Goldingay, *Isaiah*, p. 85.
82. See also Kaiser, *Isaiah 1–12*, p. 260.
83. Tucker, *Isaiah 1–39*, 142, p. 144.
84. See 1 Samuel 17:34–37. On this imagery, see Watts, *Isaiah 1–39*, p. 173.
85. Blenkinsopp, *Isaiah 1–39*, p. 265.
86. Isaiah 10:1–2. The Hebrew *shâlâl* does typically refer to the spoils of war, suggesting that a better image might be that the powerful consider the vulnerable commodities. However, in the context of Isaiah's critique, the image of predator and prey is valid. The vulnerable are both the victims of this social warfare and the spoils, much like the prey of a predator in the wild.
87. Wildberger, *Isaiah 1–12*, pp. 460–461.
88. Goldingay's argument that the connection between predator and prey in the human world and the animal world renders vv. 6–8 metaphorical backfires. Goldingay, *Isaiah*, p. 85. Rather, the connection secures the opposite conclusion. Just as disenfranchised humans are victims of their proud overlords, so also are vulnerable animals victims of their powerful predators. The comparison of victimization (and salvation) is a literal one.
89. On ch. 11 and the theme of failed kings, see Goldingay, *Isaiah*, p. 83.
90. Delitzsch, *Isaiah*, p. 282.
91. Smith, *Isaiah 1–39*, p. 267.
92. See Smith, *Isaiah 1–39*, p. 273; Berges, *The Book of Isaiah*, pp. 116–117; P. D. Miscall (2006), *Isaiah* (Sheffield, UK: Sheffield Phoenix Press), p. 58. This claim is consistent with Middleton's astute interpretation of salvation history. See J. R. Middleton (2006), "A New Heaven and a New Earth: The Case for a Holistic Reading of the Biblical Story of Redemption," *Journal for Christian Theological Research* 11, pp. 73–97.
93. Isaiah 11:8; Brueggemann, *Isaiah 1–39*, p. 103; Miscall, *Isaiah*, pp. 58–59. Miscall argues that the use of animals and children reveals the poem as myth. Miscall, *Isaiah*, p. 59.
94. Blenkinsopp, *Isaiah 1–39*, p. 263. Childs challenges this notion, noting, "References to an eschatological covenant with animals (cf. Hos. 2:18[20]) have no royal messianic component." Childs, *Isaiah*, 100.

95. Wildberger, *Isaiah 1–12*, p. 479.
96. Wildberger, *Isaiah 1–12*, p. 479.
97. See Heschel, *The Prophets*, p. 120.
98. Watts, *Isaiah 1–39*, p. 173; Brueggemann, *Isaiah 1–39*, p. 103.
99. Hans Wildberger reads the Hebrew as "will get fattened" as opposed to "the fattling." Wildberger, *Isaiah 1–12*, p. 462. Jan de Waard also acknowledges the validity and favorability of a verbal reading of "fattling." See J. Waard (1997), *A Handbook on Isaiah* (Winona Lake, IN: Eisenbrauns), pp. 55–56. Waard is here following the C rating that the Hebrew Old Testament Text Project gives this translation.
100. Wildberger takes the "will graze" of v. 7 to intimate rather "will have friendship with." Wildberger, *Isaiah 1–12*, p. 462.
101. For a view more anthropocentric than Tucker's, see J. Burton and T. B. Coffman (1990), *Commentary on Isaiah* (Abilene, TX: ACU Press), pp. 116–117.
102. Isaiah 11:9.
103. Smith, *Isaiah 1–39*, p. 273.
104. Brueggemann, *Isaiah 1–39*, p. 102.
105. See Childs, *Isaiah*, pp. 103–104.
106. R. Bauckham (2012), "Humans, Animals, and the Environment in Genesis 1–3," in *Genesis and Christian Theology*, edited by N. MacDonald, M. W. Elliott, and G. Macaskill (Grand Rapids, MI: Eerdmans), pp. 184–185.
107. Isaiah 11:9.

7 The Sacramentality of the Cosmos

1. See J. Martos (2001), *Doors to the Sacred: A Historical Introduction to Sacraments in the Catholic Church*, rev. and updated ed. (Liguori, MO: Liguori/Triumph), pp. 19–74.
2. See Martos, *Doors to the Sacred*, pp. 40–44; K. Irwin (1998), "Sacramentality and the Theology of Creation: A Recovered Paradigm for Sacramental Theology," *Louvain Studies* 23: 167–168.
3. Martos, *Doors to the Sacred*, pp. 47–69.
4. Martos, *Doors to the Sacred*, pp. 63–64.
5. See Martos, *Doors to the Sacred*, pp. 80–88.
6. For Catholics, see J. Hart (2006), *Sacramental Commons: Christian Ecological Ethics* (New York: Rowman & Littlefield); Irwin, "Sacramentality and the Theology of Creation": 159–179; D. McDougal (2003), *The Cosmos as the Primary Sacrament: The Horizon for an Ecological Sacramental Theology* (New York: Peter Lang). For an example of Protestant work in this field, see T. Runyon (1980), "The World as the Original Sacrament," *Worship* 54 6: 495–511.
7. For a clear synopsis, see K. Osborne (1988), *Sacramental Theology: A General Introduction* (Mahwah, NJ: Paulist Press), pp. 69–99.
8. See M. Kadavil (2005), *The World as Sacrament: Sacramentality of Creation from the Perspectives of Leonardo Boff, Alexander Schmemann and Saint Ephrem* (Leuven: Peeters), pp. 68–81.
9. Irwin, "Sacramentality and the Theology of Creation," 162.
10. Irwin, "Sacramentality and the Theology of Creation," 165.

11. Irwin, "Sacramentality and the Theology of Creation," 159. On the necessity of the retrieval of this notion, see K. Irwin (2002), "A Sacramental World? Sacramentality as the Primary Language for Sacraments," *Worship* 76:3 (May): 197.
12. Irwin, "Sacramentality and the Theology of Creation," pp. 163–164.
13. Irwin, "A Sacramental World?" 201.
14. Irwin, "Sacramentality and the Theology of Creation," 166, 169–174.
15. Irwin, "A Sacramental World?" 198. However, God is both revealed and hidden (see 203).
16. Irwin, "A Sacramental World?" 197.
17. Irwin, "Sacramentality and the Theology of Creation," 173.
18. Irwin, "A Sacramental World?" 199, 208–209.
19. Irwin, "A Sacramental World?" 198.
20. Denis Edwards makes a similar claim in his ecological exploration of the Eucharist. See D. Edwards (2008), "Eucharist and Ecology: Keeping Memorial of Creation," *Worship* 82: 194–213 (esp. 199–205). Edwards at times seems to overlook the anthropocentrism of his liturgical sources. See, for example, his engagement of Justin Martyr on 203.
21. See Irwin, "A Sacramental World?" 202.
22. Irwin, "A Sacramental World?" 199.
23. Irwin, "A Sacramental World?" 202–203.
24. Irwin, "A Sacramental World?" 206; italics added.
25. Edwards, "Eucharist and Ecology," 198.
26. Edwards, "Eucharist and Ecology," 199.
27. Edwards, "Eucharist and Ecology," 206.
28. Edwards, "Eucharist and Ecology," 206.
29. Edwards, "Eucharist and Ecology," 207–208; see also K. Irwin (1994), "The Sacramentality of Creation and the Role of Creation in Liturgy and Sacraments," in Kevin W. Irwin and Edmund J. Pellegrino (eds), *Preserving the Creation. Environmental Theology and Ethics* (Washington, DC: Georgetown University Press), pp. 67–111.
30. Irwin, "The Sacramentality of Creation," p. 111.
31. Edwards, "Eucharist and Ecology," 209.
32. Edwards, "Eucharist and Ecology," 209.
33. Irwin, "The Sacramentality of Creation," pp. 124–126.
34. Edwards, "Eucharist and Ecology," pp. 211–212.
35. For historical considerations, see J. Schaefer (2009), *Theological Foundations for Environmental Ethics: Reconstructing Patristic & Medieval Concepts* (Washington, DC: Georgetown University Press), pp. 65–102; Kadavil, *The World as Sacrament*, ch. 4.
36. R. Bordeianu (2009), "Maximus and Ecology: The Relevance of Maximus the Confessor's Theology of Creation for the Present Ecological Crisis," *Downside Review* 127: 103–126.
37. Bordeianu, "Maximus and Ecology," 109; also 112–114.
38. Bordeianu, "Maximus and Ecology," 104–107.
39. Bordeianu, "Maximus and Ecology," 107.
40. Bordeianu, "Maximus and Ecology," 117.
41. Bordeianu, "Maximus and Ecology," 117.
42. Bordeianu, "Maximus and Ecology," 119.

43. See A. Schmemann (1973), *For the Life of the World: Sacraments and Orthodoxy* (Crestwood, NY: St. Vladimir's Seminary Press).

44. See Schmemann's lament concerning baptism (Schmemann, *For the Life of the World*, p. 68).

45. Schmemann, *For the Life of the World*, pp. 33–34, 42.

46. Schmemann, *For the Life of the World*, pp. 34–35.

47. Schmemann, *For the Life of the World*, pp. 14–15. See also Schmemann's definition of "sacramental" (Schmemann, *For the Life of the World*, pp. 120–121).

48. Schmemann, *For the Life of the World*, pp. 44–45.

49. Schmemann, *For the Life of the World*, p. 14.

50. Schmemann, *For the Life of the World*, p. 18.

51. See D. Staniloae (2000), *The Experience of God: Orthodox Dogmatic Theology*, vol. 2: *The World: Creation and Deification*, translated and edited by I. Ionita and R. Barringer (Brookline, MA: Holy Cross Orthodox Press).

52. Staniloae, *Creation and Deification*, p. 6; see also 20.

53. Staniloae, *Creation and Deification*, pp. 62–63.

54. Staniloae, *Creation and Deification*, p. 14. Elsewhere Staniloae applies the purposelessness of existence without humanity explicitly to animals. Staniloae, *Creation and Deification*, p. 28.

55. Staniloae, *Creation and Deification*, pp. 21–27.

56. Staniloae, *Creation and Deification*, pp. 48–49.

57. V. Lossky (1976), *The Mystical Theology of the Eastern Church* (Crestwood, NY: St. Vladimir's Seminary Press), especially ch. 5.

58. Lossky, *Mystical Theology*, pp. 91–100.

59. Lossky, *Mystical Theology*, p. 101.

60. Lossky, *Mystical Theology*, pp. 111–113.

61. Lossky, *Mystical Theology*, p. 113.

62. Lossky draws on Maximus to make this point; *Mystical Theology*, pp. 108–113.

63. K. Ware (1995), *The Orthodox Way*, rev. ed. (Crestwood, NY: St. Vladimir's Seminary Press), p. 46.

64. Ware, *The Orthodox Way*, pp. 46–47.

65. Ware, *The Orthodox Way*, p. 50.

66. Ware, *The Orthodox Way*, p. 54.

67. J. Chryssavgis (2006), "The Earth as Sacrament: Insights from Orthodox Christian Theology and Spirituality," in R. D. Gottlieb (ed.), *The Orthodox Handbook of Religion and Ecology* (New York: Oxford University Press), pp. 92–114.

68. Chryssavgis, "The Earth as Sacrament," p. 112.

69. See Chapter 3 of the present work.

70. J. Meyendorff (1974), *Byzantine Theology: Historical Trends* (New York: Fordham University Press), p. 142.

71. N. V. Harrison (2008), "The Human Person as the Image and Likeness of God," in M. B. Cunningham and E. Theokritoff (eds), *The Cambridge Companion to Orthodox Christian Theology* (New York: Cambridge University Press), p. 86.

72. Schmemann, *For the Life of the World*, p. 23.

73. It is unclear whether or not Schmemann includes women in this priestly role. Schmemann, *For the Life of the World*, pp. 85, 92–93.

74. Schmemann, *For the Life of the World*, p. 75.

75. Schmemann, *For the Life of the World*, p. 75.
76. Schmemann, *For the Life of the World*, pp. 23–46.
77. Schmemann, *For the Life of the World*, p. 36.
78. Schmemann, *For the Life of the World*, pp. 75–76.
79. Schmemann, *For the Life of the World*, p. 20.
80. Staniloae, *Creation and Deification*, p. 20.
81. Staniloae, *Creation and Deification*, p. 81.
82. Staniloae, *Creation and Deification*, p. 7; italics added.
83. Staniloae, *Creation and Deification*, p. 27.
84. Staniloae, *Creation and Deification*, p. 107.
85. Lossky, *Mystical Theology*, p. 101.
86. Lossky, *Mystical Theology*, p. 97
87. Lossky, *Mystical Theology*, p. 109.
88. Lossky, *Mystical Theology*, p. 109.
89. Lossky, *Mystical Theology*, p. 111.
90. Ware, *The Orthodox Way*, pp. 50–51.
91. Ware, *The Orthodox Way*, p. 51.
92. Ware, *The Orthodox Way*, p. 53.
93. Ware, *The Orthodox Way*, p. 54.
94. Ware, *The Orthodox Way*, p. 54.
95. Ware explains the disorder of the world prior to the existence of humanity by appealing to a fall of spiritual powers prior to human sin; *The Orthodox Way*, p. 58.
96. Ware juxtaposes his view to Augustinian views; *The Orthodox Way*, p. 62.
97. Ware, *The Orthodox Way*, p. 59.
98. On this point, see A. Louth (2010), "Between Creation and Transfiguration: The Environment in the Eastern Orthodox Tradition," in D. G. Horrell, C. Hunt, C. Southgate, and F. Stavrakopoulou (eds), *Ecological Hermeneutics: Biblical, Historical and Theological Perspectives* (New York: T. & T. Clark), pp. 211–222; A. Louth (2008), "Eastern Orthodox Eschatology," in J. L. Walls (ed.), *The Orthodox Handbook of Eschatology* (New York: Oxford University Press), pp. 233–247; E. D. Reed (2009), "Animals in Orthodox Iconography," in C. Deane-Drummond and D. Clough (eds.), *Creaturely Theology, Creaturely Theology: On God, Humans and Other Animals* (London: SCM Press), pp. 61–77.
99. Ware, *The Orthodox Way*, 137.
100. See Chapter 4 of the present work.
101. Isaac the Syrian (1984), *The Ascetical Homilies of St. Isaac the Syrian*, Dana Miller (ed.) (Boston: Holy Transfiguration Monastery), p. 383; Isaac of Nineveh (1969), *Mystic Treatises*, translated from Bedjan's Syriac text with an introduction and registers by A. J. Wensinck (Wiesbaden), LXXIV.
102. Schmemann, *For the Life of the World*, p. 37.
103. For Schmemann, in the Eucharist Christians have "entered the Eschaton." Schmemann, *For the Life of the World*, p. 37. It is the Holy Spirit that "manifests the world to come" and, in doing so, "inaugurates the Kingdom" (*For the Life of the World*, p. 44).
104. Schmemann, *For the Life of the World*, p. 96.
105. Schmemann, *For the Life of the World*, p. 100.
106. Staniloae, *Creation and Deification*, p. 3.

107. Staniloae, *Creation and Deification*, p. 19.
108. Staniloae, *Creation and Deification*, pp. 4–5.
109. Such a view is, I believe, fully consistent with my depiction of "eschato-logical stewardship" in Chapters 5 and 6.
110. See Staniloae, *Creation and Deification*, pp. 108–118.
111. Staniloae, *Creation and Deification*, p. 118.
112. Staniloae, *Creation and Deification*, p. 53.
113. Staniloae, *Creation and Deification*, p. 58.
114. Staniloae, *Creation and Deification*, p. 62.
115. Staniloae, *Creation and Deification*, pp. 63, 83–84.
116. Staniloae, *Creation and Deification*, pp. 77–78.
117. Irwin, "Sacramentality and the Theology of Creation," 171.
118. Irwin, "Sacramentality and the Theology of Creation," 172.
119. Irwin, "A Sacramental World?" 199.
120. Edwards, "Eucharist and Ecology," 199.
121. Edwards, "Eucharist and Ecology," 206.
122. See Chapters 5 and 6 of the present work.
123. This reading is attested to in Romans 8, where Paul writes that all crea-tion has been "groaning" (Greek *sustenazei*), that humans bearing the Spirit "groan" (Greek *stenazomen*) inwardly, and that the Spirit intercedes in our directionless prayers with "sighs" (Greek *stenagmois*) "too deep for words." See Romans 8:22, 23, and 26. Thus, God, humanity, and the nonhuman creation are united in "groaning" (*stenazō*).

8 Alternative Traditions and Interreligious Dialogue

This chapter is a modified version of an earlier published work. See R. P. McLaughlin (2012), "Non-Violence and Nonhumans: Foundations for Animal Welfare in the Thought of Mohandas Gandhi and Albert Schweitzer." *Journal of Religious Ethics* 40, 4: 678–704.

1. R. Huntington (2002), "Jainism and Ethics," in M. Meyer and K. Bergel (eds), *Reverence for Life: The Ethics of Albert Schweitzer for the Twenty-First Century* (Syracuse, NY: Syracuse University Press), p. 197.
2. M. K. Gandhi (1959), *An Autobiography: The Story of My Experiments with the Truth*, translated by M. Desai (Ahmedabad: Navajivan), p. 11.
3. See L. Fischer (1983), *The Life of Mahatma Gandhi* (New York: Harper and Row), p. 21.
4. Gandhi, *An Autobiography*, p. 11.
5. Gandhi, *An Autobiography*, p. 11.
6. Gandhi, *An Autobiography*, p. 12.
7. Gandhi, *An Autobiography*, pp. 24–25.
8. Gandhi, *An Autobiography*, p. 25. Gandhi's interest in dietary experiments began with health concerns but ended as a religious commitment.
9. Gandhi, *An Autobiography*, p. 29.
10. See R. Johnson (2006), "From Childhood to *Satyagrahi*," in R. L. Johnson (ed.), *Gandhi's Experiments with Truth: Essential Writings by and about Mahatma Gandhi* (New York: Lexington Books), p. 4. See also Gandhi's juxtaposition of "the unadulterated esoteric teachings of not only Jesus Christ but also of

Buddha, Zoroaster and Mahomed" to "cruelly selfish" materialism. M. K. Gandhi (1999), *The Collected Works of Mahatma Gandhi* (hereafter *CWMG*), 98 vols. (New Delhi: Publications Division, Government of India), 1:206, www.gandhiserve.org/cwmg/cwmg.html.

11. F. Burgat (2004), "Non-Violence towards Animals in the Thinking of Gandhi: The Problem of Animal Husbandry," *Journal of Agriculture and Environmental Ethics* 17, 3 (May): 228–229.

12. See, for example, his views on racism, women's rights, and liberation in general. M. K. Gandhi (1962), *The Essential Gandhi: An Anthology of His Writings on His Life, Work, and Ideas*, L. Fischer (ed.) (New York: Vintage), pp. 171, 215–223, and 282.

13. See Fischer, *The Life of Mahatma Gandhi*, pp. 20–21; M. Chatterjee (1986), *Gandhi's Religious Thought* (Notre Dame, IN: University of Notre Dame Press), pp. 21–23.

14. M. Juergensmeyer (1984), *Fighting with Gandhi* (San Francisco: Harper and Row), p. 3.

15. Juergensmeyer, *Fighting with Gandhi*, pp. 18–26. For Gandhi's interpretation of the violence depicted in the Bhagavad Gita, see Chatterjee, *Gandhi's Religious Thought*, p. 38.

16. R. Johnson (2006), "*Satyagraha*: The Only Way to Stop Terrorism," in R. L. Johnson (ed.), *Gandhi's Experiments with Truth: Essential Writings by and about Mahatma Gandhi* (New York: Lexington Books), pp. 228–236.

17. Gandhi, *An Autobiography*, p. 35.

18. Burgat, "Non-Violence towards Animals," 223–224.

19. For example, in the short work, *Gandhi on Non-Violence*, Thomas Merton includes what he takes to be the main points of Gandhi's *Non-Violence in Peace and War*. The only text regarding nonviolence and nonhuman animals that Merton includes in his compendium is one in which Gandhi claims killing animals that are harmful to humans is pardonable. See T. Merton (ed., 1964), *Gandhi on Non-Violence: Selected Texts from Mohandas K. Gandhi's Non-Violence in Peace and War* (New York: New Directions), p. 87. Anthony Parel (2006) follows a similar path in *Gandhi's Philosophy and the Quest for Harmony* (New York: Cambridge University Press), p. 123. These passages do not contain Gandhi's main vision of ethics for animals. See, for example, M. K. Gandhi (1972), *Non-Violence in Peace and War* (New York: Garland), pp. 65–72.

20. Burgat, "Non-Violence towards Animals," 224.

21. Johnson, "From Childhood to *Satyagrahi*," pp. 10–11.

22. However, even in *Hind Swaraj*, Gandhi makes known the importance of cow protection, which for him extends to all animals. See M. K. Gandhi (1997), *Hind Swaraj and Other Writings*, L. Fischer (ed.) (New York: Cambridge University Press), p. 55.

23. Gandhi, *CWMG*, 19:349.

24. Gandhi, *CWMG*, 19:350.

25. Burgat, "Non-Violence towards Animals," 224.

26. Burgat, "Non-Violence towards Animals," 231.

27. This is also evident in Gandhi's practice of *satyagraha*.

28. Gandhi, *CWMG*, 1:40.

29. Gandhi, *CWMG*, 19:191.

30. Gandhi, *CWMG*, 1:91.
31. Parel, *Hind Swaraj and Other Writings*, p. 55.
32. See Burgat, "Non-Violence towards Animals," 226.
33. Gandhi, *CWMG*, 90:326.
34. Gandhi, *CWMG*, 10:73.
35. Gandhi, *CWMG*, 72:228.
36. See Gandhi, *CWMG*, 71:404; Burgat, "Non-Violence towards Animals," 230.
37. Gandhi, *CWMG*, 71:404.
38. See, for example, Gandhi, *CWMG*, 31:462.
39. Gandhi, *CWMG*, 31:462. On both Gandhi's disapproval of vivisection and the value he sees in Western medicine, see Gandhi, *CWMG*, 71:405.
40. Gandhi, *CWMG*, 50:160; see also Burgat, "Non-Violence towards Animals," 227. On the desire to end animal sacrifice, see Gandhi, *CWMG*, 60:357.
41. For a reflection on the development of the "apotheosis" of the cow, including the diversity of views that conflict with Gandhi's critical retrieval of cow veneration, see F. Korom (2000), "Holy Cow! The Apotheosis of Zebu, or Why the Cow Is Sacred in Hinduism," *Asian Folklore Studies* 59: 181–203.
42. Gandhi, *CWMG*, 37:6; C. F. Andrews (1930), *Mahatma Gandhi's Ideas (Including Selections from His Writings)* (New York: Macmillan), p. 32; Burgat, "Non-Violence towards Animals," 226.
43. Herein one sees an influence from Jainism. Perfect *ahimsa* is impossible outside of attaining the Hindu equivalent of *moksa*. See R. Huntington (2002), "Jainism and Ethics," in M. Meyer and K. Bergel (eds.), *Reverence for Life: The Ethics of Albert Schweitzer for the Twenty-First Century* (Syracuse, NY: Syracuse University Press), p. 195.
44. Parel, *Gandhi's Philosophy and the Quest for Harmony*, pp. 123–124. See also Gandhi, *CWMG*, 83:431.
45. Burgat, "Non-Violence towards Animals," 225. Again, the influence of Jainism is evident. See Huntington, "Jainism and Ethics," p. 196.
46. Burgat, "Non-Violence towards Animals in the Thinking of Gandhi," p. 225, n. 6.
47. Gandhi, *CWMG*, 90:310.
48. Gandhi, *CWMG*, 98:350; italics added. On this point, see also where Gandhi, referencing St. Francis of Assisi, writes, "I personally feel that when we rid ourselves of all enmity towards any living creatures, the latter also cease to regard us with hate." Gandhi, *CWMG*, 13:241.
49. In *Non-Violence in Peace and War*, Gandhi claims that even eating vegetables constitutes violence that is inherent to life. Gandhi, *Non-Violence in Peace and War*, p. 65.
50. Gandhi sees perfection as attainable for individual humans. See J. Brown (2006), "Gandhi and Human Rights: In Search of True Humanity," in R. L. Johnson (ed.), *Gandhi's Experiments with Truth: Essential Writings by and about Mahatma Gandhi* (New York: Lexington Books), p. 241.
51. Gandhi, *CWMG*, 50:161.
52. A. Schweitzer (1998), *Out of My Life and Thought: An Autobiography*, translated by A. B. Lemke (Baltimore: John Hopkins University Press), pp. 1–14.
53. On Schweitzer's context, see J. Brabazon (2000), *Albert Schweitzer: A Biography* (Syracuse, NY: Syracuse University Press), p. 2.
54. Brabazon, *Albert Schweitzer*, p. 16.

55. See T. Kiernan (ed., 1965), *Reverence for Life: An Anthology of Selected Writings* (New York: Philosophical Library), p. 1.
56. See Brabazon, *Albert Schweitzer*, p. 17.
57. In Kiernan, *Reverence for Life*, p. 2.
58. In Kiernan, *Reverence for Life*, p. 5.
59. See M. Meyer (2002), "Affirming Reverence for Life," in M. Meyer and K. Bergel (eds.), *Reverence for Life: The Ethics of Albert Schweitzer for the Twenty-First Century* (Syracuse, NY: Syracuse University Press), p. 30. Concerning *ahimsa*, Schweitzer writes, "The laying down of the commandment not to kill and not damage is one of the greatest events in the spiritual history of mankind." A. Schweitzer (1936), *Indian Thought and Its Development*, translated by Mrs. C. E. B. Russell (Gloucester, MA: Beacon Press), pp. 82–83.
60. Schweitzer decries the principle of *ahimsa* because, in his estimation, it fails to embody selfless love (*Indian Thought and Its Development*, p. 80). On Schweitzer's overgeneralization of *ahimsa*, see A. P. Barsam (2002), "Albert Schweitzer, Jainism, and Reverence for Life," in M. Meyer and K. Bergel (eds.), *Reverence for Life: The Ethics of Albert Schweitzer for the Twenty-First Century* (Syracuse, NY: Syracuse University Press), p. 230. His overgeneralizations notwithstanding, Schweitzer praises Gandhi's use of *ahimsa* as a call to action that extends to all living things (*Indian Thought and Its Development*, pp. 229–230); Meyer, "Affirming Reverence for Life," pp. 32, 35.
61. A. Schweitzer (1966), *My Life and Thought: An Autobiography*, translated by C. T. Campion (London: Unwin Books), p. 131.
62. Schweitzer, *My Life and Thought*, p. 129.
63. Schweitzer, *My Life and Thought*, p. 130.
64. A. Schweitzer (2002), "First Sermon on Reverence for Life," in M. Meyer and K. Bergel (eds.), *Reverence for Life: The Ethics of Albert Schweitzer for the Twenty-First Century* (Syracuse, NY: Syracuse University Press), p. 67.
65. Schweitzer, "First Sermon on Reverence for Life," p. 68.
66. "Albert Schweitzer, Jainism, and Reverence for Life," p. 222.
67. Though Schweitzer valued mysticism as a means to experience God (infinite Being), he did so only inasmuch as this experience effected ethical engagement with the world. Thus he affirms an "ethical mysticism." Barsam, "Albert Schweitzer, Jainism, and Reverence for Life," pp. 216–218.
68. A. Schweitzer (1955), *The Mysticism of Paul the Apostle*, translated by W. Montgomery (London: A. & C. Black), p. 379.
69. Schweitzer, *The Mysticism of Paul*, p. 303.
70. Schweitzer, *The Mysticism of Paul*, p. 294.
71. A. P. Barsam (2008), *Reverence for Life: Albert Schweitzer's Great Contribution to Ethical Thought* (New York: Oxford University Press), p. 24.
72. A. Schweitzer (1946), *Civilization and Ethics*, translated by C. T. Campion (London: A. & C. Black), p. 242.
73. Schweitzer, *Civilization and Ethics*, p. 254.
74. For Schweitzer, no individual was exempt from duty to other humans (*Civilization and Ethics*, p. 256).
75. Schweitzer, *Civilization and Ethics*, pp. 255–256.
76. Schweitzer, *Civilization and Ethics*, p. 243.
77. Part of Schweitzer's respect for Eastern thought is that it did not succumb to such reasoning (*Civilization and Ethics*, p. vi).

78. A. Schweitzer (1965), *The Teaching of Reverence for Life*, translated by R. and C. Winston (New York: Holt, Rinehart and Winston), p. 49.
79. Schweitzer, *Out of My Life and Thought*, p. 235.
80. Barsam, *Reverence for Life*, p. 151.
81. Schweitzer, *Civilization and Ethics*, p. 222.
82. Schweitzer, *Civilization and Ethics*, p. 223.
83. Brabazon, *Albert Schweitzer*, p. 15.
84. Schweitzer, *Civilization and Ethics*, p. 213.
85. Schweitzer, *Civilization and Ethics*, p. 243. As Barsam states, "The fundamental feature of [Schweitzer's] reverence is its boundlessness; it includes all life" (Barsam, "Albert Schweitzer, Jainism, and Reverence for Life," p. 212).
86. Meyer, "Affirming Reverence for Life," p. 23.
87. Meyer, "Affirming Reverence for Life," p. 36.
88. Schweitzer, *Civilization and Ethics*, p. 253.
89. Schweitzer, *Civilization and Ethics*, p. 246.
90. Schweitzer, *Civilization and Ethics*, p. 252.
91. In Kiernan, *Reverence for Life*, p. 5.
92. Schweitzer, *The Teaching of Reverence for Life*, p. 50.
93. Barsam, *Reverence for Life*, p. 152.
94. Schweitzer, "First Sermon on Reverence for Life," p. 68.
95. See Barsam, *Reverence for Life*, pp. 95–98.
96. Barsam, *Reverence for Life*, p. 95.
97. Barsam, *Reverence for Life*, pp. 160–162.
98. Barsam, *Reverence for Life*, p. 110.
99. Barsam, *Reverence for Life*, p. 113.
100. Barsam, *Reverence for Life*, p. 93.
101. Schweitzer, *Civilization and Ethics*, p. 245. Barsam connects the redemption of humanity with the redemption of the entire creation in Schweitzer's thought (*Reverence for Life*, p. 94).
102. Schweitzer, *Civilization and Ethics*, p. 250.
103. Meyer, "Affirming Reverence for Life," p. 33.
104. Schweitzer, *Out of My Life and Thought*, p. 236.
105. Schweitzer, *Civilization and Ethics*, p. 251.
106. Schweitzer, *Civilization and Ethics*, p. 245.
107. Schweitzer, *Indian Thought and Its Development*, p. 83. Schweitzer claims that Jainism fails to address the great problem of existence: the tragedy of will-to-live divided against itself.
108. Inevitably, such conundrums involve choosing between human and nonhuman life. Schweitzer claimed that reverence for life did not value one form of life over another (*Out of My Life and Thought*, p. 235). But as Barsam notes, practically Schweitzer did make divisions and preferences for human life over, say, bacteria ("Albert Schweitzer, Jainism, and Reverence for Life," pp. 236–237). Elsewhere, Barsam notes that Schweitzer viewed compassionate killing as acceptable for suffering animals but not for humans (*Reverence for Life*, pp. 36–37).
109. Barsam, "Albert Schweitzer, Jainism, and Reverence for Life," pp. 237–238.
110. For a good survey of Gandhi's view of Jesus and Christianity, see Chatterjee, *Gandhi's Religious Thought*, pp. 41–56.
111. Gandhi, *CWMG*, 1:311.

112. Schweitzer, *Indian Thought and Its Development*, p. 234; see also 229–238.
113. Gandhi, *CWMG*, 71:404.
114. Schweitzer, *Civilization and Ethics*, pp. 223, 245; see also Schweitzer, *The Mysticism of Paul*, p. 303.
115. Gandhi, *CWMG*, 90:310. Gandhi does, however, permit mercy killing for both animals and humans. Gandhi, *CWMG*, 37:21.
116. Gandhi, *CWMG*, 37:7.
117. Schweitzer, "First Sermon on Reverence for Life," p. 68.
118. Schweitzer, *Civilization and Ethics*, p. 242.
119. Barsam, *Reverence for Life*, pp. 35–37.
120. Schweitzer's letter to Oskar Kraus, quoted in Barsam, *Reverence for Life*, p. 28.
121. Schweitzer, *Out of My Life and Thought*, p. 235.
122. For such an evaluation, see R. P. McLaughlin (2012), "Non-Violence and Nonhumans: Foundations for Animal Welfare in the Thought of Mohandas Gandhi and Albert Schweitzer," *Journal of Religious Ethics* 40, 4: 700–701.

Bibliography

D. Alexander (2008). *Saints and Animals in the Middle Ages.* Rochester, NY: Boydell Press.

J. A. Alexander (1992/1867). *Commentary on Isaiah.* Grand Rapids, MI: Kregel Classics.

C. F. Andrews (1930). *Mahatma Gandhi's Ideas (including Selections from His Writings).* New York: Macmillan.

Apostolicam Actuositatem (1965). www.vatican.va/archive/hist_councils/ii_vatican_council/index.htm.

Augustine (1948). *City of God.* In W. J. Oates (ed.), *Basic Writings of Saint Augustine.* New York: Random House.

Augustine (1982). *Augustine on Romans.* P. F. Landers (ed.). Chico, CA: Scholars Press.

B. T. Arnold (2009). *Genesis.* New York: Cambridge University Press.

B. M. Ashley, J. K. deBlois, and K. D. O'Rourke (2006). *Health Care Ethics: A Catholic Theological Analysis.* Washington, DC: Georgetown University Press.

T. Aquinas (1265/1946). *Summa Theologica.* Translated by the Fathers of the English Dominican Province. New York: Benzinger.

T. Aquinas (1955–57). *Summa contra Gentiles.* Joseph Kenny (ed.). New York: Hanover House.

J. Barad (1995). *Aquinas on the Nature and Treatment of Animals.* Lanham, MD: International Scholars Press.

B. Bandstra (2008). *Genesis 1–11: A Handbook on the Hebrew Text.* Waco, TX: Baylor University Press.

A. P. Barsam (2002). "Albert Schweitzer, Jainism, and Reverence for Life." In M. Meyer and K. Bergel (eds), *Reverence for Life: The Ethics of Albert Schweitzer for the Twenty-First Century.* Syracuse, NY: Syracuse University Press, pp. 207–245.

A. P. Barsam (2008). *Reverence for Life: Albert Schweitzer's Great Contribution to Ethical Thought.* New York: Oxford University Press.

R. Bauckham (1998a). "Jesus and Animals I: What Did He Teach?" In A. Linzey and D. Yamamoto (eds), *Animals on the Agenda: Questions about Animal Ethics for Theology and Ethics.* Chicago: University of Illinois Press, pp. 33–48.

R. Bauckham (1998b). "Jesus and Animals II: What Did He Practice?" In A. Linzey and D. Yamamoto (eds), *Animals on the Agenda: Questions about Animal Ethics for Theology and Ethics.* Chicago: University of Illinois Press, pp. 49–60.

R. Bauckham (2012). "Humans, Animals, and the Environment in Genesis 1–3." In N. MacDonald, M. W. Elliot, and G. Macaskill (eds), *Genesis and Christian Theology.* Grand Rapids, MI: Eerdmans, pp. 175–189.

Benedict XVI (2009). *Caritas in Veritate.* www.vatican.va/holy_father/benedict_xvi/encyclicals/index_en.htm.

U. F. Berges (2012). *The Book of Isaiah: Its Composition and Final Form.* Translated by Millard C. Lind. Sheffield, UK: Sheffield Phoenix Press.

J. Berkman (2009). "Towards a Thomistic Theology of Animality." In C. Deane-Drummond and D. Clough (eds), *Creaturely Theology: On God, Humans and Other Animals*. London: SCM Press, pp. 21–40.

T. Berry (1990). *The Dream of the Earth*. San Francisco: Sierra Club Books.

B. C Birch, W. Brueggemann, T. E. Fretheim, and D. L. Peterson (2005). *A Theological Introduction to the Old Testament*. 2nd ed. Nashville: Abingdon Press.

S. H. Blank (1958). *Prophetic Faith in Isaiah*. New York: Harper and Brothers.

J. Blenkinsopp (2000). *Isaiah 1–39*. New York: Doubleday.

M. Bockmuehl (1998). *Black's New Testament Commentary: The Epistle to the Philippians*. Peabody, MA: Hendrickson.

D. Bonhoeffer (1971). *Letters and Papers from Prison*. London: SCM Press.

M. E. Boring (2006). *Mark: A Commentary*. Louisville, KY: Westminster/John Knox Press.

R. Bordeianu (2009). "Maximus and Ecology: The Relevance of Maximus the Confessor's Theology of Creation for the Present Ecological Crisis." *Downside Review*, 127: 103–126.

P. Bouteneff (2008). *Beginnings: Ancient Christian Readings of the Biblical Creation Narratives*. Grand Rapids, MI: Baker Academic.

J. Brabazon (2000). *Albert Schweitzer: A Biography*. Syracuse, NY: Syracuse University Press.

J. Brown (2006). "Gandhi and Human Rights: In Search of True Humanity." In R. L. Johnson (ed.), *Gandhi's Experiments with Truth: Essential Writings by and about Mahatma Gandhi*. New York: Lexington Books, pp. 237–252.

W. Brueggemann (1982). *Genesis*. Atlanta: John Knox Press.

W. Brueggemann (1998). *Isaiah 1–39*. Louisville, KY: Westminster/John Knox Press.

W. Brueggemann (2003). *Introduction to the Old Testament: The Canon and Christian Imagination*. Louisville, KY: Westminster / John Knox Press.

F. Burgat (2004). "Non-Violence towards Animals in the Thinking of Gandhi: The Problem of Animal Husbandry." *Journal of Agriculture and Environmental Ethics*, 17, 3 (May): 223–248.

J. Burton and T. B. Coffman (1990). *Commentary on Isaiah*. Abilene, TX: ACU Press.

Canadian Conference of Catholic Bishops (2003). "You Love All That Exists ... All Things Are Yours, God, Lover of Life ... ," www.cccb.ca/site/Files/pastoralenvironment.html.

The Catechism of the Catholic Church: With Modifications from the Editio Typica (1995). New York: Doubleday.

M. Chatterjee (1986). *Gandhi's Religious Thought*. Notre Dame, IN: University of Notre Dame Press.

B. S. Childs (2001). *Isaiah*. Louisville, KY: Westminster/John Knox Press.

J. Chryssavgis (2006). "The Earth as Sacrament: Insights from Orthodox Christian Theology and Spirituality." In R. D. Gottlieb (ed.), *The Orthodox Handbook of Religion and Ecology*. New York: Oxford University Press, pp. 92–114.

A. Y. Collins (2007). *Mark: A Commentary*. Minneapolis: Fortress Press.

D. W. Cotter (2003). *Genesis*. Collegeville, MN: Liturgical Press.

A. Clifford (1996). "Foundations for A Catholic Ecological Theology of God." In D. Christiansen and W. Grazer (eds), *"And God Saw That It Was Good": Catholic Theology and the Environment*. Washington, DC: US Catholic Conference, pp. 201–254.

D. Clough (2009). "All God's Creatures: Reading Genesis on Human and Nonhuman Animals." In S. C. Barton and D. Wilkinson (eds), *Reading Genesis after Darwin*. New York: Oxford University Press, pp. 211–227.

C. Deane-Drummond (2008). *Eco-Theology*. Winona, MN: Anselm Academic.

R. Descartes (1637/1985). "Discourse on Method." Translated by J. Cottingham, R. Stoothoff, and D. Murdoch. In *The Philosophical Works of Descartes*. New York: Cambridge University Press.

C. DeWitt (2011). *Earthwise: A Guide to Hopeful Creation Care*. 2nd ed. Grand Rapids, MI: Faith Alive Christian Resources.

D. Edwards (2008). "Eucharist and Ecology: Keeping Memorial of Creation." *Worship*, 82: 194–213.

Ephrem the Syrian (1847). *Selected Works of S. Ephrem the Syrian*. Translated by J. B. Morris. Oxford: Oxford University Press.

Ephrem the Syrian (1989a). *Ephrem the Syrian: Hymns*. Translated by K. E. McVey. Mahwah, NJ: Paulist Press.

Ephrem the Syrian (1989b). *Hymns on Paradise*. Introduction and translation by S. Brock. Crestwood, NY: St. Vladimir's Press.

Ephrem the Syrian (1994). Commentary on Genesis. In K. McVey (ed.), *St. Ephrem the Syrian: Selected Prose Works*. Translated by E. G. Mathews and J. P. Amar. Washington, DC: Catholic University of America Press.

M. Erickson (1998). *Christian Theology*. 2nd ed. Grand Rapids, MI: Baker Books.

G. D. Fee (1995). *Paul's Letter to the Philippians*. Grand Rapids, MI: Eerdmans.

L. Fischer (1983). *The Life of Mahatma Gandhi*. New York: Harper and Row.

M. Fox (1991). *Creation Spirituality: Liberating Gifts for the Peoples of the Earth*. San Francisco: HarperCollins.

W. French (1993). "Beast Machines and the Technocratic Reduction of Life." In C. Pinches and J. B. McDaniel (eds), *Good News for Animals? Christian Approaches to Animal Well-Being*. New York: Orbis Books, pp. 24–43.

T. Fretheim (1991). *Exodus*. Atlanta: John Knox Press.

T. Fretheim (2005). *God and World in the Old Testament: A Relational Theology of Creation*. Nashville: Abingdon Press.

T.Fretheim (2006). *God and World in the Old Testament: A Relational Theology of Creation*. Nashville: Abingdon Press.

M. K. Gandhi (1959). *An Autobiography: The Story of My Experiments with the Truth*. Translated by M. Desai. Ahmedabad: Navajivan.

M. K. Gandhi (1962). *The Essential Gandhi: An Anthology of His Writings on His Life, Work, and Ideas*. L. Fischer (ed.). New York: Vintage.

M. K. Gandhi (1964). *Gandhi on Non-Violence: Selected Texts from Mohandas K. Gandhi's "Non-Violence in Peace and War"*. T. Merton (ed.). New York: New Directions.

M. K. Gandhi (1972). *Non-Violence in Peace and War*. New York: Garland.

M. K. Gandhi (1997). *Hind Swaraj and Other Writings*. A. Parel (ed.). New York: Cambridge University Press.

M. K. Gandhi (1999). *The Collected Works of Mahatma Gandhi*. 98 vols. New Delhi: Publications Division, Government of India.

Gaudium et Spes (1965). www.vatican.va/archive/hist_councils/ii_vatican_council/index.htm.

J. B. Gibson (1994), "Jesus' Wilderness Temptation according to Mark." *Journal for the Study of the New Testament* 53 (March): 3–34.

I. S. Gilhus (2006). *Animals, Gods and Humans: Changing Attitudes to Animals, in Greek, Roman, and Early Christian Ideas.* New York: Routledge.

Gregory of Nyssa (1988). *On the Making of Man.* In P. Schaff and H. Wace (eds), *Nicene and Post-Nicene Fathers of the Christian Church.* Grand Rapids, MI: Eerdmans.

J. Goldingay (2001). *Isaiah.* Peabody, MA: Hendrickson.

R. M. Grant (1999). *Early Christians and Animals.* New York: Routledge.

S. J. Grenz (2001). *The Social God and the Relational Self: A Trinitarian Theology of the Imago Dei.* Louisville, KY: Westminster/John Knox Press.

D. J. Hall (1986). *Imaging God: Dominion as Stewardship.* Grand Rapids, MI: Eerdmans.

N. Habel (2011). *The Birth, the Curse and the Greening of Earth: An Ecological Reading of Genesis 1–11.* Sheffield, UK: Sheffield Phoenix Press.

J. Hart (2006). *Sacramental Commons: Christian Ecological Ethics.* New York: Rowman & Littlefield.

N. V. Harrison (2008). "The Human Person as the Image and Likeness of God." In M. B. Cunningham and E. Theokritoff (eds), *The Cambridge Companion to Orthodox Christian Theology.* New York: Cambridge University Press, pp. 78–91.

S. Hauerwas and J. Berkman (1993). "A Trinitarian Theology of the 'Chief End' of 'All Flesh.'" In C. Pinches and J. B. McDaniel (eds), *Good News for Animals? Christian Approaches to Animal Well-Being* New York: Orbis Books, pp. 62–74.

D. Hollenbach (2002). *The Common Good and Christian Ethics.* New York: Cambridge University Press.

J. A. Herdt (2008). *Putting on Virtue: The Legacy of Splendid Vices.* Chicago: University of Chicago Press.

J. Heschel (1962). *The Prophets.* New York: Harper Perennial.

M. Healy (2008). *The Gospel of Mark.* Grand Rapids, MI: Baker Academic.

R. Huntington (2002). "Jainism and Ethics." In M. Meyer and K. Bergel (eds), *Reverence for Life: The Ethics of Albert Schweitzer for the Twenty-First Century.* Syracuse, NY: Syracuse University Press, pp. 184–206.

Irenaeus of Lyons (1996). *Irenaeus: Against Heresies.* In A. Roberts and J. Donaldson (eds), *Ante-Nicene Fathers.* Vol. 1. Grand Rapids, MI: Eerdmans.

Irenaeus of Lyons (2002). *Irenaeus' Demonstration of the Apostolic Preaching: A Theological Commentary and Translation.* I. M. Mackenzie (ed.), with the translation of the text of the *Demonstration* by J. A. Robinson. Burlington, VT: Ashgate.

S. A. Irvine (1990). *Isaiah, Ahaz, and the Syro-Ephraimitic Crisis.* Ann Arbor: University of Michigan Press.

K. Irwin (1994). "The Sacramentality of Creation and the Role of Creation in Liturgy and Sacraments," in *Preserving the Creation. Environmental Theology and Ethics,* ed. Kevin W. Irwin and Edmund J. Pellegrino. Washington, DC: Georgetown University Press, pp. 67–111.

K. Irwin (1998). "Sacramentality and the Theology of Creation: A Recovered Paradigm for Sacramental Theology." *Louvain Studies,* 23: 159–179.

K. Irwin (2002). "A Sacramental World? Sacramentality as the Primary Language for Sacraments." *Worship,* 76, 3 (May): 197–211.

Isaac of Nineveh (1969). *Mystic Treatises.* Translated by A. J. Wensinck. Amsterdam 1923; Wiesbaden, reprinted 1969.

Isaac the Syrian (1984). *The Ascetical Homilies of St. Isaac the Syrian.* Dana Miller (ed.). Boston: Holy Transfiguration Monastery.

D. Jackson (2007). *Marvelous to Behold: Miracles in Medieval Manuscripts.* London: British Library.

W. Jenkins (2008). *Ecologies of Grace: Environmental Ethics and Christian Theology.* New York: Oxford University Press.

J. Jensen (1984). *Isaiah 1–39.* Wilmington, DE: Michael Glazier.

J. Johnson (2005). "Genesis 1:26–28." *Interpretation,* 59 (April): 176–178.

R. Johnson (2006a). "From Childhood to *Satyagrahi.*" In R. L. Johnson (ed.), *Gandhi's Experiments with Truth: Essential Writings by and about Mahatma Gandhi.* New York: Lexington Books, pp. 3–14.

R. Johnson (2006b). "Introduction: Gandhi's Experiments with the Truth: Private Life, *Satyagraha,* and the Constructive Programme." In R. L. Johnson (ed.), *Gandhi's Experiments with Truth: Essential Writings by and about Mahatma Gandhi.* New York: Lexington Books, pp. xi–xviii.

R. Johnson (2006c). "*Satyagraha:* The Only Way to Stop Terrorism." In R. L. Johnson (ed.), *Gandhi's Experiments with Truth: Essential Writings by and about Mahatma Gandhi.* New York: Lexington Books, pp. 228–236.

M. Juergensmeyer (1984). *Fighting with Gandhi.* San Francisco: Harper and Row.

M. Kadavil (2005). *The World as Sacrament: Sacramentality of Creation from the Perspectives of Leonardo Boff, Alexander Schmemann and Saint Ephrem.* Leuven: Peeters.

O. Kaiser (1983). *Isaiah 1–12: A Commentary,* translated by John Bowden. Philadelphia: Westminster Press.

E. Kant (1785/1998). *The Groundwork of the Metaphysics of the Moral.* Translated by M. Gregor. New York: Cambridge University Press.

B. Kent (2002). "Habits and Virtues (Ia IIae, qq. 49–70)." In S. J. Pope (ed.), *The Ethics of Aquinas.* Washington, DC: Georgetown University Press, pp. 116–130.

R. J. Kernaghan (2007). *Mark.* Downers Grove, IL: Inter-Varsity Press.

D. Kinsley (1995). *Ecology and Religion: Ecological Spirituality in Cross-Cultural Perspective.* Upper Saddle River, NJ: Prentice Hall.

E. J. Kissane (1941). *The Book of Isaiah.* Dublin: Browne and Nolan.

F. Korom (2000). "Holy Cow! The Apotheosis of Zebu, or Why the Cow Is Sacred in Hinduism." *Asian Folklore Studies,* 59: 181–203.

T. Kronholm (1978). *Motifs from Genesis 1–11 in the Genuine Hymns of Ephrem the Syrian.* Lund, Sweden: Gleerup.

C. M. LaCugna (1993). *God for Us: The Trinity and Christian Life.* San Francisco: Harper.

W. S. Lasor, D. A. Hubbard, and F. W. Bush (1996). *Old Testament Survey: The Message, Form, and Background of the Old Testament.* 2nd ed. Grand Rapids, MI: Eerdmans.

C. Leget (2005). "Eschatology." In R. V. Nieuwenhove and J. Wawrykow (eds), *The Theology of Thomas Aquinas.* Notre Dame, IN: University of Notre Dame Press.

A. Linzey (1995). *Animal Theology.* Chicago: University of Illinois Press.

A. Linzey (1998). *Animal Gospel.* Louisville, KY: Westminster/John Knox Press.

A. Linzey (2009). *Why Animal Suffering Matters: Philosophy, Theology, and Practical Ethics.* New York: Oxford University Press.

V. Lossky (1976). *The Mystical Theology of the Eastern Church.* Crestwood, NY: St. Vladimir's Seminary Press.

A. Louth (2008). "Eastern Orthodox Eschatology." In J. L. Walls (ed.), *The Orthodox Handbook of Eschatology.* New York: Oxford University Press, pp. 233–247.

A. Louth (2010). "Between Creation and Transfiguration: The Environment in the Eastern Orthodox Tradition." In D. G. Horrell, C. Hunt, C. Southgate and F. Stavrakopoulou (eds), *Ecological Hermeneutics: Biblical, Historical and Theological Perspectives*. New York: T. & T. Clark, pp. 211–222.

Lumen Gentium (1964). www.vatican.va/archive/hist_councils/ii_vatican_council/index.htm.

J. Martos (2001). *Doors to the Sacred: A Historical Introduction to Sacraments in the Catholic Church*. Rev. and updated ed. Liguori, MO: Liguori/Triumph.

K. A. Matthews (1995). *Genesis 1–11:26*. Nashville: B&H.

A. MacIntyre (2007). *After Virtue: A Study in Moral Theory*. 2nd ed. Notre Dame, IN: University of Notre Dame Press.

D. McDougal (2003). *The Cosmos as the Primary Sacrament: The Horizon for an Ecological Sacramental Theology*. New York: Peter Lang.

A. McIntosh (2009). "Human and Animal Relations in the Theology of Karl Barth." *Pacifica* 22, 1 (February): 20–35.

R. P. McLaughlin (2011). "Evidencing the Eschaton: Progressive-Transformative Animal Welfare in the Church Fathers." *Modern Theology*, 27, 1 (January 2011): 121–146.

R. P. McLaughlin (2011). "*Noblesse Oblige*: Theological Differences between Humans and Animals and What They Imply Morally." *Oxford Journal of Animal Ethics*, 1, 2 (Fall): 132–149.

R. P. McLaughlin (2012a). "Non-Violence and Nonhumans: Foundations for Animal Welfare in the Thought of Mohandas Gandhi and Albert Schweitzer." *Journal of Religious Ethics*, 40, 4: 678–704.

R. P. McLaughlin (2012b). "Thomas Aquinas's Eco-Theological Ethics of Anthropocentric Conservation." *Horizons*, 39, 1: 69–97.

R. P. McLaughlin (2013). "Jonah and the Religious Other: An Exploration in Biblical Inclusivism." *Journal of Ecumenical Studies*, 48, 1 (Winter): 71–84.

J. McKeown (2008). *Genesis*. Grand Rapids, MI: Eerdmans.

J. Meyendorff (1974). *Byzantine Theology: Historical Trends*. New York: Fordham University Press.

M. Meyer (2002). "Affirming Reverence for Life." In M. Meyer and K. Bergel (eds), *Reverence for Life: The Ethics of Albert Schweitzer for the Twenty-First Century*. Syracuse, NY: Syracuse University Press, pp. 29–36.

J. R. Middleton (2004). "Created in the Image of Violent God? The Ethical Problem of the Conquest of Chaos in Biblical Creation Narratives." In *Interpretation*, 58/4 (October): 341–355.

J. R. Middleton (2005). *The Liberating Image: The Imago Dei in Genesis 1*. Grand Rapids, MI: Brazos Press.

J. R. Middleton (2006). "A New Heaven and a New Earth: The Case for a Holistic Reading of the Biblical Story of Redemption." *Journal for Christian Theological Research*, 11: 73–97.

D. Minns (1994). *Irenaeus*. Washington, DC: Georgetown University Press.

P. D. Miscall (2006). *Isaiah*. Sheffield, UK: Sheffield Phoenix Press.

R. W. L. Moberly (2009). *The Theology of the Book of Genesis*. New York: Cambridge University Press.

J. Moltmann (1992). *The Spirit of Life: A Universal Affirmation*. Translated by M. Kohl. Minneapolis: Fortress Press.

J. Moltmann (1993). *The Crucified God: The Cross of Christ as the Foundation and Criticism of Christian Theology*. Translated by R. A. Wilson and J. Bowden. Minneapolis: Fortress Press.

J. Moltmann (1996). *The Coming of God: Christian Eschatology*. Translated by M. Kohl. Minneapolis: Fortress Press.

J. Moltmann (2009). "Horizons of Hope." *Christian Century*, (May 20): 31–33.

A. Motyer (1999). *Isaiah*. Downers Grove, IL: Inter-Varsity Press.

M. Northcott (2009). "'They Shall Not Hurt or Destroy in All My Holy Mountain' (Isaiah 65.25): Killing for Philosophy and a Creaturely Theology of Non-Violence." In C. Deane-Drummond and D. Clough (eds), *Creaturely Theology: On God, Humans and Other Animals*. London: SCM Press, pp. 231–248.

Nostra Aetate (1965). www.vatican.va/archive/hist_councils/ii_vatican_council/index.htm.

K. Osborne (1988). *Sacramental Theology: A General Introduction*. Mahwah, NJ: Paulist Press.

A. Parel (2006). *Gandhi's Philosophy and the Quest for Harmony*. New York: Cambridge University Press.

N. Phelps (2002). *The Dominion of Love: Animal Rights according to the Bible*. New York: Lantern Books.

S. Pinckaers (2002). "The Source of Ethics of St. Thomas Aquinas." In S. J. Pope (ed.), *The Ethics of Aquinas*. Washington, DC: Georgetown University Press, pp. 17–29.

J. Porter (1990). *The Recovery of Virtue: The Relevance of Aquinas for Christian Ethics*. Louisville, KY: Westminster / John Knox Press.

Pope Benedict XVI (2011). "If You Want to Cultivate Peace, Protect Creation: Message for the 2010 World Day of Peace." In T. Winright (ed.), *Green Discipleship: Catholic Theological Ethics and the Environment*. Winona, MN: Anselm Academic, pp. 61–71.

Pope John Paul II (1979). *Redemptoris Hominis*. www.vatican.va/holy_father/john_paul_ii/encyclicals/documents/.html.

Pope John Paul II (1990). *Peace with God the Creator, Peace with all of Creation*. Message on World Day of Peace. www.vatican.va/holy_father/john_paul_ii/messages/peace/index.htm.

Pope John Paul II and Patriarch Bartholomew I (2002). *Common Declaration on Environmental Ethics*. www.vatican.va/holy_father/john_paul_ii/speeches/2002/june/index.htm.

Pope John XXIII (1963). *Pacem in Terris* www.vatican.va/holy_father/john_xxiii/encyclicals/index.htm.

Pope Paul VI (1967). *Populorum Progressio*. www.vatican.va/holy_father/paul_vi/encyclicals/index.htm (accessed August 2009).

S. J. Pope (2002). "Overview of the Ethics of Thomas Aquinas." In S. J. Pope (ed.), *The Ethics of Aquinas*. Washington, DC: Georgetown University Press, pp. 30–53.

G. V. Rad (1961). *Genesis: A Commentary*. Translated by John H. Marks. Philadelphia: Westminster Press.

J. Ratzinger (1988). *Eschatology: Death and Eternal Life*. 2nd ed. Translated by M. Waldstein. Washington, DC: Catholic University of America Press.

J. Rickaby (1919). *Moral Philosophy: Ethics, Deontology and Natural Law*. 4th ed. New York: Longmans, Green.

E. D. Reed (2009). "Animals in Orthodox Iconography." In C. Deane-Drummond and D. Clough (eds), *Creaturely Theology, Creaturely Theology: On God, Humans and Other Animals.* London: SCM Press, pp. 61–77.

R. R. Reno (2010). *Genesis.* Grand Rapids, MI: Brazos Press.

R. R. Ruether (1992). *Gaia and God: An Ecofeminist Theology of Earth Healing.* New York: HarperCollins.

T. Runyon (1980). "The World as the Original Sacrament." *Worship,* 54, 6: 495–511.

R. D. Ryder (1989). *Animal Revolution: Changing Attitudes towards Speciesism.* Cambridge, MA: Basil Blackwell.

P. Santmire (1985). *The Travail of Nature: The Ambiguous Ecological Promise of Christian Theology.* Minneapolis: Fortress Press.

N. M. Sarna (1989). *The JPS Torah Commentary: Genesis.* Philadelphia: Jewish Publication Society.

J. Schaefer (2005). "Valuing Earth Intrinsically and Instrumentally: A Theological Framework for Environmental Ethics." *Theological Studies,* 66: 783–814.

J. Schaefer (2009). *Theological Foundations for Environmental Ethics: Reconstructing Patristic & Medieval Concepts.* Washington, DC: Georgetown University Press.

A. Schmemann (1973). *For the Life of the World: Sacraments and Orthodoxy.* Crestwood, NY: St. Vladimir's Seminary Press.

E. Schockenhoff (2002). "The Theological Virtue of Charity." In S. J. Pope (ed.), *The Ethics of Aquinas.* Washington, DC: Georgetown University Press, pp. 244–258.

A. Schweitzer (1936). *Indian Thought and Its Development.* Translated by Mrs. C. E. B. Russell. Gloucester, MA: Beacon Press.

A. Schweitzer (1946). *Civilization and Ethics.* Translated by C. T. Campion. London: A. & C. Black.

A. Schweitzer (1955). *The Mysticism of Paul the Apostle.* Translated by W. Montgomery. London: A. & C. Black.

A. Schweitzer (1965a). *Reverence for Life: An Anthology of Selected Writings.* T. Kiernan (ed.). New York: Philosophical Library.

A. Schweitzer (1965b). *The Teaching of Reverence for Life.* Translated by R. and C. Winston. New York: Holt, Rinehart and Winston.

A. Schweitzer (1966). *My Life and Thought: An Autobiography.* Translated by C. T. Campion. London: Unwin Books.

A. Schweitzer (1998). *Out of My Life and Thought: An Autobiography.* Translated by A. B. Lemke. Baltimore: John Hopkins University Press.

A. Schweitzer (2002). "First Sermon on Reverence for Life." In M. Meyer and K. Bergel (eds), *Reverence for Life: The Ethics of Albert Schweitzer for the Twenty-First Century.* Syracuse, NY: Syracuse University Press, pp. 62–69.

C. Seitz (1993). *Isaiah 1–39.* Louisville, KY: John Knox Press.

L. H. Sideris (2003). *Environmental Ethics, Ecological Theology, and Natural Selection.* New York: Columbia University Press.

P. Singer (1975). *Animal Liberation: A New Ethics for Our Treatment of Animals.* New York: Avon Books.

G. V. Smith (2007). *Isaiah 1–39.* Nashville: B&H.

D. Staniloae (2000). *The Experience of God: Orthodox Dogmatic Theology.* Vol. 2, *The World: Creation and Deification.* Translated and edited by I. Ionita and R. Barringer. Brookline, MA: Holy Cross Orthodox Press.

M. C. Steenberg (2008). *Irenaeus on Creation: The Cosmic Christ and the Saga of Redemption.* Boston: Brill.

G. Steiner (2005). *Anthropocentrism and Its Discontents: The Moral Status of Animals in the History of Western Philosophy.* Pittsburgh: University of Pittsburgh Press.

Theophilus of Antioch (1880). *Letter to Autolycus.* In A. Roberts and J. Donaldson (eds), *Ante-Nicene Christian Library: Translations of the Writings of the Fathers,* Vol. 3. Edinburgh: T. & T. Clark.

W. S. Towner (2001). *Genesis.* Louisville, KY: Westminster/John Knox Press.

W. S. Towner (2005). "Clones of God: Genesis 1:26–28 and the Image of God in the Hebrew Bible." *Interpretation,* 59: 341–356.

G. M. Tucker (1994). *Isaiah-Ezekiel.* Nashville: Abingdon Press.

US Conference of Catholic Bishops (1991). *Renewing the Earth.* www.usccb.org/sdwp/ejp/bishopsstatement.shtml (accessed September 2009).

W. E. Vine (1971). *Isaiah: Prophecies, Promises, Warning.* Grand Rapids, MI: Zondervan.

T. Vivian (2003). "The Peaceable Kingdom: Animals as Parables in the *Virtues of Saint Macarius.*" *Anglican Theological Review,* 85, 3 (Summer): 477–491.

J. Waard (1997). *A Handbook on Isaiah.* Winona Lake, IN: Eisenbrauns.

B. K. Waltke with C. J. Fredericks (2001). *Genesis: A Commentary.* Grand Rapids, MI: Zondervan.

J. D. W. Watts (1982). *Isaiah 1–33.* Waco, TX: Word Books.

K. Ware (1995). *The Orthodox Way.* Rev. ed. Crestwood, NY: St. Vladimir's Seminary Press.

K. Ware (1999). "The Soul in Greek Christianity." In M. James and C. Crabbe (eds), *From Soul to Self.* New York: Routledge, pp. 49–69.

G. J. Wenham (1982). *Genesis 1–15.* Waco, TX: Word Books.

R. N. Wennberg (2003). *God, Humans, and Animals: An Invitation to Enlarge Our Moral Universe.* Grand Rapids, MI: Eerdmans.

C. Westermann (1984). *Genesis 1–11: A Commentary.* Translated by J. J. Scullion. Minneapolis: Augsburg.

L. White (2000). "The Historical Roots of Our Ecological Crisis." Reprinted in J. Berry (ed.), *The Care of Creation: Focusing Concern and Action.* Downers Grove, IL: Inter-Varsity Press, 2000, pp. 31–42.

H. Wildberger (1990). *Isaiah 1–12.* Translated by T. H. Trapp. Minneapolis: Fortress Press.

E. Wolde (1995). *Stories of the Beginning: Genesis 1–11 and Other Creation Stories.* Ridgefield, CT: Morehouse.

M. Wynn (2010). "Thomas Aquinas: Reading the Idea of Dominion in the Light of the Doctrine of Creation." In D. G. Horrell, C. Hunt, C. Southgate, and F. Stavrakopoulou (eds), *Ecological Hermeneutics: Biblical, Historical and Theological Perspectives.* New York: T. & T. Clark, pp. 154–167.

D. Yarri (2005). *The Ethics of Animal Experimentation: A Critical Analysis and Constructive Proposal.* New York: Oxford University Press.

Index